I've travelled the world twice over,
Met the famous: saints and sinners,
Poets and artists, kings and queens,
Old stars and hopeful beginners,
I've been where no-one's been before,
Learned secrets from writers and cooks
All with one library ticket
To the wonderful world of books.

© Janice James.

The wisdom of the ages
Is there for you and me,
The wisdom of the ages,
In your local library.

There's large print books
And talking books,
For those who cannot see,
The wisdom of the ages,
It's fantastic, and it's free.

Written by Sam Wood, aged 92

RUFFLES ON MY LONGJOHNS

Isabel Edwards was in her early twenties when she and her husband Earle began homesteading in British Columbia's remote Bella Coola Valley. Born in Britain and raised in quiet Victoria, young Isabel had only notions of wilderness life when she and Earle left their home and edged closer and closer to the wilderness. What was to be one winter spent in the northern coastal mountains has become almost fifty years. Mrs. Edwards spins yarns about those early days and tells of the isolation and loneliness of being the only woman in a world of men.

ISABEL EDWARDS

RUFFLES ON MY LONGJOHNS

Complete and Unabridged

ULVERSCROFT
Leicester

First published in Great Britain in 1980 by
Hancock House Publishers Limited
Surrey

First Large Print Edition
published 1997
by arrangement with
Hancock House Publishers Limited
Surrey

British Library CIP Data

Edwards, Isabel
　　Ruffles on my longjohns.—Large print ed.—
Ulverscroft large print series: non-fiction
　　1. Edwards, Ralph 2. Ornithologists—Biography
　　3. Canada Goose 4. Large type books
　　I. Title
　　598.4′178′092

　　ISBN 0–7089–3752–7

Published by
F. A. Thorpe (Publishing) Ltd.
Anstey, Leicestershire
Set by Words & Graphics Ltd.
Anstey, Leicestershire
Printed and bound in Great Britain by
T. J. International Ltd., Padstow, Cornwall

This book is printed on acid-free paper

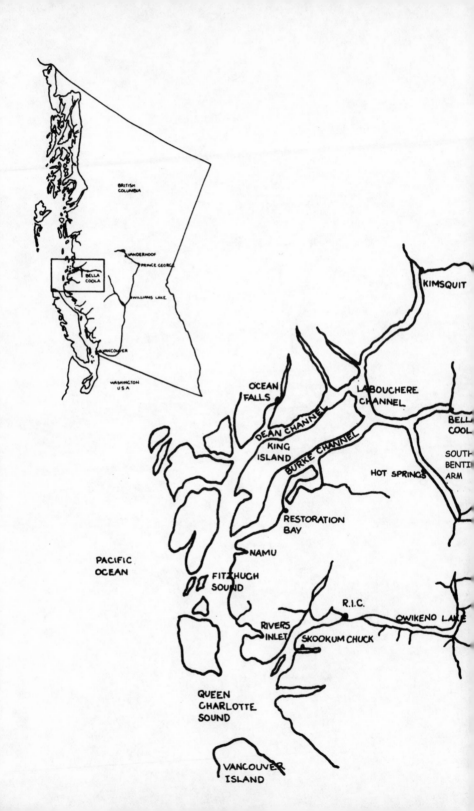

BRITISH COLUMBIA

VANDERHOOF
PRINCE GEORGE

BELLA COOLA

WILLIAMS LAKE

VANCOUVER

WASHINGTON USA

KIMSQUIT

OCEAN FALLS

LABOUCHERE CHANNEL

BELLA COOL

DEAN CHANNEL

KING ISLAND

BURKE CHANNEL

SOUTH BENTII ARM

HOT SPRINGS

RESTORATION BAY

NAMU

PACIFIC OCEAN

FITZHUGH SOUND

R.I.C.

OWIKENO LAKE

RIVERS INLET

SKOOKUM CHUCK

QUEEN CHARLOTTE SOUND

VANCOUVER ISLAND

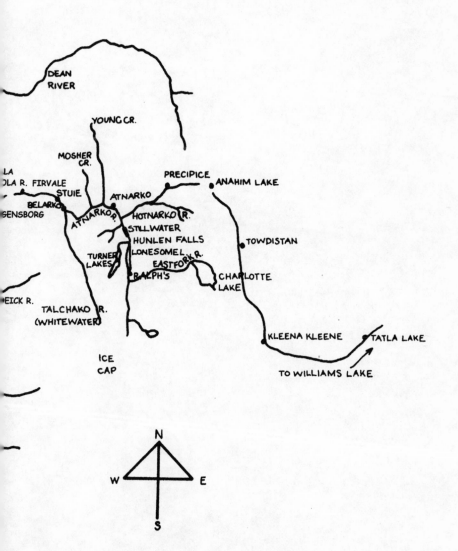

For Earle

Introduction

EARLE looked up from the letter he was reading, "How would you like to go north for the winter?"

This was my fond husband, asking me if I'd like to leave the pleasant climate of Oregon to spend a winter in snow and ice.

"North!" My voice almost cracked in reply. "Are you joking?"

Ever since I could remember, I had suffered from "snow-phobia." The sight of falling snowflakes filled me with unreasoning terror and the thought of spending a winter in a snow-bound wilderness was unbelievable.

Still holding the letter scrawled in his brother's bold handwriting, Earle went on, "Ralph has invited us to spend the winter at Lonesome Lake. He thinks it might help my asthma."

There was a pause as Earle's eyes searched my face. "You'd really like it there. The air is so clear." Then as a final assurance he added, "We'd only stay for the winter."

In January of 1913, Earle's brother had taken up a preemption in the uninhabited forest at the head of a seven-mile lake which he named "Lonesome." It was in West Central British Columbia and part of a tributary of the Bella Coola River which flows through the snow-capped mountains of the Coast Range to the sea. Ralph thought it was little short of paradise, with unlimited building material in the cedar forest, fish in the river and plenty of wild game in the woods. He and Earle spent several winters together, trapping and working on Ralph's homestead.

"It was wonderful up there," Earle reminisced, "hiking on snowshoes above timberline, carrying a heavy pack in the deep snow. It didn't matter if we got wet or chilled, there weren't any germs to give us colds. Perhaps it really would help cure my asthma."

How could I resist this appeal? Before autumn came Earle had persuaded me and we arranged our affairs and

2

were on our way north.

Earle was as happy as a schoolboy turned loose; but this was a voyage into the snowy wilds for me and I was filled with trepidation.

1

Going North

IT was early September in 1932 when we left Portland with the little Studebaker coupé piled high with camping equipment. Its rumble seat was open and filled with everything we would need for spending the winter at Ralph's, except for food, foot gear and woolen underwear. We would get these in Vancouver after we reached British Columbia.

"People in the north all wear woolen longjohns in the winter," Earle advised me.

I never questioned him. After all, he had lived there and should know.

As we crossed the border in Blaine, the customs official looked askance at the size of our bulging load, covered snugly with a tarpaulin and lashed down securely with rope. After asking a few perfunctory questions, he waved us through.

It was the immigration official who held us up. He had the fixed idea that I wasn't married to Earle and he wanted to see our marriage license. Without thinking, I had packed it in a suitcase which was buried somewhere in the load, along with my British birth certificate, Earle's Canadian Naturalization papers and his honorable discharge from the Canadian army in 1918. The gold wedding band I was wearing, engraved with our names and the date of the wedding over six years ago, didn't count. We had to unload everything.

Earle released the knots he had tied so securely, then pulled the rope free and dropped it to the ground. Next came the heavy tarpaulin, followed by the folded tent. Then came the mattresses and bedding, followed by dunnage bags

6

and suitcases of clothing. Light-weight camping gear and feather-weight winter apparel hadn't been thought of in those days. There was also a portable, hand-winding phonograph and some records, a carton of books and a typewriter, tools, a gun and axe, and on the bottom, a sheet of metal to make an air-tight heater when we reached Ralph's.

It was an impressive pile and I began to wonder how we had been able to get it all in to begin with; but we produced our wedding certificate!

Burning with mortification as we exposed our worldly goods to public gaze, I marveled at Earle's self-control. However, we weren't finished yet. Now came the questioning.

"Where are you going?"

"To Lonesome Lake."

"Where is that?"

"At the head of the Bella Coola River."

"Where is that?"

"In West Central British Columbia." We produced a map.

"There aren't any roads marked into Lonesome Lake," the official commented.

"There aren't any," Earle replied.

7

"Well, how do you expect to get in there?"

"Hike." Earle was getting irritated.

"You'll get lost," was the observation.

"Not very likely," Earle rejoined. "I'm an experienced woodsman and have trapped furs in that country."

On and on it went. "What do you intend to do when you get in there? Are you going to work?"

"Well, I don't intend to sit around and watch my brother do everything."

"What does he do?"

"He has a farm and goes trapping in the winter." Earle's voice was getting a little edgy. I wondered if the official was becoming interested in the people who lived so far away from roads and wanted to hear more about them or whether this was a routine interrogation.

By this time the customs official had sauntered over. He began to inspect the pile of things lying on the pavement, curious about why we had a portable typewriter, a record player, and a rifle. Were we bringing them in to sell? Where did we get the rifle? Why did we need it?

Earle answered him as best he could, saying these things were part of our equipment. The rifle was needed to protect us from bears and it had been bought from a sporting goods store. It was an 8mm Lebel made by the Remington Arms Company for the French army, near the end of the First World War. The armistice was signed before the rifles were delivered and they were now being sold as army surplus. Earle had remodeled it into a sports gun.

"Military guns are not allowed into Canada," the official told Earle, "It will be necessary for you to take the rifle to the chief of the Customs Bureau in New Westminster for inspection and possible confiscation."

They finally finished with us and we reloaded. We drove to New Westminster in silence and outside the customs building I waited in the car, slumped down in misery, wondering how much a new rifle would cost if they confiscated the Lebel.

The wait seemed interminable as I sat in the car, imagining the worst and it was almost a shock when I saw

9

Earle bouncing cheerfully down the steps carrying the gun. He smiled as he opened the car door and gave a chuckle, "Nicest chap, in there. No problem. Nothing to it. Our rifle is a sports gun."

We spent a day in Vancouver and went shopping for the underwear and boots. Parking the little coupé outside one of the large general stores in downtown Vancouver, we closed and locked the rumble seat but forgot to lock the car doors.

The clerk in the men's department had the woolen underwear we wanted and after Earle had ordered his he asked for some for me.

We were informed that Stanfield's didn't make one-piece woolen longjohns for ninety-five pound women, so we ended up by holding the garment in front of me and guessing whether it would fit or not.

Then we found the leather shoepacks, made by Palmer, which Earle insisted were the best foot gear available. They were beautifully made but had stiff, slippery leather soles. Earle said they were made that way so they could be fitted with screw-caulks, so we bought some of them too to take with the boots. Earle said he would attach them later.

The car was not there when we came out of the store with our purchases.

"We must have come out of the wrong door," I suggested, so we walked around the block. Still no coupé. It was a sickening feeling.

Numbed, we found a policeman who directed us to the police station.

The officers were sympathetic, and after asking a lot of questions they told us to go back to our motel and wait until they phoned.

"What will we do if they don't find the car," I asked Earle.

He made an unconvincing joke about the mounties always getting their man. However, two hours later there was a call. The coupé had been found undamaged, and the rumble seat was still locked and intact. Could we come to the station and pick it up? Could we!

We thanked the officers profusely and taxied to the station to claim our car. It was scarcely believeable but everything was as we had left it in the locked rumble seat. It was as if someone had played a bad joke. Secretly, I wondered if a guardian angel wasn't reaching out a staying hand; but Earle's enthusiasm was undiminished. He thought that as long as our shopping was finished and the afternoon was still young we might just as well pack the car and begin the journey north.

Going out the highway we drove behind a truck full of mounties in their scarlet uniforms, seated upright on benches on either side of the open vehicle. I was thrilled and for a while thought this might be an escort provided as an extension of the marvelous courtesy the police had shown us. But they turned off on a side road and we were alone heading for the wilderness.

Out we drove through the rich farm lands of the Fraser River Delta, warm in the late afternoon sunshine. Mile after mile we were surrounded by this peaceful beauty with its backdrop of snow-capped mountains. But I sat there with the gnawing recollection of that roadless map of Lonesome Lake.

"Do you suppose Ralph knows we are

coming?" I asked Earle.

"Probably not. Very likely he's still busy getting in the last of the second crop hay or harvesting the garden," he replied.

Possibly Ralph hadn't made the long trip out for his mail in a couple of months so would have no idea yet that we had accepted his invitation to spend the winter, or that we might come in by any other way than up the coast by steamer from Vancouver to Bella Coola. The Union Steamship made a weekly trip north from Vancouver carrying mail, passengers and freight to the isolated hamlets, canneries and logging camps that dotted the rugged coast. This was the only contact Bella Coola had with the outside world except for the packhorse trail from the interior which followed a branchline of the Yukon Telegraph through the mountains, down from the jack-pine, slough-grass interior to the heavily forested, verdant valley — the route Earle was planning to take.

I would have preferred the coastal route. While I was still in high school I had made the boat trip and spent two summer holidays with my sister after she had gone to Bella Coola as a bride to live. She had married Vincent Clayton, the first white child to be born in the Bella Coola Valley, and they continued living in the rambling old twelve-room house with its thick log walls and hand-hewn beams where Vincent had lived all his life. It was part of the fur-trading post his father, John Clayton, had built on the bank of the Bella Coola River.

The house was still filled with Victorian furniture, most of which had come around the Horn in sailing ships, finishing the journey up the coast from Vancouver to Bella Coola in Clayton's own side-wheeler.

It was a romantic holiday for me, but a day's horseback ride up the sparsely settled valley was as far as I had gone and I scarcely knew there was a hinterland or what a long way it was from the sleepy little fishing village to Lonesome Lake.

This is the route we would have taken if my sister had still been in Bella Coola but the year before she and Vincent had taken the children to Victoria to put

14

them in school and the old house was unoccupied.

Back in Portland when Earle had decided on the Cariboo-Chilcotin route, it had seemed easy to plan on getting horses at Anahim to take us down the telegraph line into the valley to where Ralph's trail branched off to the Stillwater. There we could leave our things at Frank Ratcliff's trapping cabin while we hiked up around Lonesome Lake to Ralph's.

2

Cariboo Country

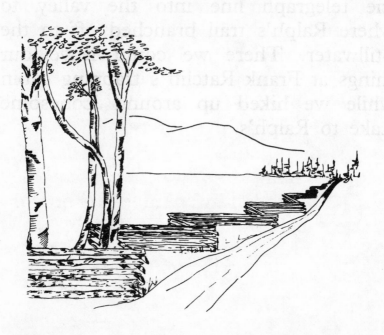

AT the end of our first long day
out of Vancouver, it was growing
dark before we came to a place
where we could camp. Earle turned off
the highway onto a narrow dirt road until
he found a grassy clearing near a small
creek. There was no sight of human
habitation and we were far enough from

the highway not to hear any of the few cars that were traveling. It was secluded and quiet and we were alone.

Then around the corner of the road, out of the dusk came the jingling of harnesses, followed by a team of horses and a wagon driven by two young ranchers. They pulled up in the grassy clearing with only one glance at us when Earle said, "How do you do."

They replied, "Howdy," and unhitching their horses they tied them to the wagon where they had hay. Wordlessly they made a small fire, warmed something over it, ate and crawled into their bedrolls beside the fire and went to sleep.

So much for the social life, I thought, but at least they were there and we were less apt to be disturbed by wild animals. It never occurred to me that these young chaps had taken one look at our Oregon license plate and regarded us as the interlopers.

Inside our tent I could hear the gurgling of the creek and occasionally, far off, the maniacal call of a coyote; but above it all was the incessant munching of the horses.

Earle slept like a baby, but in the morning, hollow-eyed, I complained about the horses chewing their cud all night and he replied, "Oh, for heaven's sake! Don't you know? Horses don't chew cud, they just chew their food thoroughly. If you were a rancher, that would be music to your ears."

The second day took us up the awesome Fraser River canyon with its water raging through Hell's Gate; the road high above it, blasted out of sheer rock. I thought of the prospectors who had traveled this treacherous route in the goldrush days and wondered why the unknown was a challenge to some and a threat to others.

At Lytton the highway turned to take us over into the arid lands of the Thompson River, so different from the fresh green fields we had driven through the day before. We were held up for two hours in the dusty sunshine while the road was being rebuilt with antiquated machinery; but by late afternoon we reached Williams Lake, a cow town where we bought gas and inquired about the road to Anahim Lake. The attendant could tell us about

18

it as far as Tatla Lake, about two-thirds of the way to Anahim, but from there he was mercifully vague.

It was not far from Williams Lake to the Fraser. The air was warm and filled with the aromatic fragrance of the sun on sage brush which dotted the hillside near the bridge. We had to wait until a herd of cattle was brought across the swaying suspension bridge, a few animals at a time, to reduce the vibrations of too many hooves. There were corrals at the other end to hold the cattle and we could see the cowboys working in the dust, slapping their rein-ends against their leather chaps and shouting with voices hoarse from days on the trail.

We sat in the quiet September sunshine, its peacefulness accented by the sounds of the cattle crossing the bridge, muted by the murmur of the river. All around us the undulating sidehills flowed steeply to the river, covered with dry autumn grass interspersed by dark evergreens which lined the timeworn gullies. Here and there a dark green conifer escaped its gully and stood in splendid isolation, casting a long afternoon shadow on the

19

golden grass. This was the beginning of the unforgettable beauty of the Chilcotin, and some of its tranquility seeped into our souls. The city tensions were beginning to melt away.

After the cattle had crossed the bridge and been herded together they passed us in a cloud of dust on the last lap of their journey to the stockyards in Williams Lake. We ventured out onto the bridge ourselves and actually felt it sway and vibrate as we drove cautiously across. On the other side we climbed the long, steep Sheep Creek Hill and found a delightful spot off the road near a creek where we could spend the night. This time I slept soundly.

All the following day we drove through picturesque rolling range, covered with bleached grass and accented by black snake fences along the winding dirt road. Occasionally there were little islands of trees and unexpected lakes which reflected the blue sky, their margins filled with reeds and water lilies.

We passed through several small settlements, each with a combined store and post office; a church and a school, surrounded by outlying ranches. Most of the buildings were made of logs and some of the cabins had window boxes filled with flowers and there were vines trailing over the doors. It was an enticing country at this time of year but we heard it was bitterly cold during the winter.

It was evening by the time we reached Tatla Lake and a September mist rose from the lake with the tops of golden birches floating above it. I thought of the words of a lovely Scottish song, "The mist is in the gloaming." We turned off the motor. From somewhere on the lake a loon called, then a coyote howled. Two haunting sounds that left me quivering.

It was late and we were tired, so to save time we looked for a place to sleep without having to pitch the tent. There was a small, partially-finished log structure with walls and a roof which looked sturdy enough to keep out wild beasts and I pleaded with Earle to put our beds in there. He looked at me in horror and said, "We'd never live it down! That is going to be a two-seater outhouse for the log school over there.

The door and fixtures haven't been put in yet."

There was a depth to Earle's knowledge which surprised me more than once in the days to come.

There were no other travelers on the winding road the next day until we neared Kleena Kleene, where we met Sam Colwell, the telegraph operator who had a relay station. He stopped his car to chat and we enquired about the road ahead. Looking at our bulging load, he shook his head and long after we had said good-bye I could see him in the rear-view mirror, leaning out of his car window, still shaking his head and calling, "Take it easy! Just take it easy!"

The road wound among trees and boulders. Anything calculated not to rip out an oil pan had been left where it was. Toward evening there were so many rabbits on the road it was hard to distinguish them from rocks and the effect was that of ancient cobblestones suddenly starting to hop.

There seemed no end to the jack pines and boulders, but by nightfall we came to the place marked on the map as

Towdistan, a single log cabin whose owner was away. The place had an air of indescribable loneliness. The side of the house facing the road had a door in the center, flanked on either side by a small window, and over one window the sod roof had come loose from its moorings, dropping down over one eye with a dissolute expression.

The unadorned aspect of the cabins seemed cheerless at first but before long I grew accustomed to their lack of color and began to associate the weather-beaten look with warm hospitality.

But the cabin at Towdistan was empty and we camped by a creek that night, building a blazing fire to keep out the cold and loneliness. The elevation at Towdistan is four thousand feet and though the day had been hot, the night was freezing and there was ice on our water pail in the morning.

We were near the end of the useable car road and very soon we were going to have to find a place where we could store the car for the winter. This seemed the point of no return. This is where we would sever the ties that bound us to our familiar world and I was obsessed by a gnawing fear of the unknown that lay ahead of us.

We also had to find someone with horses to take us over the trail from Anahim Lake, down into the Bella Coola Valley where we could cache our belongings at the Stillwater cabin. From there we would have to make our way on foot to Lonesome Lake and Ralph.

Here at Towdistan we could see a telephone line going from the pole at the road to the cabin and assumed there was a telephone inside, and we desperately needed to use one. The cabin was locked but Earle thought if we left a note explaining our plight, it might be all right if he boosted me up and in through a small, partly-opened window so we could use the phone.

The goose-neck, crank-operated telephone on the wall had a list of users between Anahim and Tatla Lake. There weren't many and their rings were listed beside the names in a variety of dot and dash arrangements.

We rang everyone in the Anahim area to enquire about horses but there was no one who wasn't busy putting up hay in the last of the fine weather. Every horse was in harness, pulling either a mower, rake or slip. We were going to have to walk. But, there was one other suggestion. Due west of us was a sleigh road into Charlotte Lake, and a rancher there by the name of George Powers was said to have a boat with an outboard motor. If we could manage to get our car over that road, where no car had ever been before, we might be able to hire Powers to take us down the lake. From there we could hike down the East Fork, then down the Atnarko to Ralph's place. Earle voted to try the Charlotte Lake route. We had just enough gas to get us in to the Powers's ranch but not back out again.

The trees on the sleigh road must have been cut in winter when there was about a foot of snow on the ground. It was probably smooth for a sleigh or a high-wheeled wagon but it was almost impassable for a car with a low clearance. We wove our way among stumps, chopped some and put the wheel over others. It took the whole day to make fifteen miles. We spent part of the time in a spring hole where we had to cut jack pines and pry each wheel into the air to put logs under it, making a sort of corduroy road before we were back on dry land again. It was evening by the time we approached the lake and the first glimpse of it through the jack pines was like a light in a window.

The wagon tracks we were following crossed a sandy beach at the head of the lake and went through a tiny creek into which we eased the car and became well and truly stuck. It was too late to do anything but unpack and make camp. By now we were out of gasoline for the camp stove, so I was going to have to cook our meals over a campfire. I still remember the sadness I felt watching my shiny utensils turn black, and I only hope Earle felt the same way about my once-polished fingernails, most of which were now swathed in bandages.

Problems always seem a disaster to me but to Earle they are a stimulating challenge. However, this time it looked as though we were going to need help to extricate the car and in the morning we planned to hike to the Powers's ranch and try to get someone to pull us out with a team.

Charlotte Lake is a large, pear-shaped lake, about fifteen miles long and five miles across in the widest place, lying in the heart of uninhabited country. The Powers's ranch was the only one between Towdistan and Ralph's place, a distance of more than fifty miles.

Just as we were finishing breakfast the next morning, we looked up to see a horse and rider emerging from the trees on the wagon road from Towdistan. We greeted him and he introduced himself as Eddie Collett, George's partner, coming home to check on their ranch before returning to finish the haying. He told us there was no one at the ranch, nor any gas, nor any boat either. My heart sank.

"Looks like you're stuck there," he observed, "I'll give you a hand."

Taking his lariat, he attached one end to the car and the other to his saddle horn. With Earle using the motor, the noise added impetus to the horse, and we were soon out of the sand.

It was not far to the ranch and Collett told us we were welcome to leave the car there and we spent the morning preparing to leave it for the winter.

Back at camp Earle announced, "There's only one thing we can do. We'll go down the lake on a raft. We can cache our things at the foot of the lake and hike on down the Eastfork to Ralph's. I'll get horses and come back over Mt. Kappan with them."

I looked at the lake. It seemed so vast. But Earle was already on his way with the axe to a grove of dead jack pines nearby. He chose five tall, straight trees that were uniform in size to fell onto the sandy ground where we could drag them to the water.

Cutting the logs about thirty-five feet long, he notched them for cross-ties. We had no nails, but ample rope to lash the raft together, hoping the rope would tighten when it was wet and hold the logs snugly together. Earle was going to make a sail out of the huge tarpaulin we bought to protect the car from the sun when we were camping in the desert the winter before. It was large enough to cover the car completely, right to the ground. Fortunately it had grommet holes all around the edge so it could be tied to a crossbar which Earle made of a twelve-foot, dry jack pine pole. A mast had to be made, but before it was raised and guyed to the raft, Earle fixed a loop of stout rope to the tip through which a rope could be pulled to hoist the sail.

At the end of the second day all was ready. We noticed there was a light, off-shore breeze in the evening and thought we should take advantage of it so we quickly broke camp and carried everything to the raft. Earle loaded the things securely aft of the mast which was about a third of the way back from the bow. There must have been six hundred pounds of freight and our combined weight added at least two hundred and fifty pounds more.

It was dark before we were finished but we made a bonfire at the edge of the water to give us light to see by. Earle stood on the stern with the steering oar and I sat in the empty space in front of him. My job was to manipulate the sail when directed by the skipper. Pulling up the sail with the rope, Earle fastened it as the gentle breeze filled the canvas, and it took only a light push with the pole to pry the raft from the shore. We were away! The raft began gliding down the lake; this was better than walking!

All went well for about half a mile when we noticed water lapping over the logs. We were sinking! It was not far to shore but before we could beach the raft, many of our belongings were wet, mostly the bedding. Despite the huge fire we built to dry things out, I woke in the morning to find my pillow had frozen, leaving a thawed hole where my head had rested.

The following day we discovered the cause of our trouble. Under the bark of the jack pine logs were myriads of wormholes which had acted as a sponge and quickly filled with water under pressure of the load. There were dry jack pines available everywhere and Earle soon had two more logs added to the raft to increase its buoyancy. This time there was no need to wait until evening for the offshore wind, for we discovered it had been only a draft coming from the stream and had died about the time we started to sink.

It was the middle of the next day before we were loaded and ready to set sail once more. There was a light breeze blowing in the right direction and confidently we pushed off from shore. The full sail billowed and the heavy raft began to move slowly at first, and then with accelerating speed. Before we knew it we were in the middle of the lake, when suddenly a strong gust of wind caught us and the nose of the raft ploughed under.

"Grab that sail!" Earle yelled.

No sailor ever leapt into the rigging faster than I climbed over the duffle piled around the mast. I gathered the tarpaulin in my arms while Earle backed as far to the stern as he could. In another moment we would have been standing on end in the widest part of Charlotte Lake.

I clung to the sail for dear life to keep the wind from filling it again and slowly the nose of the raft stopped its plunge, but it seemed to take forever before it started coming back to the surface.

Terrified, I was beyond reason and

begged Earle to go to shore, which was probably the worst thing we could do for Charlotte Lake was about five miles wide where we were and the only shore we could go to was a wind-swept bay. The waves caught us broadside as they broke on boulders the size of a kitchen stove and we were soon in danger of breaking up.

We were safe from drowning, but the only way to save the raft from disintegrating was to keep it away from the boulders. It was impossible to use the sail and we had only one pole, so I was going to have to go ashore and tow the raft with a long rope attached to the bow while Earle kept it off the rocks with the pole.

It was hazardous getting from the bouncing raft onto the slippery rocks but I made it, falling in once, just to the waist. Then, leaping and sliding, I tugged on the towline and we began to move. For what seemed an eternity, we pulled and poled. I began to feel I was doing penance, but at last we were around the point at the end of the bay, out of the waves and the wind which by then had died down as suddenly as they came.

We were still too distraught to talk and from there to the foot of the lake we sailed in idyllic tranquility, with only a gentle movement of air which kept the sail filled. We seemed more to be standing still while the mountains and trees glided past. The only sound was the lonely call from a loon far away. The deep blue of the sky and the gold of the autumn leaves were reflected in the lake and a September silence enveloped us. After such a perilous beginning, the serene ending to our voyage down the lake was a soothing balm. It ended all too soon.

Charlotte Lake pours down a swift chute through rocky walls to a little gem of a lake below and then on to another small lake which empties into the turbulent Eastfork, then into the Atnarko, which flows into Lonesome Lake. The chute was much too swift to try to navigate so we moored the raft nearby and unloaded our belongings, carrying them to a perfect campsite with a view of both lakes, the one over which we had just come and the jewel that lay below us. We sat in the deep, dry moss for a long time and stored the beauty in our memory. As far as we knew the little lake had no name and Earle suggested we call it Lake Isabel. We still do, to ourselves, but we never did anything about it.

We dismantled the raft that evening to save the ropes, then put up the tent so we could sleep in it. Drifting off to sleep after a long day, a thought crept into my mind — scarcely a week away from home and already the car had been stolen and we had almost been drowned. What else could happen? Well, there were still bears and blizzards. But I settled into a sound sleep in the deep, soft moss, lulled by the sound of flowing water.

In the morning we stored our belongings in the tent before starting out on foot for Lonesome Lake. Earle estimated it to be about twenty miles and thought we could make it in a day, although there were no trails and in places he said we would very likely have to cut footlogs and cross back and forth over the creek which had carved its way through high bluffs. Earle had made the trip several years before when he trapped in this country, so he had some idea of what we were going to run into.

Tying the flaps of the tent, Earle shouldered the packsack which had spare socks and enough food for a couple of days, then picked up the rifle and axe, and we were on our way.

The first trial came after we had been hiking for a few miles through park-like jack pines, following the creek. We came to an old burn where the dead trees had fallen in a dense network of knee-high criss-crossed poles. There was no way through, under, or around them so we had to walk on top. It was September and dry and they were slippery; and so were my boots. Earle hadn't been able to put the caulks in them and with the stiff leather soles, I skated off of every log, bruising my shins and almost weeping in frustration. The exertion warmed me so much in the growing heat of the sun that finally I had to take off the heavy pants and shirt that I had found so comforting in the early morning frost and continue in the woolen longjohns.

Unaccustomed to wool my skin began to itch and I felt an acute distaste for the hideous garment. Earle had been so proud of getting something to keep me warm in the winter, how could I tell him I loathed the things? They were heavy and confining and too warm.

We stopped to rest for a moment and Earle must have noticed the distress on my face. "You all right?" he asked.

"Oh fine," I panted. "It's just that I itch all over. I'm a bit too warm. These things aren't very feminine, are they?"

"You'll get used to them," he answered cheerfully, "And you can sew some ruffles on them, or something, when we get there."

There seemed no end to the fallen trees, but finally we did come to the other side where we decided to have a rest and some lunch. Earle mixed some powdered milk with water from the creek and this was all I wanted. The rest of the afternoon we followed the Eastfork, at times climbing over logs, at others crossing the stream on a footlog to the other side to avoid a bluff. This was a new experience for me and no matter how often Earle demonstrated how easy it was to stand upright and walk a footlog with assurance, the only way I ever made it was by crawling on my hands and knees, with my excess clothing tied around my waist and hanging down my back. Invariably, in the middle of the footlog, I would look at the turbulent water below and feel the need to lie flat on the log and wrap my arms around it until the panic passed. The only time I tried to walk upright I fell into the water which fortunately wasn't deep just there. Looking back on it, it seems remarkable that Earle didn't hold me under instead of pulling me out.

Once, after he had helped me across still another footlog, I wanted to make amends and offered to carry part of the load for him. He let me have the axe and I hadn't had it five minutes before I split my knee open. Having no bandages, it made a sticky mess, with the woolen underwear keeping the wound from closing.

By evening we weren't half way to Ralph's and there were beginning to be signs of bears. There were no salmon spawning in the Eastfork for them to feed on but after gorging on fish in the Atnarko, I suppose the bears liked to take little side trips up the Eastfork looking for berries. At any rate, Earle thought it safer to camp on an island, so he felled a footlog onto one that was large enough to have trees for a fire and evergreen boughs for a bed. I was too tired to want food and what little I did try to eat didn't stay down. Earle made a roaring fire and a comfortable bed in front of it but I had been properly trained to be careful with matches in the woods and all I could think about was the hazard of a forest fire. I spent the night going back and forth between the creek and the fire with a cup, getting water to keep things under control. Earle slept soundly.

By noon the next day we reached the junction of the Eastfork and the Atnarko where one could begin to smell the rotting fish. The riverbank was littered with the remains of dead salmon, many with just the throats bitten out of them, thrown there by the bears. They must have heard us coming, or smelled us, since there were no bears in sight but we could hear them in the brush not far away. Oddly enough, I felt no fear whatever but Earle was aware of the danger and checked his gun. I begged him not to shoot any bears as I wanted to get to Ralph's and soak my blistered feet and go to bed.

It was growing dusk and starting to rain when we reached The Birches.

3

The Birches

THE Birches. A little world of its own in the midst of a vast wilderness. A mile to one side or the other and we could have passed it by without knowing it was there.

We had been following a trail that must have been used by bears since fish began spawning in this river. Then came the first evidence of man's habitation; an axe mark, a tree felled with a saw, cow droppings, then the haunting fragrance of woodsmoke, then a fence and a clearing, a barn and a cabin, a cow bell and children's voices, and we were there.

Sixty miles from the nearest settlement, completely isolated, without radio or telephone, this family lived in contentment with what they had, which by our standards was all too meager.

Ralph had left that morning for Atnarko, more than twenty miles away, to get the mail and see if there was any word of us. I had never met my brother-in-law or his family, but Ethel made us warmly welcome and almost the first thing she did was give me a basin of hot water for my tortured feet.

After a welcome supper, she took bedding out to the barn where we made a bed in the fragrant hay and when night came we were glad to crawl into it. Sleep came swiftly and nothing could have disturbed it.

In the morning Earle was full of the excitement of being back again and restless to see Ralph. He decided to hike around the lake and intercept him somewhere, probably at the Stillwater. This is where they did meet, to Ralph's amazement, and while they sat talking on a log, Earle couldn't resist demonstrating his prowess with the rifle he had brought in. He took the head off a goose that was swimming in the reeds about fifty yards away. Ethel roasted it for dinner that evening.

The beautiful home which Ralph had built his heart into had burned to the ground in the autumn just a few years before. Trudy, a baby then, was four when we arrived, John six, and Stanley eight. After the fire they had taken refuge in the small trapping cabin Ralph made when he first came to Lonesome Lake. It was only big enough for one but they crowded in and Ethel managed to cook over the stone fireplace in the corner until Ralph had time to put up the present cabin. This was a log structure with a spacious roof which they intended only for a temporary home but they had grown attached to the site and remained there.

While we were there Ethel slept in the house and Trudy slept in a crib on the porch, summer and winter. The boys slept in the hay and Ralph had a bunk in his workshop. We continued to sleep in the barn until Earle was able to take two of Ralph's horses and pack in our belongings over the mountain on an old Indian trail.

There is an adage in this country: never borrow a man's horses, his dog, his gun or his wife. We broke the first rule immediately. Ralph let Earle have Ginty, his faithful partner, and Ethel let him have her pet mare, Queenie.

The weather held fine, although the higher peaks were white with fresh snow and Ralph thought there might be some for the horses to go through but it wouldn't be deep yet. It was a steep climb for them, going up Mt. Kappan, but once on top it was open going and soon they were into a couple of inches of powdery snow. Crossing one smooth patch the mare suddenly caught her hind foot in a wedge-shaped crack in what turned out to be a large, flat rock. She seemed unable to release herself and Earle tried to help but in her distress she kicked at him with the other foot and even bit him. Finally, she did manage to extricate the imprisoned foot but the tissue was torn and obviously painful, as she wouldn't use it at all. In this open place there was a scant amount of feed showing through the snow but in her condition there seemed only one thing Earle could do, leave her until the leg had healed sufficiently for her to get home. He went on alone and brought back a pack load with Ginty.

Earle led him among the trees and once when they emerged into an open space, they surprised a huge bull moose with an enormous set of antlers, about fifty yards away. It began shaking its head and acting belligerent. Earle had no rifle and wasn't anxious to get into a mix-up between a moose and a horse so he led Ginty quietly behind a large rock and kept out of sight until he was well away from the moose.

Everyone at The Birches was distressed to hear about their injured pet. This didn't ease our own discomfort, but after resting Ginty for a day, Earle returned for the remainder of the things. As he approached the open space where he had left the mare, Ginty whinnied and out of the brush on the far side of the clearing trotted Queenie, breaking into a gallop and whinnying back, apparently recovered from her injury and happy not to be alone any more.

She wasn't the only happy one. There was great rejoicing when they returned to the farm. Ralph was going to have to use the horses during the next month for packing in the yearly supplies and having a lame horse would have upset his plans.

The children were fascinated by the pack Earle unloaded in the woodshed. They were unaccustomed to visitors, as the only outsiders who came to The Birches were occasional bear hunters and the inspector of spawning grounds from the Department of Fisheries, whom Ralph escorted from the end of the road to the head of the river and back each autumn.

The children were not shy but quiet and reserved. They didn't play organized games the way children do who attend school, but were small adults in their activities. They had a curiosity about us and the things we brought in and the day Earle came back with the first load from Charlotte Lake was a red-letter day for them. They discovered the box of toiletries and used the lipstick and tooth paste to make decorations. The hair brush was used to scoop out a jar of cold cream. They weren't being willfully destructive, I tried to tell myself as I washed the greasy mess out of the brush, they were just trying out new materials in an imaginative way. But it tried my patience when Stanley, who loved hiding things, cached our supply of first aid equipment and medicines, then wouldn't tell us where they were.

One day, when my feet were healed, the boys took me to visit their trapline. On the way we had to stop and see everything of interest in this private world of theirs; the eagle's nest, the squirrel cache of coneflowers and the intricate engineering projects of Stanley's, scattered along the way. Coming back, in exchange for their courtesy, I tried to teach them about marching in time to music which I whistled while waving an imaginary baton and stepping high like a drum major. I have never been made to feel more foolish by the silent looks of children. Life was real and earnest for them and hiking with trail-covering strides was something they could understand. Learning to march in step with others seemed unnecessary and senseless.

There was a similar reaction when Earle produced the comic books we had brought in for them. City children seemed to like colored comics but here they drew only empty stares. In the evenings, six-year-old John read Dickens aloud to the other two who listened with rapt attention. He needed only occasional help with pronunciation.

In this northern latitude winter dusk came at four o'clock and the evening meal was eaten in the light of one small candle set in the middle of the table. This may have been because there was a shortage of coal-oil until the supplies were brought in, but the hours of reading were limited and bedtime came early.

The dark, unpainted walls of the hewn logs absorbed the light, so Earle and I were pleased we had brought in a carton of white, powdered casien paint, somewhat like calcimine or whitewash. Mixed with water it went a long way and we put two coats of it on the kitchen and dining area of the cabin, with amazing results; everything seemed much brighter in the light from the solitary candle.

Now that the supplies were down from Charlotte Lake we were able to put up the tent, which we enlarged with the tarpaulin. Earle began to work on the heater which he made from his own design with the roll of eight by four, twenty-gauge sheet metal which we brought in, riveting the parts together with cut nails. It made an excellent, oval-shaped air-tight heater with a hinged lid and a spark-proof damper in front. The fire was easily controlled and we were comfortable all winter in the tent. Later it was used for years in a cabin.

By the time the heater was made and our sleeping quarters arranged, Queenie's leg had healed completely and Ralph was ready to begin his yearly freight packing. This was a rough, arduous trip, taking the horses through the woods to the lake and swimming them across the narrows because of rock-slides and bluffs farther on. Then Ralph had to continue on down the other side of the lake to where the trail through the Valley of the Shadow began.

From the foot of the lake to the end of the road at Belarko, each round trip with the three horses would take five days. Barring mishaps, the freighting would take three or four weeks to complete.

While Ralph was gone Earle was busy cutting and splitting wood for Ralph's cookstove and heater, as well as some for our own, stacking it in the woodshed attached to the house. Ethel was occupied from morning until bedtime with household duties and outside chores. There were cows to milk and stock to be fed in addition to the feeding of mink, which was a new project on the farm.

Ralph had built about twenty pens of sturdy, fine-mesh wire and had caught wild mink in special cage traps. He brought the mink in from the trapline in the box traps and in transferring them to the pen he would reach into the trap and grasp the mink swiftly by the back of the neck with his bare hand, then lift it gently into the pen. Once, his timing was out and he was soundly bitten in the thumb by the mink. He said it felt like red-hot needles being driven into his hand.

The experiment of raising mink in captivity was succeeding but it entailed a great deal of work. Each evening Ethel had to scrub vegetables and grind them in a hand-operated meat grinder, as well as fresh meat when they had it, or canned meat when they hadn't. They also saved all the bones from their butchering and meat canning operations, grinding them in a hand-operated bone grinder that made them into bonemeal, an important ingredient in the mink diet. Sometimes it would be dark before Ethel would go out with the lantern to feed the mink, laden with a huge dishpan full of correctly balanced feed for them.

Looking back over the years, I seem unable to remember being much of a help in this busy household. Born in a small English town and brought up in gentle Victoria, B.C., the closest I ever came to a farm was in the bedtime stories my mother read to her five children as each grew old enough to sit by the fireside and listen. Farming in the books was a sentimental gathering of eggs in a basket or riding on a pony.

Even after Earle and I were married and had gone to Portland to live there were still no farms in my life. Nothing in my upbringing had trained me for life on a farm, and day after day I was more of a hazard than a help. I couldn't be trusted with sharp knives or axes because I would cut myself, and a rope in my hands could have been lethal to livestock. It was years before Earle finally could trust me to make a bowline instead of a slip knot.

I couldn't milk a cow, and even the strong laundry bar soap peeled the skin from my hands. However, before the winter was over, I did have an opportunity to demonstrate one accomplishment. I could swim well, and clad in an improvised bathing suit, one bright January day I dove off a thick block of river ice into the frigid water and swam a little before climbing out and running barefoot in the snow, across the fields to the warm tent. Not many people this far north learned to swim where the water is cold, even in summer, and mosquitoes are an additional deterrent. So I suppose this bit of exhibitionism was balm for my ego.

To our surprise, Ralph returned from the packing trip after just a few days. The boys heard him coming and raced to the house yelling to Ethel, "Daddy's coming! Daddy's coming with the horses!"

Ethel's face grew tense with concern. Nothing short of disaster would turn Ralph back from his task. Wiping her hands on her apron, she and the children ran to meet him.

"Are you all right?" she called. "What's wrong?"

"They've had some heavy rains down the valley and a bridge washed out! They couldn't haul our freight until a new one is built."

"But we are nearly out of supplies. What will we do?" Ethel asked.

"I managed to borrow some flour and sugar and candles at Atnarko," Ralph replied. "Enough to keep us going until the lake freezes hard enough to take the horses across it — maybe in February."

Turning to Earle, he inquired, "How would you and Isabel like to do the packing for us then?"

The weather turned cool and Ralph thought there was time to butcher the bull and can the meat in glass sealers before he left to begin trapping. Preparations were made to do the butchering one morning and the animal was penned but not fed his evening meal. This seemed inhumane to me but Ralph explained it was to prevent excess gas forming from undigested food, making it difficult to remove the bloated paunch from the carcass.

Women and children were banished from the scene. In a harsh land where survival depended on the taking of life, Ralph protected his children as much as possible from witnessing the death of domestic stock. But there seemed no sensitivity about messing around in the gore after the animal was dead. The children ate the cooked liver and heart as soon as the meat was chilled and Stanley, who had been admonished not to poke a hole in the bloated stomach, escaped from the dinner table with a knife and made a generous slash in the distended paunch. It must have been satisfying to him to hear the gas escaping, but in the house not too far downwind, we became all too aware of the offensive odor.

In the background of all this farming activity were the trumpeter swans. In October they were beginning to come back from their summer in the north, returning to their winter feeding grounds in the open water at the head of Lonesome Lake, as well as the adjacent Stillwater. Wheeling out of the sky and calling in melodious harmony, they returned each year as the lakes in their nesting grounds to the north began to freeze. It was a thrilling experience to see them.

Settling in the shallow waters of the lagoon opposite the farm clearings, they were where Ralph was able to keep watch over the little flock, and long before he persuaded the Canadian Government to help save them from extinction, he was buying barley for them and packing it in with his own supplies.

It was 1925 before the Canadian Wildlife Service became aware, through Ralph, of this small band of almost extinct trumpeter swans and when it was learned that Ralph was buying feed with his own money and packing it in at his own expense, they finally authorized him to spend twenty-five dollars a year for feed if he would continue to pack it in without charge. 1932 was the first year of this program and Earle and I were going to pack up the barley with the other supplies from the end of the road with Ginty, Queenie and Old Blue in February.

The grain was to be used when the weather became extremely cold and the birds were unable to obtain their natural feed of roots and minute crustaceons which they found when they tipped up and reached down into the water with their long necks. They also fed on a fern-like moss that grew under water in the open water holes at the upper end of each of the string of lakes on the Atnarko River. In a moderate winter there was enough natural feed in this area to support a small flock but in severe weather there were losses, and this is when Ralph fed the grain. He was so successful in increasing their numbers, the government eventually appointed him Keeper of the Swans, giving him a moderate stipend and paying for an increased amount of feed and the packing of it.

The swans were shy of anyone except Ralph and even he had always to be careful to wear the same clothing or they became alarmed and stayed away. No one else was allowed to go near them while they were feeding, or to make a noise in that area. The preservation of these magnificent birds was a dominant theme in the winter lives of this family.

Earle told me of an experience he had in saving a swan during the early part of the First World War when he was the telegraph lineman and operator stationed at Mosher Creek about halfway between Atnarko and the end of the road. It was early spring and he had an urgent message for Frank Ratcliff who was trapping at the Stillwater. Taking his horse, Dan, Earle rode up to find Frank. The message requested that he come down the valley immediately, but before Frank could leave he would have to pull up all his traps, so Earle decided to stay over a day and help him.

When they were returning from the end of Frank's line near Lonesome Lake they saw a swan swimming all alone in a pool among some logs, apparently unable to get out. The water was about fifteen feet deep and the area between the logs was probably about thirty by twenty feet, with the surrounding barrier high enough so the bird had no room to make a run and become air-borne. It would be impossible for it to climb out over the logs to escape. Earle found it hard to imagine how it got there in the first place but very likely it had been weak and might have been attacked by an eagle, dropping into the pool in its fright.

Earle and Frank went over to see the emaciated bird. There was no available food within the pool and it was obvious that it would starve to death if left there. Earle decided to rescue it and take it home with him on the horse. Fortunately he was wearing caulks in his boots and could run on the logs, but the swan darted from side to side of the pool as Earle tried to catch it. Finally, with all his clothes on, Earle took a run and jumped as far as he could, catching the swan in his arms as he landed in the water and went under. With one arm around the swan, he swam to the logs where Frank helped him to get out. A mature swan has a wing spread of eight feet and weighs as much as thirty-five pounds, but this one was weak and light and offered very little resistance.

Frank rowed the boat down the Stillwater to the cabin while Earle held the bird in his arms. At the cabin he tied the swan in a large gunnysack with its head and long neck sticking out, then getting his horse from the meadow, Earle saddled it and stuffed two sacks with loose hay to make a soft bed for the swan to ride on. Dan was curious about the long white neck that kept waving about on the saddle but he was not excited and the swan was quiet and gentle and made no outcries. Earle led the horse down the twenty miles of trail to his cabin at Mosher Creek.

There was a slow-moving spring creek flowing through the woods on Earle's place and he hurriedly fenced the creek and part of the woods with wire mesh he had bought for a chicken run, giving the swan a pool of running water about two hundred feet long. Both sides of the stream were rough with logs and brush so there was little danger of the bird trying to escape by land.

Earle had no idea what to feed it. He knew what their natural food was, but since he had none he broke up some fresh cabbage and sprinkled it with oats and wheat, then left the bird alone.

In the morning the food was gone. Each day Earle increased the amount of feed and each morning it had disappeared. The swan began to grow stronger and was swimming more vigorously. At the end of ten days Earle was thinking of turning it loose when one morning he heard a family of wild ones bugling overhead. Running out, he saw them flying over the pen so he raced to pull the posts from the mud and take away the wire on the downstream end of the pen. Then he herded the swan quietly down the stream to the river, about one hundred feet away. There he left it to join the others. With a strong current and a brisk west wind, the bird had perfect conditions for a takeoff. Earle never saw it again.

4

Christmas

THE trapping season had begun. Ralph was gone for days at a time, hurrying away with his fast walk, carrying a heavy pack on his back. When he returned there were furs to be skinned and stretched then hung to dry in the cabin which began to have a musty, wild-animal smell. Furs were his only reliable source of revenue, but with the country still in the midst of the depression he felt fortunate to have even this meager income.

Christmas was approaching and we had our first gentle snowfall. It gave quietness to the land and everyone seemed happy, except me. Ever since the lake began freezing and became impassable I was haunted by the feeling of being cut off from the world. Now the snow emphasized it still more, and no matter how much Earle told me what a friend the snow was and how it was a blanket to the land, I didn't believe him. I hated it. To help cure me of my phobia, he encouraged me to go walking in the gently falling flakes, but it didn't work. It just made my feet cold.

There wouldn't be any Christmas mail until after the lake froze hard in January and we were able to go down with horses to pack in mail and freight. Ethel was getting short of supplies so there wouldn't be any Christmas baking.

The children had never had a festive Christmas. There was nothing to set this day apart from any other, no Christmas music, no decorated Christmas trees, no colored lights, none of the things I had always associated with the festive season.

Except for the date on the calendar no one was aware that it was Christmas, but because we were there it was decided to have a tree and presents. This was to be a surprise for the children.

Ethel bleached some flour sacks and then dyed them, making a quilt for Trudy, embroidering a design with colored wool that she had stored away, and I helped renovate an ancient teddy bear. Earle made a sled and some wooden guns for the children and Ralph spent his evenings making moccasin boots and leather mittens for the three of them from hides he had tanned with hemlock bark. All these preparations had to be done at night when the children were in bed.

On Christmas Eve Ralph brought in the Christmas tree and stood it in one corner of the cabin. Earle cut a star for the top from an empty tomato tin and we made a paper chain from colored strips cut from advertising letters sent out each fall from fur buyers; it looked cheerful wound around the tree. Ethel even found a little tin foil and colored bits of wool and a few Christmas cards, saved since their other house burned down. We even squandered some absorbent cotton from the first aid kit to make tufts of artificial snow.

In this country nothing was ever wasted and Ethel had a small hoard of brown paper which we pressed with the heavy flat-iron to use for wrapping the gifts. We wrote little verses on gift cards made from writing paper and decorated them with crayons. Bits of colored yarn made marvelous wrapping twine and could be saved to be used afterwards for darning socks.

There was quite an impressive pile of gifts at the foot of the tree before we pinned a sheet across the corner in front of it. Ethel wound the portable record player and placed a Christmas carol on it, ready to play in the morning.

Everyone was up as usual with daylight the next day. The children were curious about the sheet stretched across the corner and kept wanting to peek but Ethel kept them away from it. They had to wash and brush their hair before breakfast and when we were all seated around the table, Ralph asked the blessing, which he did before every meal.

When the bowls of porridge and milk were finished, Ethel started to play the Christmas carol, then dropped the sheet which hid the tree. The children were speechless. They stood there in bewilderment, not knowing what to do, and darted glances at their parents for some clue to this new experience.

They made no effort to go near the tree until Ethel spoke to them, "Those are Christmas presents. Bring one over to the table and we'll read the card."

The two younger children moved slowly toward the tree but it was a long time before Stanley could be urged to pick up one of the gifts and bring it to the table so the tag could be read. He did it slowly and cautiously as though this strange behavior were some sort of hoax. I felt a lump in my throat and my eyes began to sting.

Ethel had made me a bag for my knitting from the same dyed flour-sacking as Trudy's quilt and Ralph had made Earle a leather case for the round pocket whetstone all men carried in their pockets in this country. Everyone received something that someone else had made and each parcel was opened slowly and carefully.

When we were finished, Ethel folded all the wrappings and saved the scraps of colored yarn. The children took their guns and sled outside while they helped Ralph feed the animals, taking carrots as a special treat for the cattle and horses.

There were the usual chores to be done and the animals to care for but there were no best clothes to get dressed up in, no church bells, no radio music, no colored lights, no turkey and plum pudding. But after supper, Ralph read Dickens' *Christmas Carol* aloud.

Lying in bed that night, with the moonlight outside on the silent snow, I thought about the children and what this day had meant to them. Had they been confused by the tree and the unexpected presents? Did Christmas fit into their lives? I didn't know the answers but I needn't have worried. The children were capable of rejecting whatever had no place in their scheme of things. They would sort things out for themselves.

In many ways the winter solstice was more significant to this family than

Christmas. It marked the beginning of longer days, and in a land where winter was five months long it already seemed to have been winter for the full span of its tenure. In reality, the coldest days were still to come when they began to lengthen with the returning sun. Each day of the year was carefully crossed off on their calendar so there would be no confusion about the date. This was important only because of going down for the mail and arriving at Atnarko on the same day as the mail carrier on his bi-weekly packhorse trip.

As the days grew shorter toward the solstice and the hours of sunlight even less among the high mountains, there was a growing anticipation of December twenty-first, knowing that soon after, the days would begin to lengthen. They quoted the old saying, "As the days begin to lengthen, the cold begins to strengthen." The days were colder in January, which means the ice on the lake was getting thicker and safer for travel.

One of the loveliest things in the sub-zero weather was the pattern of minute hoarfrost feathers that grew on the surface of the snow in the windless shelter of the homesite. They grew singly as well as in corsage-like clusters, sparkling like jewels in the noonday sun and shattering like glass when touched. Even the cabin windows had frost ferns on the inside in the mornings before the warmth of the fires melted them or the children scraped them off. Sheltered from the wind that sometimes roared on the river, the hoarfrost and snow remained for a long time on the bushes and trees in the still, cold air by the house and creek, and the ugly scars of man's habitation were transformed into beauty.

We were busy stoking fires and keeping warm after Christmas. The children spent most of their mornings at lessons on one end of the kitchen table. The boys were learning by correspondence through the Department of Education and could go at their own pace. Ralph was also building up his library again after the disastrous fire, spending more money than he could afford on books for both the children and Ethel and himself.

He was making shorter trips on his

trapline now that the weather was so cold. One pleasant day he asked Earle if he would like to go down the lake and tend the traps for him while he went up the line. I was delighted when Earle asked me if I would care to go too. This would be my first trip away from the farm since we arrived; my little world had been confined to the narrow paths in the snow within the clearings.

Halfway down the frozen lake we were startled by a sudden loud report like a rifle shot close by, and then the ice seemed to heave beneath our feet. Alarmed, I dropped to my knees and Earle laughed, "Don't be frightened. It's all right. It's just the ice expanding. You should have been with me the first time I heard the ice groan and pop."

A crack had appeared not far from us, all across the ice which was eighteen inches thick by then. We were completely safe but I was convinced the ice would open up and swallow us.

Helping me to my feet, Earle told me about the first time he had come up the lake after it had frozen. Having no horses then, he had been backpacking supplies from the end of the road, making a cache in a small supply cabin at the foot of the lake until he had a sled load which he could drag up on the ice. On the last trip up from the Stillwater, it was late and he decided to stay for the night in the little shelter along with the supplies. There was no door or any way to warm himself inside the tiny cabin, so he found an extra coat to wrap up in, then lit a candle, sticking it with candlewax to a chip of wood. On the dirt floor he found an old western pocket book and settled himself to read during the long hours of darkness.

Earle was not long out of Boston and the strange noises he heard made it hard to concentrate on the book. There were sounds like rifle shots. Then he was sure he heard wolves fighting with grizzly bears, accompanied by roars and howls. Then there was a weird moaning and groaning. Suddenly the light tipped over and went out. He groped for the candle, lit it again and stuck it tightly once more to the chip of wood. He resumed reading and once more the candle fell over and went out. This time he was convinced something must have knocked it over but he hadn't seen anything. Puzzled, he decided to hold the lighted candle in his hand, and before very long it was struck again but this time he saw it was some sort of flying animal that had put out the light. Lighting the candle again, he began searching for the creature and finally spotted two large, bright eyes on the top log of the cabin wall. As he watched it, the animal sailed past him and out through the door opening. It was a flying squirrel.

It was a long night and when daylight finally came Earle decided to find the source of the groaning and shooting he had heard in the dark. Walking out on the ice he stood there looking about him when suddenly there was a loud, sharp sound and a crack appeared quite near him, all the way across the lake. It was open at the top of the thick ice but still closed at the bottom and Earle thought the ice might be expanding in the cold; cracking under pressure. The groaning could be caused by the ice being forced up the shore of the lake, one side having a perpendicular bluff and the other a sloping rockslide. There were more cracks all the way up the lake.

5

Packing in Freight

BY the end of January Ralph had a large parcel of furs ready to go out. The weather had settled and the ice was thick enough to be safe for the horses to travel on with their caulked shoes. It was decided that Earle and I should take the three animals and start the packing trip.

The frozen lake seemed enormous when we walked out onto it, Earle went ahead, leading Ginty and carrying an axe with which he checked the density of the ice near familiar spring holes. I stayed farther back with Old Blue while Queenie went free. This kept the weight of the horses from being concentrated in one spot. The ice was about two feet thick, so there was no need for concern.

I never grew used to how great the distances seemed that we were going to travel. Standing on a spot where we could see for miles down the valley, I would ask Earle, "How far is it now?"

He would reply, "Do you see that sharp-peaked mountain down there? Well, it's the one beyond that." And on we would go, one step after another, always managing to get there when Earle said we would.

The lake was seven miles long and by the time we reached the far end, it was a relief to leave the unbroken expanse of snow and ice and enter the green timber that sheltered the three-mile stretch of trail down to the Stillwater. Ralph called this the Valley of the Shadow and it was notorious for its mosquitoes in summer and grizzlies in the fall. This is where Earle had experienced his first encounter with a mother grizzly. It almost turned out to be his last, and seeing the place where it happened made the story very real to me.

Staying with Ralph one autumn before the First World War, Earle was making a trip down for supplies and mail. He was hiking along the narrow Valley of the Shadow trail between the lake and the Stillwater with a packsack on his back and a .35 Remington rifle in his hand when he came to a place where the trail skirted a spawning stream on one side and a steep bank on the other. There was a movement in the trail and he noticed a young grizzly cub about the time the cub saw him. It started scrambling up the hillside but slipped and skidded backwards, letting out a cry of alarm for its mother. With a roar she charged like a locomotive out of the brush near the creek and landed in the trail about fifteen feet from Earle, her hackles up and her eyes blazing. She reared to her hind legs with her arms extended and her mouth wide open in a hideous roar. Charging at Earle, she was almost upon him as he swung the rifle around and shot from the hip. Ducking his head he dodged to one side to avoid being struck as she lashed out with her powerful arms, and in the encounter she knocked the rifle from his hands. Simultaneously, Earle turned and ran for his life.

He still doesn't know whether he shed his packsack or whether she took it from him, but the next day when he returned to the scene he found it in shreds and the rifle bitten through the outer protective barrel as well as the stock. No doubt she associated the scent of the recently fired rifle with the cause of her distress, and returned to fight it. There was blood on the trail so Earle knew he must have shot her.

Earle said the trip down the trail had been arduous and slow but going back he literally flew over fallen trees and obstacles that had to be detoured before. With frequent glances over his shoulder he finally discovered the bear was no longer chasing him and was able to stop and rest.

There was only one trail between the lake and the Stillwater and this was where the bear was. A wounded grizzly is a dangerous animal and Earle had no way of knowing if this one had died or would live and be a menace. Johnnie Ratcliff and Walter, who lived in the nearest cabins, were away but Frank Ratcliff was staying in his cabin at the foot of the Stillwater and Earle decided to get him to help in tracking down the wounded bear.

The coho were spawning and there were bears everywhere, so Earle decided his safest course was to get as far away from the river as possible, climbing up the hillside on the other side of the valley where it was open going and there was better visibility. This meant crossing branches of the river on foot logs and going through the timber to the hillside.

After traveling a safe distance down valley, Earle returned to the river again which was one hundred feet wide and about ten feet deep at this point. He swam over to Johnnie's cabin and found a shotgun and ammunition and from there he hiked the two miles down to Frank's cabin at the foot of the Stillwater. On the way he saw three more grizzlies but they were without cubs and ran from him.

Frank was at home and surprised to see Earle. After giving him some dry clothes he asked him if he had had any supper.

"No," Earle replied, "But I almost made supper for a grizzly."

Frank was distressed by the news of a wounded bear and the two of them decided to track her down in the morning.

Frank had his Mannlicher rifle and Earle had Johnnie's twelve-gauge shotgun when they rowed up the Stillwater the next morning. They found the torn-up packsack and chewed rifle where the bear had left them. There was a light trail of blood into the brush but they lost it when the bear had crossed the creek.

After searching for awhile, both men became thirsty but only one at a time dared drink from the stream, while the other stood on guard. Grizzlies are notoriously cunning and can be noisy or absolutely silent while escaping from a man. They are also known to hide and pounce on their victim, so both men were on the alert.

They came to a dense cedar thicket and Frank thought they should search it, when suddenly a tremendous roar and bellowing came from its center and the men stood with their firearms ready. Then all was silent. They stood waiting until Frank finally thought they should go in after the bear. They moved cautiously forward into the thick growth of evergreens, Frank in the lead with Earle close behind him. There was no further sound from the bear, but they came upon a scene of havoc and destruction. The bear must have spent the night in there, biting and chewing the trees in her anger until she had torn down everything within an area of a very large room. Roaring when she heard the men, she then slipped silently away. There was no blood but they were able to track her to the mountainside where they lost her trail and never found it again.

Standing in the snow with Earle and the horses, looking at the place where the horrendous encounter took place, it became so real I couldn't refrain from looking around for bear tracks and half expected to see a cub come sliding backwards down the steep sidehill.

It was a relief when we came out of the Valley of the Shadow into the clearing of Johnnie Ratcliff's cabin. It was on the bank of the tranquil Stillwater and everything a frontier cabin should be; peeled logs, shake roof and stone fireplace.

The horses had to cross the river here and be taken around the edge of the meadow the next day, to the foot of the Stillwater where the "ding-blasted" trail began. There were another eight miles of trail from there before reaching Atnarko, a "stopping place" run by Max Heckman, a one-armed trapper. Earle thought we had gone far enough for one day so he swam the horses across the quiet river at Johnnie's to where they could rustle in the partly snow-covered tall grass. They were familiar with this sort of feed and wouldn't be apt to run away while we spent the night with Frank.

We loaded the gear into a clumsy dug-out which was stabilized by an improvised cedar pole outrigger, and paddled on down the two miles of winding, peaceful Stillwater to Frank's cabin. Warmed by the protecting ice on the lake, this water rarely froze, making it a natural feeding ground for the swans. We startled a family of them as we glided around a bend and came upon them in a pool. I hadn't realized how big they were until we were close and I saw what a long time it took them to become air-borne. Flying low over our heads they called to each other in their alarm; their trumpeting a harmony of tone, ranged from high to low in pitch, according to age; beautiful and stirring.

I had met Frank once before, on his honeymoon in Portland, and he welcomed us royally. He had married attractive Laura Hober, the sister of Ralph's wife, and they lived on a large farm not far from Bella Coola. Frank spent his winters alone, trapping at the Stillwater. He was a handsome man with a deep voice and ready laughter. Over six feet tall, he carried himself with the bearing of a senator.

Trapping is a lonely life and Frank's

only companion while he was at the Stillwater was a friendly Airedale named Curley. They both seemed as happy to see us as we were to be there.

The log cabin had an unusually picturesque setting among quaking aspen and birches, with a backdrop of dark evergreens. There was a grassy clearing that sloped gently from the cabin to the water and the view, stretching up the Stillwater to the mountains around Lonesome Lake and the snow-clad peaks beyond, was fascinating. One of the windows in the cabin looked out on this scene.

There was a cast-iron cookstove in the cabin as well as a heater. The stove had beautiful embossed clusters of grapes on the oven doors, as well as on the two smaller ones in front which opened to expose the glowing fire. In front of this opening was a sort of hearth which actually was a covered place to collect ashes. The curved legs of the stove left a space beneath it for storing wood or for warming slippers. These stoves seemed to be in every cabin in the north where supplies had to be packed in on horseback. The moveable parts could all be taken off and packed separately, lightening the load of the main body. They were easily reassembled.

The cast-iron heater was built on the same principle. It also had an embossed design and it took larger pieces of wood which kept burning all night. Frank had a large wood box as well as a special box for holding the pitch wood he brought home in his packsack from each trapping trip. He found the pitchy wood, which never rots, in fallen dead fir trees. It was his evening chore to shave strips of it ready for lighting the fire quickly in the morning. He never left the cabin without leaving some shavings ready in case a fire was needed in a hurry on his return.

The table was in front of the window. Over it was a small shaving mirror, and tacked to the hewn log wall nearby was a picture of "September Morn," a painting of a modest young lady, ankle-deep in a vast ocean — the innocent pin-up of that period. It had probably been clipped from a magazine advertisement about the time of the First Word War — a picture of feminine grace and charm to cheer the bachelors in this womanless wilderness.

Near it, on the wall where it would illuminate both the table and the stove was a coal-oil lamp in an ornate wrought-iron bracket holder, with a polished reflector. There was also a calendar, with crosses marking off the days Frank had been there, away from his family. Behind the stove were nails driven into the logs for hanging frying pans and a griddle iron, as well as for drying socks. There were nails in the wall around the heater in the other corner, for drying heavier clothing, and this is where the ladder, attached to the wall, led up through the trapdoor to the attic, or ram pasture, as it was referred to by the bachelors.

In the third corner was a wide bunk made of peeled cedar poles which held a pallet filled with dried slough-grass, covered with Hudson Bay blankets and a dark, patchwork quilt. Hanging on nails around the walls near this were the pelts of Frank's fur catch, drying on stretchers. Under the bunk were the mouse-proof grub-boxes.

Between the bed and the remaining corner was the second window and cupboards with shelves which held dishes and food in mouse-proof containers. Mice were an ever-present menace and while we were there Frank was constantly inventing a better mousetrap.

The floor of the cabin was of hewn logs with a trapdoor in the center, leading to an excavation under the floor where the vegetables and perishables were kept from freezing.

Frank was preparing supper when we arrived and I was initiated into the art of making sour-dough biscuits. "Starter" was kept in a small earthenware crock near the stove to encourage fermenting and was poured into a mixing bowl. Flour was added as well as soda, salt and sugar. This was stirred, then kneaded and shaped. Venison tallow was melted in a baking pan and each biscuit was dipped into it, then flipped upside down so the coating of fat would brown the top to a crisp crust. Nothing ever tasted more wonderful with farm butter and homemade strawberry jam. We had mowich (venison) steaks and boiled potatoes as well. The table was covered with a washable checkered oilcloth and we sat on ladderback chairs that Frank had made by hand from birchwood. They were fitted together perfectly with wooden pins and had woven rawhide seats.

After supper we sat and talked and talked. Anyone who has been living alone for some time has a compelling urge to talk and Frank was no exception. He and Earle had a lot of catching up to do and I kept falling asleep in my chair from sheer exhaustion but would wake to hear them still talking. Finally Earle and I climbed the ladder to the attic where there was a bed among the overflow of snowshoes and trapping equipment.

In the morning we washed in the basin on a little shelf behind the cabin door and had a huge breakfast of sourdough hotcakes with farm butter and syrup, and more venison steaks. No one knew about cholesterol in those days and fuel was needed to provide heat and energy for a hard day on the trail.

We took the dugout and the saddles across to the opposite side of the river from the cabin, where the trail to Atnarko began, so we could pick them up when we came down on that side with the horses.

The Stillwater was created by a bottle-neck made by a steep mountain creek on the cabin side which rolled boulders against a high bluff near the outlet of the quiet water. This was where Ralph's notorious "ding-blasted" trail began to climb a forty-five degree rockslide up to the solid rock wall where the trail was supported on a cribbing of cedar logs and poles three hundred feet above the river. There was just room for a pack horse to manipulate his pack around the corner, and was no place for a skittish animal.

After saddling the horses at the Stillwater we climbed the rocky trail and descended to a willow flat where there was evidence of moose feeding on the willows.

The Atnarko River sidehills, facing the sun, are the winter feeding grounds of the mule deer which range in the adjacent mountains during the summer. Every day on this packing trip we saw them, singly or in groups, on the sidehills feeding on bunchgrass and kinnikinnick. There are two types of kinnikinnick, one a low-growing evergreen vine with red berries and the other a three-foot bush with similar dark green leaves which are more available to the deer through the snow. Foraging for food, the deer came down off the mountainside to move from one good feeding ground to another and in places they kept the trail padded down into a well-traveled thoroughfare.

About three miles from the Stillwater we came to the Smokehouse, where the Hotnarko from the interior joined the Atnarko. Crossing over the Hotnarko on a narrow bridge, we went on down the valley on the trail that followed the single strand of telegraph line which extended from the interior, all the way to Bella Coola.

It was another five miles over the winding horse trail to Atnarko and I began asking Earle again, "How far is it now?" It felt wonderful when we finally came over a ridge and looked down on a long, snow-covered hay field with a barn at the other end and a cabin on a wooded knoll beyond it. Smoke was coming out of the chimney and Maxie and his Airedale, Rex, came out to greet us.

Max was a tall, angular man of Swiss origin, clean-shaven and with a fringe of gray hair around a sun-tanned head. He was smoking an ancient corn-cob pipe and his left forearm was encased in a moosehide sheath; he had lost his hand in a mining accident. In time, I was to find the stub was used for everything, including plugging it into the mouthpiece of the party-line telephone while he "listened-in" on the receiver; or placing it in an inverted cup while wiping the outside after dishwashing.

Earle fed the horses at the barn while I sat by the stove and watched Maxie prepare supper. I had been warned that bachelors resent women interfering with their domestic arrangements, swearing they could never find anything after a woman had been around, so I didn't try to help on this first meeting. Again we had venison and boiled potatoes and some of Maxie's inimitable sourdough muffins. He kept chickens and had eggs to use in his baking.

Maxie's cookstove was a larger version of the one at the Stillwater and the airtight heater stood back to back with it in the center of the room, the single stovepipe going up through the ceiling and "ram pasture" above. Over the years enough smoke had escaped while stoking the fires to stain the walls and ceilings of the entire cabin a dark chocolate brown but there were two large, small-paned windows downstairs to let in light, although the glass was somewhat murky. Max had a ladder-like rack suspended from the ceiling near the stove where he dried his damp clothes. Socks hung from the rack on letter "S" hooks made of telegraph wire. The spacious table was covered with green battleship linoleum, an expensive improvement over oilcloth, and one could place hot pans on it without damage. The sturdy white dishes were kept in a rack on the wall handy for the next meal and Max sat on a stool at the head of the table while guests ranged themselves on a long "grub-box" on the side of the table opposite the wall, facing a large moosehead calendar from an ammunition company.

This is where Earle and I sat after supper while Max began one of his long, spell-binding yarns. It was about a bear hunt in winter after he had discovered a bear's den high up the mountain in the deep snow on his trapline. He contacted an eager sportsman who flew with a friend all the way from New York to the West Coast and then came up by boat from Vancouver to Bella Coola. From there, by car and saddlehorse they arrived to climb the snowy mountain on snowshoes in the middle of winter to rout a grizzly bear from its den.

We listened, fascinated, while Maxie filled in every colorful detail, building up the suspense so that when he removed an imaginary pipe from his mouth, put it down and picked up an imaginary pair of binoculars, put them down and picked up an imaginary rifle, I jumped when he pulled an imaginary trigger and nearly fell off the end of the grub-box.

It was remarkable that we were able to sleep after listening for four hours to this yarn, but a day on the trail promotes sound sleep and we were glad to climb the steep stairs to the guests' sleeping quarters. In the flickering light of our single candle the smoke-begrimed woodwork seemed even darker up there and the bedding Earle took down from a hanging rod made me shudder. One could only guess when it had been washed last or how many tired trappers or horse wranglers had slept in it. I looked at the blankets in dismay but Earle whispered to me that it probably wouldn't hurt us, so we spread our mackinaws on the pillows and climbed between the blankets with all our clothes on, wrapping part of our coats under our chins so that no exposed skin came in contact with the grime. No one could have slept more soundly in sterile hospital sheets.

The next day's journey was about fifteen miles through the snow on the narrow trail to Belarko, a farm at the end of the road. This time the trail was broken by the mail carrier's horses. Most animals flatten a trail in snow by walking behind each other, but horses make a step trail with widely spaced, alternate holes, each horse stepping precisely in the holes made by the preceding one. Using these makes traveling on foot extremely tiring for a man, especially when the snow has been soft and then freezes hard. Stepping on the icy rim of the hole he slides down into it, repeating the jolting experience with each step and catching his toe on the frozen rim as he lifts his foot out again. For a small woman it was exhausting.

Belarko was a farm and a stopping-place where one could buy meals and a bed as well as feed for the horses. It was less colorful than Maxie's but warm and comfortable and our host entertained us by demonstrating his skill at making alcohol from grain. He had an elaborate contraption of glass battery jars and tubes, and metal containers with inverted lids which he kept filling with snow to hasten the condensation. Apparently the end product was worthy of the effort.

Our horses were stabled during the night along with the other horses at Belarko and in the morning Earle noticed that Old Blue seemed gaunt and empty. On our return trip in four days' time the horses were stabled the same as before and Earle observed that Blue was in the stall next to a large, aggressive-looking horse. During the night, he decided to take a lantern and go out to check on

Blue. Sure enough, out at the barn he found all of the horses with hay in their mangers, except Blue. As he suspected, the horse next to him had an unusually long halter rope and had been reaching across, eating Blue's hay first, before his own.

Earle went in alongside of Blue to transfer some of the hay back into his manger when something grabbed him between the shoulder blades, lifted him off his feet and hurled him back underneath Blue. He could have been kicked to death but Blue didn't move. Crawling cautiously out from underneath the horse, Earle stood for awhile to regain his composure and then decided to wait and see if the neighboring horse would try to bite him again. He kept his back turned, inviting an attack, but watched out of the corner of his eye and as the horse reached out with his mouth wide open and ears back, Earle whirled and struck him a hard blow on the nose with his fist. After that there was no more trouble and he was able to transfer the hay and shorten the halter rope.

Returning to the bedroom, Earle

removed his upper garments and turning his back to me said, "Take a look at this, will you." Between his shoulder blades, as large as a saucer, was what looked like raw hamburger. The horse had bitten right through the heavy mackinaw and woolen shirt.

The next morning, for the first time, I began to feel helpful. There is a special technique in packing a horse which Earle had learned years before. When I understood his reason for painstakingly balancing the loads and carefully securing the ropes, I began to admire his skill, for our loads never became loose or had to be repacked, nor did the horses ever develop sore backs from improperly balanced packs which swayed from side to side.

I felt a sense of importance leading Blue back up the trail, with Queenie following and Earle bringing up the rear with Ginty. The step tracks were hard for me to reach and I was tired by the time we finally got to Atnarko where we unloaded the horses at the woodshed before taking them to the barn to be fed. Max had been fishing and had supper waiting for us. This time it was steelhead steaks and nothing ever tasted better. My cheeks were rosy after a day in the open, and sleepy though we were, we listened to yet another of Maxie's stories before going to bed.

The next morning we were on our way back to the Stillwater, taking some mail and parcels for Frank. With the horses settling into the routine of packing, we were back there early enough for Earle to take the freight up the two miles of Stillwater in Frank's boat, caching it in the Johnnie Ratcliff cabin, then bringing back hay to feed the horses. This was the hay that Ralph had cut with a hand scythe and stored in the cabin on his mail trips during the summer. Earle also fed oats which we had just packed up.

Staying with Frank was as enjoyable as it had been the first time. The men spent a pleasant evening exchanging yarns and it warmed the heart to hear Frank's frequent, deep chuckle. This time, however, we were tired after the long days on the trail and were glad to get to bed early.

The next day was Sunday and Earle

thought we would have a day of rest for ourselves as well as the horses. He turned them loose to rustle in the meadow, pawing the snow for the tender hearts of the long slough-grass.

There was a relaxed and leisurely feeling at breakfast as we sat at the table eating hotcakes and watching a family of swans feeding on the aquatic moss that grew abundantly in the river at the foot of the cabin clearing.

As we watched, suddenly an eagle flew past the cabin from one of the tall trees near it and dove directly at the swans. They were alarmed and tried to escape but their takeoff was slow and cumbersome and the eagle struck one of the cygnets. However, it was necessary for the predator to rise in the air again for another strike and it was then that all three of us burst out of the door, yelling to scare him.

Curley was barking fiercely and Frank had grabbed his shotgun from the rack as the eagle prepared to dive at the swans again. Frank fired and the bird dropped into the water. By this time the swans had become air-borne and had flown away in panic and Frank assumed that the eagle was dead. It was lying motionless in the water with its wings outspread, and when Curley plunged into the river to retrieve it, Frank let him go. As the dog reached out to take the bird in his mouth, a talon suddenly flashed out and fastened on Curley's nose, forcing it underwater. All the while they were drifting slowly downstream toward the swift outlet of the Stillwater.

Frank realized that the dog would soon drown so he ran to the boat with his gun and cast off without waiting for Earle. Reaching the dog, he put out his hand to try to release the claw and get the dog's muzzle to the surface again when the eagle seized Frank's hand with the other talon, sinking the claws deep into the flesh. Frank let out a yell and we could see he was in trouble but there was no way of getting to him. Somehow he managed to reach the gun with his free hand but couldn't shoot because of Curley so he used the gun as a club and struck the eagle on the head with a blow that knocked it senseless, relaxing its talons. Both Frank and Curley had nasty wounds which were deep and took a long time to heal.

For a time Curley didn't want to go near the water again but he had enjoyed going out in the boat with Frank and before long was back out with him once more. He would stand on the front seat with his feet up on the very tip of the bow and gaze into the water for fish. Sometimes, if the weather wasn't too cold, Frank would give the boat an unexpected twist with the oars, throwing Curley off balance. Usually he ended up in the water, but if he managed to maintain his balance he would look around at Frank with a grin. It was a game they both enjoyed.

The weather held fair and Earle thought we should make the best of it by traveling every day for as long as we could, so we repeated the pattern of two days down from Frank's cabin and two days back, with the little extra trip up the Stillwater each time to cache the freight in Johnnie's cabin. Sometimes there was fresh snow in the mornings and once there was a two-day thaw that softened the snow and soaked my leather boots which I had failed to change to rubber ones. My feet were wet and cold for two days and so swollen with chilblains I had to rest for a day at Maxie's while Earle went on alone to the Stillwater with the horses. Max was away all day on his trapline and I was able to spend most of the time sleeping.

By now we had made six round trips with the horses and moved about a ton and a half of freight, some of it light but bulky. There were several cases of new glass sealers for preserving food, which Ralph had advised us to put on Ginty as he thought Blue couldn't be trusted. But Earle had established a rapport with the horse and found him docile, so he put the lighter load on him and let the younger Ginty carry the heavier load of grain. There were no mishaps and Blue seemed to be aware of his fragile load, stepping widely around any obstructions in the trail.

The landmarks and distances seemed less awesome now that I had grown familiar with them and each morning there were new animal tracks in the snow, a sort of daily newspaper in the animal world. When we were close to the river I watched the mergansers and the cheerful little water ousel bobbing up and down on a rock and diving into the icy water for food. The mergansers were quite numerous and were a spot of color in a white landscape. Occasionally there were a few swans in a bend of the river but for the most part they remained feeding at Lonesome Lake or the Stillwater.

With the last load moved to the upper cabin on the Stillwater, the horses had to be taken around the meadow and across the river again to Johnnie's cabin where the three-mile trail to the lake began, the Valley of the Shadow trail, where we actually saw a huge grizzly track in the snow during a spell of warmer weather. Earle said they sometimes left their dens high up on the mountainside for a little jaunt toward spring and then went back to bed again.

In the area between the Stillwater and the lake the river was broken up into three or four shallow channels and from early summer until late fall these contained easily accessible spawning salmon for the bears.

This is where the big grizzlies fed and Frank had shot an enormous one in self-defense when hiking the trail in August of 1913, a couple of years after he had taken up his preemption at the Stillwater.

He skinned the bear and measured the hide. It was sixteen feet from the tip of the nose to the hind feet but the summer fur was sparse and short; however, Frank dried the skin and kept it in his farm home for years.

He gave the skull to Earle who cleaned and boiled it, then sent it to the Smithsonian Institute in Washington, D.C. They wrote him that it was the largest grizzly on record and named it the Ursus Atnarko sub-species.

We made several round trips between Johnnie's cabin and the lake and then tied the horses to trees near the cabin for the night, feeding them hay and oats. Frank invited us to stay with him instead of camping at the upper cabin, so we returned each evening in the dugout.

He was anxious to build another boat

for the Stillwater and asked Earle if he would come down and stay with him after the packing was finished, and Earle had agreed. Of course I was included.

Frank had taught me how to make sourdough biscuits like his and I was also learning to catch trout. It didn't take much skill to catch them in the deep hole not far from the cabin. I would go out on the raft and anchor it with a rock tied to a rope and in no time have enough for a meal, looking down into the clear water and jerking the hook away from anything that wasn't large enough. The biggest trout I ever caught was a Dolly Varden, thirty-six inches long and eighteen inches in circumference. Most of them were a little smaller and it didn't seem to matter much what I used for bait; a piece of mouse flesh or a red kinnikinnick berry.

Just above the fish hole was a patch of aquatic moss that was a lovely thing to see, floating gracefully underwater with delicate fronds and tiny white blossoms where it reached the surface. The swans seemed to like this and there was more of it farther up the Stillwater. Paddling quietly in the dugout, we often surprised a flock of the huge birds feeding on it as we rounded a bend in the river. Somehow the peacefulness of the scene induced silence and we rarely talked while on the water or on the trail. It seemed an offence to nature. Ralph's children never shouted or squealed the way urban children sometimes do, not from lack of zeal but because the environment was quiet; also because a cry for help might go unheeded.

Earle arranged the packs so that the last loads from the cache at Johnnie's cabin would go on up the lake to the Birches with the horses. There was great rejoicing when we arrived with mail and some of the more urgently needed supplies.

The next morning we left Ginty and Queenie at the farm and returned to the foot of the lake with Blue, carrying harness instead of a packsaddle. Earle had nails and spikes and a hammer and axe to make a sturdy sled that would carry all the freight on the ice, behind the horse. There was plenty of material available near the frozen lake for making one, and before long it was ready to load. It was a rough job but Earle made the runners as smooth as he could so the horse was able to pull the heavy sled without too much effort. An old Cariboo Road coach horse, Blue seemed to be glad to be traveling without a load on his back and moved freely, his mane and tail flowing in the breeze.

Ralph had large, mouse-proof cedar boxes in the shelter of the barn where he kept the swan barley and the surplus household supplies. Everything was stored away after the sacks and cases had been sorted out. The family was happy to have something sweet again beside home-canned fruit. They loved hot chocolate made from shaving a bar of cooking chocolate and heating it in milk but their supply of it, as well as sugar, had run out nearly a month before. Everything possible was ordered in compact bulk to reduce the size of the packhorse loads, and Ethel never used powdered laundry soap from a carton, but always soap in a bar.

The freight was all up and the horses were back home again, but even with a month's freedom from feeding them, Ralph was going to be short of hay before spring. Blue was getting old and near the end of his useful days so Ralph decided to butcher him to feed themselves and the mink. This was distressing to us and we wished we could have left before it happened. We had grown attached to the horse, but frontier life was a hard and sometimes cruel one and the mink in the pens had to be fed. Horse meat was served on the table but it was a long time before I could bring myself to take a bite. Unable to swallow it, I rushed outside to be sick under a tree.

6

Building the Stillwater Boat

THE weather was beginning to turn mild and Earle thought we should try to get back down to Frank's before the rain started and the snow turned to slush. We were too late. By the time our clothes were washed and we had packed a few things, the snow on the lake had melted and there were two inches of water all over the surface.

Ralph gave us about fifty pounds of potatoes to take with us, so Earle built a small sled to carry them, as well as our pack of clothing. Out on the ice there was a strong wind blowing down the lake and Earle found he was unable to hold his footing with his rubber boots. The sled blew ahead of him and the pack on it acted as a sail. Fortunately I was wearing my leather boots which by now had caulks in them, so Earle sat on the pack and I held the rope, letting the sled pull me down the lake. We made record time, with spray flying up from the bow. It was quite exhilarating and we were across the seven-mile lake in no time. The trail to the Stillwater was too rough to drag a sled over so we cached it in a safe place, and having only one packsack, decided to tie the sack of potatoes under water in the outlet from the lake where the water was just above freezing and free from ice. It was nearly a week before Earle went back for the potatoes and he found them undamaged. When we cooked them they tasted like sweet potatoes and were delicious.

Settling in with Frank was a pleasant experience; his genial nature made me feel less inexperienced, less of a "chechako," and I was beginning to learn how to do things. At least my fingers were in bandages less of the time. Having learned how to anchor the raft at the fish hole and catch trout, as well as having mastered the art of sourdough biscuits, I was able to take over the cooking and housework, leaving the men free to get on with the boat building.

At the upper end of the Stillwater they had found the perfect cedar for making the lumber. It was dead and dry and still standing, about eighteen inches in diameter, with its bark off. Growing in a dense cedar grove, there were very few branches, or knots, in the lower portion.

The men felled the tree and cut a log about twenty-five feet long which they dragged on the snow to the river. They towed it behind the boat to the foot of the Stillwater and after dragging it up to the cabin, hoisted it up onto the uncovered ceiling joists of the woodshed, adjacent to the house. There they fastened it into place with dogs, a tool something like a heavy iron staple, which measured about two and a half feet between the points. One point was driven into the joist and the other into the log to hold it from moving.

With the log held steady in a position to saw they marked the four outside slabs with a chalk line colored with powdered charcoal from the stove, leaving the center of the log a timber of uniform thickness the full length. This was the portion they were going to cut into lumber.

The chalk line was powdered again and attached to the horizontal timber at each end, then snapped like elastic to mark the cutting line for the planks which were to be five-eighths of an inch thick. With the dogs holding the timber steady and the weight of the saw keeping the cut vertical, the planks were a uniform thickness.

Frank stood on the platform he had made on the ceiling joists of the shed and Earle stood below. Frank lifted the saw and Earle pulled it downward as it cut the wood. It was hard, tiring work for both men even though they kept the saw sharp to make the cutting easier.

The tree was dry so there was no need to store the lumber before using it. Earle dressed it by hand with a plane, making the correct bevel on the edges to create a tight joint for holding the caulking.

This was to be a flat-bottom boat, nineteen and a half feet long and four feet wide, with a transom stern, so Earle laid the boards on saw-horses and shaped the outside to the design. Then he nailed the ribs to the bottom, using burned nails so they could be clinched.

The sides were approximately two feet high and he placed them so they were standing on the planks of the bottom which were flush with the outer edge of the sides. The ribs on the sides were tied to the ribs of the bottom with natural crooks cut from sound, tough roots of old fir stumps. They were fitted to the angle between the ribs and fastened tightly together with four screws in each crook.

There were three seats which rested on strips of two-inch cedar, running the length of the boat, and there was a rubbing strip around the upper edge on the outside. The slat floor was made of two-inch wide cedar strips, separated with one-quarter inch spacing, resting on the floor ribs. The stem was made of fir and the planking was caulked with rags which became saturated with green paint when we painted the boat; and tar, when we coated the bottom.

After the whip-sawing was finished, Frank resumed his trapping while Earle worked on the boat. In the long evenings we would relax in the warmth of the cabin and sometimes Frank would get out his mandolin or fiddle and play until bedtime. It was melodious and cheerful in this setting and we enjoyed it.

At other times he spun yarns about hunting and trapping. The Ratcliffs were frontiersmen, and dogs, particularly hounds, had been an important part of their life here at the Stillwater. Frank talked a lot about one old hound, Whitey, who was very clever at tracking coyotes; and the dog loved biscuits. Whitey used to sleep outside on a pile of gunnysacks to one side of the cabin door and Frank thought the dog must have listened to everything that was said. When the other men were there and they were talking inside the cabin in the evenings, Frank, without a change in tempo or tone used to interject the words, "My dog, Whitey, likes biscuits," and the hound would set up a baying that brought laughter and a reward of a biscuit.

Frank was given a young Airedale named Curley while he still had Whitey, and after Curley matured the men often took him with their hounds on a coyote hunt. Coyotes were numerous in those early days and their pelts were valuable. They were also a menace to the deer. So the hounds would get the scent of a coyote and chase it until it took refuge in a hole in a rockslide. They bayed, but wouldn't go in after it; however, Curley would come dashing up and dive in without hesitating, tackling the coyote and dragging it out.

When Curley first came to the Stillwater he was inexperienced and Frank wanted to take him out on the trapline for company, but it wasn't safe until the dog had been trained to keep away from the traps. Most of them were baited with duck which the dogs didn't seem to care for, and duck feathers were used to conceal the trap. However, occasionally other meat was used and Frank decided to bait a couple of traps with venison, to teach Curley a lesson.

On the next trip over the trapline, Frank took Curley with him and when they came to the trap baited with venison, Frank walked on past, paying no attention, and then stepped behind a tree to see what would happen. The dog did just what Frank hoped he would; he reached for the bait and put his foot in the trap.

It wasn't a big trap but it must have been pinching painfully. Frank waited behind the tree for about fifteen minutes, long enough for the dog to feel helpless and deserted, then he walked back and released Curley. In his relief and delight, the dog licked Frank's hands and face and as they walked on up the trail, Curley stayed close behind him.

Shortly they came to the second trap that had been baited with venison. It was getting ripe and must have smelled enticing. Curley went over to the bait and stood there for a minute, then decided not to take a chance. Never again did he attempt to take a bait from a trap-set. Frank had a satisfied smile on his face when he finished his story.

Evening after evening I listened to the

two men as they sat and talked about the days when they first came to live in this wild country. Frank and the other two Ratcliffs, Walter and Johnnie, had come first and taken up the three Stillwater preemptions. It was Frank who had taken Ralph to see the long, narrow lake at whose head Ralph had found what he was searching for.

It was a bachelor's world and except for the few years when Earle's mother and younger brother lived with him at Mosher Creek, there were no other women beyond the Seventh Day Adventist colony at Firvale, about thirty miles from Bella Coola. All of the settlers were bachelors, most of them young men in their prime, eager to carve a home for themselves out of the dense forests.

There were a dozen of them, all immigrants who had come to the Atnarko Valley to trap and open up the frontier. The government encouraged them to come, wagering them the quarter-section of land they chose, against their ability to put up a dwelling, clear a few acres, and have the land surveyed within five years.

No one understood the real reason

for their coming. Was it a sense of adventure, a yearning to explore the unknown and develop the frontier; a need to have space around them; or were they escaping from a life where they didn't belong?

Gyllenspitz was a Swedish aristocrat and a political refugee. Creswell was an Oxford University graduate and the youngest son of a titled and wealthy English family whose oldest son would inherit the title. There were many of these young Englishmen in Canada, seeking adventure and living off an allowance from an estate which had no place for them in England. They were referred to as "remittance men."

Max Heckman and his brother, Lou, were from the shores of Lake Lucerne in Switzerland and had been miners when they came to Canada. George Young was also a miner. Mark Marvin, who first developed the place where Maxie now lived, claimed to be an English diplomat but was thought to be Italian.

Frank, Walter and Johnnie Ratcliff were frontiersmen from Oregon. The two Chadwell boys were from Oregon as well, and both Earle and Ralph came from the eastern states.

All of these men left a mark on the land they adopted; a cabin, a clearing, but only at The Birches, Ralph's homestead, where there was a woman and a family did the farm continue as an established home. In the end, the other clearings were either left unoccupied or undeveloped.

At the Stillwater, Johnnie and Walter had both left their preemptions and were living elsewhere and Frank used his cabin only in the wintertime when he trapped. With the exception of Ethel, women didn't seem to want to live in isolation.

This gave me food for thought and on the nights when I went to bed early, climbing the ladder to the attic and leaving the men talking happily about the past, I lay there listening to their voices drifting up to me, feeling myself trapped as surely as Curley had been.

"Only for the winter," Earle had promised back in Portland.

The winter would soon be over but neither of us had talked of returning to the city. Earle's asthma was leaving him; he seemed relaxed and happy and I had almost forgotten to be afraid of snow.

Most of the talk between the two men was of their trapping experiences, something Earle had rarely mentioned to me, or at least it hadn't meant much to me if he had, but lying in the attic bed, surrounded by trapping equipment, it became very real and I listened intently to Earle's story as his voice went on. He was talking about the days when he and Ralph were trapping out of The Birches after the First World War. They had returned to the valley and Earle had stayed in Bella Coola to fish for a season while Ralph had gone directly to Lonesome Lake to continue developing his farm. After fishing was over, Earle joined him and they prepared to go trapping for the winter; Ralph on his established trapline which ran up and down the Atnarko valley from his homestead, and Earle on a new line that crossed Ralph's.

On both of these lines the men found evidence of old Indian deadfalls for bears, made of cedar logs and weighted down with stones. The good-sized logs were completely rotten, indicating they had been cut forty or fifty years before; there were decayed remains of traps for smaller animals as well.

About the first of October, before the snow came, Ralph and Earle went together to build a cabin on Earle's new trapline, about a day's hike from the farm. They found a suitable site on a level place about forty feet square, near a sizeable stream running down the mountain where the shoulder of Mt. Monarch came down toward the Whitewater, or Talchako River.

The next day they set to work building the cabin. Making it eight by twelve feet with a sloping roof, they used jack pine poles as logs for the walls and placed them with the thick end up on the two sides to give the roof a pitch and then chinked the cracks with moss. The roof was covered with poles pressed together tightly, then covered with jack pine branches laid on like shingles. Ralph thought this would shed any water from melting snow on the roof but even in zero weather with the cabin buried in sixteen feet of snow, water dripped through the fronds when Earle built a fire in the stone fireplace. Finally he had to tie a heavy canvas beneath the roof to lead the water to the wall, away from the bunk which had a sleeping pad made of evergreen fronds, about two feet deep.

The corner fireplace was made with a hearth backed by stone slabs placed one on top of the other as high as the roof, with a smoke hole which they covered with more branches to keep out the snow until they returned.

Later, Earle built another cabin near Circle Divide, using a different method for making the roof. He hollowed the poles with his axe so they could be fitted together, one facing up and the other down, like roof tiles, so the melting snow ran off the roof instead of dripping inside. And instead of a corner fireplace, he packed up two four-gallon coal-oil tins whose open ends he forced together to make a heater that took two-foot long pieces of wood giving him steady, smokefree heat all night. One square end of the heater he opened on three sides with a knife, leaving the third side intact, to be used as a hinge, making a door on the opening of his fire box. He also packed up several lengths of stove pipe, enabling him to have a smokeless fire.

Returning to the Lonesome Lake cabin, they spent several weeks packing supplies to Ralph's trapline cabins, stocking them for the winter. By the time they had finished it had snowed deeply on the mountains and was time for Earle to set traps on his line. Ralph was going to go with him to help pack in the supplies.

Before they left they baked a batch of what they called their trapline biscuits. They were made of ground roast venison, oatmeal, dried fruits, and flour and venison fat. These were nourishing and sustaining and easy to carry in their packs.

Arriving where they had thought the cabin should be they found the snow about twelve feet deep, enough to bury it completely, and they could find no sign of it.

It was getting dark so they gave up their search for the cabin and looked for a place to camp. Going to the edge of a ravine, they saw evidence of a huge snowslide which had left a dense tangle of logs sticking up through the snow. The sidehill was fairly steep, but adjacent to the dry logs was a thicket of young balsams about forty feet high with eighteen inch trunks, close enough to the ravine so the men would feel the warmth if they set fire to the old snowslide logs. The wood burned well and threw out a lot of heat, so the two of them propped themselves against tree trunks on the steep slope and spent the night without blankets in below zero temperature.

In the morning they had a cold breakfast of biscuits and melted snow before going on. Taking turns at breaking trail with their snowshoes, they climbed above timberline, and crossing a ridge, looked down into a beautiful valley about a thousand feet below them.

Traveling westward, they came at last to the brink of the Whitewater canyon. The river seemed no more than a stream four thousand feet below them and as they stood on the brink looking down, they heard what sounded like cannonading in the distance. They decided to investigate. The sides of the canyon were steep but the men made their way cautiously through the balsam and jack pine until they came out onto a smooth, treeless slope. They thought it might be snow-covered rock and Ralph decided to slide down it onto the ledge below. Afraid of damaging his rifle while he was sliding, he threw it down ahead of him into the deep snow, then slid safely down onto the ledge. Earle followed, relieved to find there was still another ledge below the one on which they were standing that could be reached by sliding again, and from there it was not difficult to reach the bottom.

Turning to their left they soon came to the source of the noise they had heard. It was ice falling from a spectacular three-hundred-foot wall all the way across the canyon, the vertical face of a glacier flowing down for fifteen or twenty miles from a gigantic ice field. They had never heard of this glacier before and thought perhaps they were the first white men ever to see it. While they stood watching, great chunks of ice fell onto the boulders, the sound reverberating in the canyon.

In the center of the wall of ice was a large opening about fifteen feet wide and eighteen feet high, and from the center of this cavern came a stream of water thickened with pulverized rock and glacial silt. This was the source of the Whitewater, which turns the Bella Coola River white with glacial silt in hot summer weather, coloring the inlet for ten miles out.

There was just enough fluid in the dense stream to keep it moving. On each side of it was a dry strip of silt where the men could walk, so they decided to go into the cavern and investigate. Under the icy canopy everything was a beautiful, delicate blue, turning gradually to a dark purple as they went farther in. Finally, it was black.

Having no light with them they could see nothing in the total darkness so decided to return. At the face of the glacier they saw standing dead trees on either side of the canyon about one hundred and fifty yards from the ice, indicating that the glacier had advanced beyond where it now was, the grown trees having been killed by the cold from the glacier. But no dead trees stood close, showing there had been no recent advance, or that perhaps there may have been a receding.

Leaving, they went on down the Whitewater about a quarter of a mile and climbed out of the canyon by way of a fir ridge that led up to the beautiful valley which they named Sunshine Valley. They spent the night under a huge, solitary balsam fir whose branches extended at least twenty feet all the way around. The tips of the branches were weighted under the heavy snow and formed a snug canopy into which they made their way, finding only a foot of snow within the shelter.

They decided to make camp and chopped down a dead, standing balsam which they cut into three-foot lengths for firewood. Next, they chopped a hole in one side of the large tree, which must have measured about three feet in diameter at its base. The sap was frozen but the heart wood was dry. Splitting kindling from the dead balsam they had cut, they started a fire in front of the hole. After about an hour the dry wood in the heart of the tree was burning and the hole became a glowing mass of hot coals which reflected the heat and kept them warm all night. They slept comfortably without blankets on a thick bed of boughs, taking turns changing places so each could be thoroughly warmed by the fire.

Starting out on snowshoes for home, they hiked through the deep snow till they reached the Turner Lake watercourse which led in the direction of Lonesome Lake, but twelve-hundred feet above it. At the far end they cut across from the frozen lakes to the rim of the Atnarko valley overlooking Ralph's clearings. From there they slid down the snow-covered mountainside to the river which they crossed on a raft, then hiked up the meadow to home.

On the second trip over the trapline, Earle went alone. The weather was getting cold and he had a heavy pack with more traps and bait as well as food, and he also carried a rifle and an axe. Taking the same route that he and Ralph had used, he found he had to break trail again as the old snowshoe tracks were obliterated by fresh snow. However, Earle found the lost cabin this time.

There was dry wood inside for the fire and he had brought a goat-skin sleeping bag. Tired, he lit the fire and had something to eat, then crawled into the bag to sleep. He had no idea of how long he had been asleep when he woke suddenly to find the walls of the cabin on fire. Diving through the door, he used a snowshoe to shovel snow onto the fire and extinguished it quickly. When the smoke had cleared away, Earle realized the cabin logs had pitch blisters on them that had vaporized when heated from the warmth of the fireplace. The gas from them had ignited and the surface of the poles had burst into flame spontaneously all over the interior of the cabin. He was fortunate to be alive.

The next day Earle continued to follow the same route he and Ralph had taken, but about halfway up a gentle slope he suddenly found himself hanging upside down with his snowshoes caught on branches near the top of a tree that had been buried in snow. In a moment of panic he realized there was no one to help him and his body would hang there until spring if he didn't get out by himself. The next snowfall would obliterate his tracks and cover him completely.

Choking with snow and with the heavy pack and rifle dangling around his ears, he seemed unable to move, but slowly he began pulling up his body by taking hold of his pant legs and gradually lifting his head and shoulders. Impeded by the heavy pack, it seemed an age before he could reach the snowshoes with his hands. After this, he transferred his hold to the trunk of the tree, and grasping it with one hand, he released the buckle on his snowshoes with the other. Free of these, he was able to stand upright on the sturdy branches, holding on to the tree with one hand and with the other he used a snowshoe to beat a packed area around him in the dry, fluffy snow. Then placing both snowshoes on the packed snow, Earle carefully rolled over onto them and managed to get his feet in the harness. Fortunately he had been carrying his rifle with the strap over his shoulder so nothing was lost. On his feet once more, he noticed there was a slight rise in the snow where he had fallen through, indicating a tree completely buried in the snow. From then on he avoided snow mounds in the high country.

Going on up above timberline Earle found all the snow had been blown off the ridges and the bare rocks were covered with lichens. One lone male cariboo with enormous antlers stood looking at him, showing no fear, but curious. He whistled to it and left it there as he went on down into Sunshine Valley where he saw large numbers of ptarmigans. Then he found the fire tree and spent the night.

The next day Earle went down into the Whitewater to set traps, then climbed out of the canyon and headed for a low pass that would bring him out onto the Turner Lake watercourse. Halfway there it began snowing heavily. Rather than make camp he decided to keep going until he reached a certain level place which he knew would lead him to the far end of the Turner Lakes overlooking Ralph's place. He found the level area then started descending slowly in the blinding snow, expecting to hit the lake, but before long he ran across a snowshoe track. For a moment he wondered who else was hiking in the snowstorm, but the tracks fitted his. He backtracked on them until he found another good balsam which made a shelter similar to the one near Sunshine Valley; but by this time he was growing tired so he made a fire and bough bed and had a meal before resting. Wolves howled all night. He was apprehensive so he slept lightly, with his rifle ready.

By morning the snow had stopped and after a breakfast of biscuits, Earle snowshoed down onto the first of the Turner Lakes and started walking the fifteen miles of smooth going in the soft snow. With each step he sank to his knees and the tip of the snowshoes caught in the snow as they came back up. Earle took two stout cords out of his packsack and tied one to the tip of each snowshoe so he could help lift it out of the snow. This helped, but trudging on the monotonous smoothness of the lakes and using the same muscles with each step without relief was exhausting. The temperature was below zero, and weary from his restless night he longed to lie down and sleep for awhile. He didn't dare, so instead, leaned over frequently and rested with his elbows on his knees. This gave him the relief he needed without the hazard of falling asleep which would have been fatal in sub-zero temperatures.

Finally toward evening, he neared the rim of the Atnarko canyon above Ralph's place. He kept going, down the hillside, falling and rolling until he slid into a tree. Getting up with his feet still in the snowshoes, he slid for another fifty yards. Everything was snow-covered but thoughts of a good meal and warm bed kept him going until he reached the bank of the river opposite Ralph's cabin. It was dark now and he was disappointed not to see a light in the window and assumed Ralph was away on his trapline. The river was chest deep and fifty yards wide at this spot, flowing with slush ice. Earle put his rifle and snowshoes in a safe place under a tree and sliding into the water, he waded across. It was perishing cold and he was numb when he climbed out of the river and walked to the cabin. Before reaching it his clothes were frozen stiff and he was scarcely able to bend his knees.

Crawling up the steps, he could see candlelight through the window. Ralph was home. He had heard Earle and opened the door to the frozen apparition who stumbled in. When Ralph asked him if he was hungry Earle replied that all he wanted was lots of strong, hot coffee with sugar in it.

While Ralph made the coffee Earle stripped off the frozen clothes, but when he came to his boots he found the socks were frozen to them and the skin of his feet was frozen to the socks. Ralph helped him pull off the boots but it was necessary to thaw the socks by immersing them in warm water, an excruciatingly painful process. In dry clothes, he drank the coffee until his thirst was quenched, then climbed in between four double Hudson Bay blankets and slept for forty-eight hours. When he woke he felt fine.

Always afterwards, both Ralph and Earle referred to the area where he met his own snowshoe tracks as Circle Divide.

7

Making Packsaddles

W E continued to spend the evenings in companionable relaxation with Frank, but his trapping was about finished for the season and it was almost time for him to return home.

It took Earle two weeks to build the boat and Frank had to leave before it was completed. This left the two of us to launch it.

We did this the day the paint had

dried and the tar was still fresh on the bottom. The boat was upside down on the sawhorses and Earle got underneath the center seat while I held the bow and steered toward the water. It was muddy and slippery on the river bottom but Earle had instructed me on what to do. We were to flip the boat in unison when Earle gave the signal, landing it right side up in the water.

Wading out almost to my waist, Earle gave the signal, "Now!" I was still slow in my reaction. While he flipped his end, I still hung onto mine and went under with it. I found myself sitting on the bottom of the river underneath the bow of the boat. The boat was safe, floating high and dry and right side up when I emerged, dripping mud and moss. It was a beautiful boat and we were as proud as if we had launched an ocean liner. Oddly enough, nobody ever gave it a name.

Spring came and the weather warmed. The alder catkins turned a rosy color and the fragrance of the cottonwood buds filled the air. They were dark chestnut-brown and sticky with a substance the Indians used in healing skin disorders or wounds. The scent was so delightful, I kept a bud in the pocket of my shirt. One of the names for cottonwood is the Balm of Gilead. The blossoms open into grape-like clusters of small green fruit which the black bears eat. With their long, sharp claws they are often seen climbing high into a cottonwood tree in spring before the fruit ripens and bursts into a white fluff that looks like snow as it floats down and covers the ground.

We made many trips to the upper end of the Stillwater in the new boat, just for the sheer pleasure of it. Neither of us ever mentioned that winter was over and that it was time to return to Portland.

Not far from Johnnie's cabin was an open spot, free of brush, where the soil was deep and rich and high enough to be safe from spring flooding. One day, as we passed it, Earle remarked, "That would be a good place for our garden."

It was as easy as that. We both knew we would never go back to the city again. This was where our hearts were.

"We could have a small garden down at Frank's cabin," Earle went on, "And this one would be large enough for potatoes and carrots and roots for winter storage. We'd better get busy and find some poles for fencing it."

Keeping the deer out of gardens and orchards was a problem in this country. All Ralph's fences were unusually high with the rails close together and the bottom ones near to the ground so the smaller deer couldn't crawl under or through between them.

By the time our garden plot was dug and fenced the ice had gone from the lake and it was time to make a trip to Ralph's to get some seed potatoes.

Earle made a raft at the foot of the lake and rigged it with oars to save the long, rough hike around the lake.

It was good to see the family again and Ralph seemed pleased when we told him we were not going to return to Portland but were going to find a farm of our own.

The next day Ethel made a cake and ice cream in celebration, then we began packing our things to take to the Stillwater. Ralph offered to take us down the lake in his boat, but before we left there was something Earle wanted to do.

On the way down the Eastfork in September, Earle had caught the leather strap of his wrist watch on a branch and weakened the fastening, so he removed it and placed it in his shirt pocket. Somewhere along the way he lost it. It was a valuable watch and he frequently wondered if he would find it if he went back to search for it.

Leaving me at Ralph's, he left quite early in the morning and began his search after reaching the rough terrain of the Eastfork. The leaves were still on the trees when he lost the watch and his chances of finding it somewhere on the ground under ten or fifteen miles of leaves were slim indeed.

He concentrated his search on the roughest part of the trip, where we climbed up and down over the precipitous bluffs. On the steep slope of one of these, the leather straps eaten away by mice and lying half hidden by a fallen leaf, lay the watch.

It was incredible. Earle picked it up and wound it and it still ran. It was still ticking when he placed it against my ear on his return to the tent at Ralph's that night.

The following day we sailed down the lake in Ralph's boat. With the three of us and all our belongings, there was very little freeboard and the water grew a bit rough. The men were enjoying it, but conditioned by the Charlotte Lake experience, I was frightened and begged to be put ashore to walk the rest of the way through the trees and across the rockslide to the foot of the lake. At least this lightened the load a bit.

With such awkward packs, Earle and I had to make several trips over the Valley of the Shadow trail between the lake and Johnnie's cabin at the Stillwater, but finally everything was rowed down in the boat to Frank's cabin and we settled in for the spring and summer. Frank had invited us to use it for as long as we wanted.

It was peaceful at the Stillwater; there was a tranquility about the place that made us want to spend the rest of our lives there. Every day was filled with work which wasn't work, but pleasure, and we went to bed to sleep soundly.

We've always looked back on this interlude as the happiest time of our lives and even now, nearly fifty years later, there comes a day in winter when the light from the newly fallen snow combines with quietness and transports the senses back to the cabin at the Stillwater. It is almost a physical sensation, coming without bidding; and then it is gone, leaving pleasant recollections of our life there.

I only remember wishing for one thing I didn't have, some fresh green vegetables in the spring. After the snow had gone, I found some clover growing along the trail and we cooked and ate it but it tasted horrible. Another time on our way to Atnarko to get the mail, I saw what looked like young mint near an old cabin. I plucked it with delight and crushed it to my nose to inhale its fragrance before I discovered it was stinging nettle.

Near the end of May we had an unexpected visitor at the Stillwater. One afternoon there was an unusual sound from somewhere and we discovered it was a call from an Indian on the trail across the river. Going over in the boat we talked with him and found his name was Frank Sill from Algatcho, a remote Indian settlement to the north of Anahim. He said he was camping about five miles down the trail with his large family, "hiyu kids" was the way he put it, and they were trying to catch spring salmon. They weren't having much luck and were "broke grub." He was out hunting for mowich (deer) and he had just run into a huge grizzly, "all the same big like horse." He seemed somewhat shaken so we took him across to the cabin and made him a cup of tea. When he left we gave him some smoked trout from the smokehouse and he went away happy.

Looking out of the cabin window the next morning, we saw a bull moose in the brush across the river from the cabin. It was a beautiful animal, wading in the shallow water in the early morning mists. We watched it as it fed, then Earle said, "You know, those people need that meat. I really should get it for them."

I didn't want him to destroy anything so beautiful but he persuaded me that people were hungry. In a frontier life there was little room for sentiment, and men survived by eating wild game. I was unhappy to see him reach for his gun but afterwards I was proud of his marksmanship, and a few days later I even enjoyed eating some of the meat.

Getting the carcass across to the cabin might have been a problem but the moose dropped in shallow water and we were able to get it out to where the water was deep enough for it to float so we could tow it behind the boat.

At the grassy shore by the cabin I wondered how we would get it up onto dry land for dressing, but Earle explained that he would make a Spanish windlass. I had never heard of one before but he said he had often used one for moving heavy objects.

Taking a heavy rope and attaching one end to a stump in the direction he wanted to go, and tying the other end to the moose, Earle adjusted the rope so there was a little slack. Then he cut two poles about six feet long and three inches in diameter. One pole was placed on the ground about half way along the rope and through a loop made by twisting the rope snugly. Then this pole was placed vertically, with the tip slightly embedded in the ground. The end of the second pole was inserted under the rope leading to the stump and then both poles were pivoted, so the rope wound around the vertical one. As the rope wound, it shortened; one turn of the pole took up about ten inches of rope, and slowly the moose moved up out of the water onto dry land.

I was impressed by Earle's engineering ability but more concerned that the rope would break under the strain and cause an accident, or else Earle would lose his grip on the pole and it would swing around and clout him on the side of the head. But all went well and before long we were ready to cut up the meat.

The mosquitoes and flies were troublesome but we made a smudge and Frank had an excellent smokehouse, so by cutting the meat in pieces and hanging them in the smoke we were able to protect it all before Earle hiked on down the trail the next day to ask the Indian to come and get three-quarters of it.

Sill and his wife rode up with a couple of packhorses to get the meat. They had seen the bear again and were extremely excited. We could hear his wife's high-pitched yelling at the horses long before they came into sight.

"Hope that grizzly doesn't smell the meat and chase you back to camp," Earle joked as they packed the horses.

We had no idea who Frank Sill was or that he would play a role in our lives one day.

There were a lot of empty glass sealers in the woodshed as well as a big copper boiler, so I preserved all the meat I could in them and we made jerky of the rest. These were strips of lean meat, smoked until dry. They seemed to keep forever and were not unpalatable; certainly they were marvelous exercise for the teeth and the meat was a change from our almost constant diet of fish.

Earle decided to tan the moose hide while I was busy canning the meat. With the hide stretched over a smooth log, he started scraping the inside of the skin and removing all the surplus fat with one of Frank's scrapers. Next, he tied the hide in the river to soak until all the hair slipped from it. Then the cleaned hide was soaked in a wooden tank which Earle made for the purpose with some planks left over from boat building. Again he caulked the joints with rags so they wouldn't leak and filled the tank with an alkaline solution of lye.

The hide soaked in this for two weeks with occasional stirring, then was washed again and returned to the tank, this time to soak in an acid solution made from boiled hemlock bark chips. We made enough to cover the hide and left it to soak for about a month until the beautiful dark tan color of the solution had penetrated the thickest portion of the hide.

Washed again, the hide was ready to be stretched on a frame and "worked" to soften it as it dried. Earle cut small holes all around the edge of the hide and laced it to a pole frame with wet rawhide strips which tightened as they dried. He had put the frame in a place where there was a breeze but no sun, and then with a blunt stick about four feet long and an inch in diameter he pressed and stroked the drying hide, flexing it until it became soft and pliable. When it was finished he worked some neetsfoot oil into it. This oil never became rancid and was used to keep leather soft and waterproof.

We were proud of the leather when it was finished. Earle decided to make something he had observed there was a real need for — a comfortable-fitting packsaddle that would not make sores on a horse's back. The Anahim Lake country was opening up for cattle ranching and in the fall packtrains traveled the trail from the interior to the end of the road for winter supplies. At the end of the six-day pack trip, down and back, there were many sore backs from ill-fitting saddles.

Frank had a comfortable riding saddle which fitted a horse's back perfectly and Earle used this as a pattern for the sidebars of a packsaddle. He carved them from dried cottonwood, using Frank's bench vise and shaping the wood with a spoke-shave to fit the curves of a horse's back. The forks were made from dried birch and we even found discarded metal rings for the cinch which Earle made of washed gunnysacking.

About the first of July the lodge at Stuie, near the end of the road, organized a stampede. Most of the interior Indians were already down and were fishing in the river, and after a long, lonely winter the cattle ranchers were glad of a chance to bring a string of weather-beaten horses down into the luscious valley for a feed of green grass before their own haying began. They were able to visit with friends, have a feed of salmon and take back supplies for the summer when they returned. Probably they were also glad to escape the mosquitoes and flies that were troublesome in the interior during the spring and early summer.

Earle had finished a couple of saddles and we decided to hike down to the stampede and take them with us. They were an immediate success and after watching the stampede, Earle traded them for a little mare he fell in love with who was in the wild bucking horse bunch.

After unloading her rider, no one could catch her. She had come from Nemaia Valley near Chilko Lake in the interior where there were some fine horses. She had a certain air about her and Earle wanted her. We probably wouldn't have been able to afford her but she had once been creased in the neck, either by a bullet or a snag. It hadn't damaged her, but had left a small scar. Earle named her Maryanka after a high-spirited heroine in the Tolstoy novel he was reading.

Returning to the Stillwater after the stampede, Earle put the mare on a long rope and toggle in the clearing by the cabin. A toggle is a moveable wooden anchor made of a short length of log. There was plenty of feed and she had access to water, but best of all, she was near us and we could go out frequently and curry her and get her used to being handled.

In no time she was tame and Earle was getting ready to break her to the saddle when she disappeared. She simply was gone one morning. We hunted for her everywhere, up the Stillwater and down the trail. With the long rope and toggle we didn't see how she could get very far without leaving some trace in the brush or long grass, but there was none. In the end, after a week's searching, we had to conclude she must have become entangled in the rope while swimming and been carried helplessly down the river and been swept under a logjam. We were heartsick and much of the joy seemed to be gone from our lives.

One morning, about three weeks after her disappearance we were rowing up the Stillwater to tend the garden when a whinny and a slight movement from the far side of the wide meadow caught our attention. There, in the edge of the brush was Maryanka, her rope wound tightly around a tree. She had been able to reach some feed, and until recently, there had been water.

She whinnied to us again and we were choked with emotion. Earle petted her, unwound the rope and led her to the open water where she drank. Then we led her to the boat and while Earle rowed, I sat in the stern and held the rope as she swam strongly to the clearing at the cabin. From then on, there was never a trace of wildness and Earle trained her to the saddle without difficulty. She was one of the family and responded to our affection.

With Maryanka safe and back in the clearing at the cabin we were happy again, but the summer was passing and we realized that before long we were going to have to leave this idyllic spot and establish ourselves on a place of our own.

A mile or so down the trail from Max Heckman's was an unoccupied clearing with an abandoned cabin and fences, known as the old George Young place, the only other preemption in Atnarko. We both had admired it each time we passed and Earle had written to the owner inquiring if it was for sale. He was a former friend of Earle's and had replied that he was willing to sell; however, nothing had been settled yet. We had the summer in which to make the decision and in the meantime we had accepted an invitation to join my sister and her husband at a ranch they were going to develop near Anahim Lake. They had left the old house in Bella Coola and gone to Victoria but Vincent disliked city life and wanted to start cattle ranching. Earle was going to help him build the cabin and I was going to teach the children. We planned to join them at Anahim in August but not before we had to make a trip to Prince George, about five hundred miles away, in the north central part of the province.

We had brought our car into Canada through the border customs at Blaine on a visitor's permit which lasted for twelve months, and the year would soon be up. It was necessary for us to go through certain formalities to satisfy the Canadian Customs and they insisted the car be taken to Prince George, the nearest customs office. There seemed no reason why all this business couldn't be transacted by mail but no amount of explaining would make the authorities change their minds. This seemed an expensive and unnecessary trip to us, one that would take the best part of a week's travel, even after we had reassembled the car at Charlotte Lake and driven it back out to the road at Towdistan again. After writing innumerable letters, we resigned ourselves and prepared to leave the Stillwater to make the trip.

Maryanka was still in the clearing at the cabin and during the fly season we kept her comfortable with a smudge and rubbed her with a pinetar solution which repelled the blackflies and mosquitoes. There was still plenty of feed and there seemed little danger of her running away again so we felt free to leave her for a day and make a long-anticipated trip into Hunlen Falls before we left. They were considered to be the second highest falls in Canada and I had heard their roar from the trail at the foot of Lonesome Lake. The falls themselves were obscured by canyon walls and the heavy timber growing near the trail, so I had never seen them.

Earle had promised to take me into the basin at the foot of the falls after they were free from their enormous burden of winter ice and the high water of the spring run-off was over. They dropped a spectacular thirteen hundred feet into a basin they had worn for themselves in a chasm not far from the outlet of Lonesome Lake. They were named after Old Hunlen whose trapline had run through this area long years before.

Getting an early start, we rowed up the tranquil Stillwater in the morning sunshine, then left the boat and hiked up the mosquito-infested trail through the Valley of the Shadow until we came near the outlet of the lake. Earle walked ahead with the rifle in case of bears while I followed behind, waving a cedar frond to brush away the thick cloud of mosquitoes that settled on our clothing and skin. We were accompanied by their constant hum.

As we neared the lake, the trail wound its way through the boulders of the estuary of the Hunlen stream, then we left the trail and followed the cataract for half a mile until we came to a bluff and rocky outcropping. Climbing around these obstacles with some difficulty, we came out on the edge of a mist-filled basin into which the water plunged with an earsplitting roar. It fell from a sloping ledge at the foot of Turner Lake, thirteen hundred feet above, and we were drenched in spray and deafened by the noise. There was no desire to stay in this awesome spot for long and it was a relief to turn away and begin the descent into the quiet safety of the valley again.

Away from the noise, we sat in the sun and Earle told me about the time he and Ralph had once gone to the top of the falls where the water pours over the smooth edge. The bare rock of the rim sloped slightly downward and was empty of trees or brush. To be able to see the falls below, it was necessary to go out to the edge and look over. The men had no rope, so Earle lay down and crawled over the smooth slope to the rim to peer down at the spectacle. Reaching for a large stone, he dropped it over the rim and watched it falling until at last it seemed to stand still, diminishing in size until eventually he could no longer see it at all.

He was spellbound for a long time, mesmerized by the roar and the tremendous fall of water constantly moving away from him. Earle felt slightly dizzy and was aware of an almost uncontrollable urge to let his body follow the water into the chasm. With his last bit of will he resisted the desire but found himself unable to back up. The slightest movement of his body rolled him farther over the ledge on the tiny pebbles covering the smooth, sloping rock. He had reached the point of balance between life and death and knew he had to remain motionless and call to Ralph for help.

Cautiously Ralph stepped forward, was able to take hold of Earle's feet and pull him gently backward until they were both well out of danger. It was a long time before either man spoke.

8

Old Young Place

THE last few days at the Stillwater were beautiful but it was time to leave for Prince George and we packed Maryanka to begin the three-day trip to Charlotte Lake where we would get the car going again. We hoped to be able to leave her in pasture there until our return.

George and Jessie Powers were at home this time when we arrived at Charlotte Lake, but they were about to leave as Jessie had picked up a splinter in the

154

palm of her hand while pitching hay and had developed blood poisoning. The hand was greatly swollen and an ugly color, with dark streaks going up her arm and a swelling in the armpit. She was in great pain and unable to sleep.

It was going to take two or three days in the wagon to reach medical aid, and since we had a first aid kit with us, Earle asked George to let him try to help. We sterilized a sharp knife as well as a hypodermic needle and Earle injected some analgesic into the hand. With Jessie panting on the bed, he made a slit around the base of her thumb and let the pus pour into a dish. Each time it slowed, Earle pressed gently in other areas and the draining began again. When it had finally finished, her hand was soaked in hot water then bandaged with antiseptic. Jessie was able to sleep at last after several wakeful nights.

We waited a couple of days to be sure of Jessie's recovery and Earle spent his time getting the car running again.

Jessie fell in love with the coupe and wanted to trade a team of horses for it. I would have liked to trade something for their beautiful old Edison cylinder-record gramaphone, with the morning-glory horn. It had a large stock of cylinder records and one of them was the ubiquitous "Red Wing." One heard it blaring forth everywhere there was a gramaphone: "Oh, the moon shines bright on pretty Red Wing . . . "

George rode out to Towdistan with us to make sure we made it over the sleigh road safely. Somehow the trip didn't seem to take as long as it had when we drove in nearly a year ago.

We thought it foolish and a waste of time to have to make this trip to Prince George; it took us three full days of driving to get there. The customs official who took care of Earle was apologetic about our having been forced to make the trip, saying the papers could easily have been filled out in Bella Coola.

However, the journey to Prince George was not entirely wasted. My older sister, whom I hadn't seen for years, lived in Vanderhoof, seventy miles west of there. She had no idea we were making the trip and as there was no telephone connection between the two places, I sent her a telegram from Prince George, "Fill up the golden bathtub. We'll be over this evening." She, too, had lived through times without running water and had often written, "When we get rich, I'm going to have a golden bathtub in the middle of the drawing-room."

She and her husband had a wonderful party for us in their charming home and I wore a dress for the first time in a year. It felt strange to be out of overalls, and the shoes I brought, which hadn't been worn since we left Portland, pinched my feet. Moccasins and boots had given them room to spread.

It was pleasant to be among friendly people with gracious manners but I felt slothful not to be working or doing something useful. Idleness was something that had no part in frontier life and I felt a restlessness to be away and about the business of carving a niche for ourselves in the wilderness.

In the morning, laden with cakes from the party, we were away again, back to Anahim where we were going to join Vincent and my other sister, and Earle was going to begin work on their log cabin.

August and September are wonderful months in the interior. The air is like wine and everyone is busy haying. It seemed more like a picnic than a work party, living in tents while the cabin was being built. The children were having a marvelous time riding horses and had no interest in lessons. Even Vincent seemed to prefer to sit in the shade for hours, talking to his two old friends. Cahoose and Capoose — interior Indians who had taken packtrain loads of furs to the Clayton trading post in Bella Coola when Vincent was a lad. He talked to them now in their own Stick Indian language and they loved it.

Vincent had hired a rancher with a team to come and haul logs for the cabin and before the middle of October the walls were up; but it was beginning to be obvious that it would never be completed in time for the cold weather.

The sky was gray and lowering, with a few snowflakes in the air when Earle and I realized we were going to have to get back down the valley before the snow came. We knew now that what we really wanted to do was go back to Atnarko and make our home on the old George Young place. Max might not be happy about losing his free pasture but he could get along without it as he had another large pasture of his own.

We made plans to leave Anahim and get down into the valley before it snowed. and Vincent decided to take his family back to Victoria again for the winter.

On the thirteenth of October, we drove the coupe through the long grass across Cless Pocket meadow to the Squinas ranch where there was a shed in which we arranged to store our car. It stood where the road through the Chilcotin ended and the horse trail to the valley began. That night it snowed eighteen inches all the way down to Atnarko. Coming early, the snow was a harbinger of a hard winter which lasted for six months.

Ralph had asked us to bring down an old horse he had bought from a rancher to use for mink feed, so when we picked up Maryanka from the Powers ranch we had two horses for the trip.

About halfway between Anahim Lake

and Atnarko, there was a stopping place called the Precipice, with pasture or hay for horses. It was a day's journey for a horse from a stopping place in either direction, and in the fall there was excellent deer hunting. The ranch was owned by Jack Weldon, a friend of Earle's and we decided to accept his invitation to stay over a day and get some venison. Then we would have meat to go with our rice and tea. Earle shot a large buck and we were fortunate to have the extra horse to carry it.

It was tiring to walk through the deep snow, which continued all the way down the trail to Atnarko. By the time we reached Maxie's it was dusk and we were fatigued and hungry. We couldn't help wishing he would invite us to stay for the night but when we told him we were planning to buy the Young place which he had been using as a free pasture for years, he merely jerked his head in that direction and muttered, "There's a stove down there."

Two more miles down the trail and no light in the window! There weren't any windows for that matter, except a small

160

one in the lean-to kitchen; the glass had long since been broken or carried away from the others. There was a small, rusty cast-iron stove in the kitchen that stood on four rocks instead of legs. The place smelled of pack rats but there was a bed frame made of cedar poles in one corner, and a rickety table. In the larger room, both windows were gone and the snow had blown in. There was a tent belonging to the trail crew hanging on a rod suspended from the ceiling, and we used this to help pad the bare boards of the bed in the kitchen.

There was no fuel for the stove but Earle pried loose a top rail from the fence and chopped it into firewood while I took pages from an ancient rat-chewed mail order catalogue to plug the obvious cracks between the logs.

The horses had been unpacked and turned to rustle in the snow. They were able to find some feed in the long grass around the edges of the field which was fenced so they couldn't run away.

We melted snow for tea, then boiled some rice and fried two large venison steaks. But before we did this, there was

161

one awful moment of depression when I wanted to go home to mother.

The pack rat kept us awake most of the night, so we lay in the darkness and talked about what we would do.

"I'll make arrangements with Max to feed the horses on a monthly rate," Earle planned. "Then I'll cut a supply of wood and leave you in the cabin while I go to Hagensborg and buy enough supplies to last us the winter."

In the morning when Earle went to see Max about the horses, he found him still a little hostile but he did agree to feed the animals. We borrowed one thing from him — a trap to catch the rat.

The snow stayed on the ground and settled, but there was still a foot of it by the time Earle came back with the winter supplies. We hadn't dug the potatoes at the Stillwater yet and there was also a packhorse load of our things at Frank's cabin that had to be brought down.

Taking the two horses we went up to the Stillwater, and borrowing Frank's shovel and mattock, we rowed up the river to dig the potatoes. Earle shoveled the snow off the fenced garden plot and we dug through the frozen ground with the mattock and salvaged the deepest of the potatoes, hoping they weren't frozen. There were four sacks of them, but by the time they had warmed up in the cabin, half of them turned to watery mush and had to be discarded. We did save enough for the winter though.

We brought down the things we had stored at Frank's: the heater Earle had made at Ralph's and two folding camp cots with mattresses and chintz covers, along with a small bookcase and the typewriter.

The depression of the first night in the George Young cabin had given way to a home-making instinct and before long the living room was cosy and warm and pleasantly comfortable.

The cabin stood in the field not far from the river, with a beautiful view up and down the valley. It was made of cottonwood logs, hewn with a broad-axe and gray with age. Each log was more than two feet wide and so neatly fitted, the inside walls had a smooth surface. The living room was almost square and the kitchen was a lean-to on the side next to the trail. On the wall behind the front door there was a ladder to an attic bedroom. This was for guests. Earle and I slept on the twin cots which were chintz-covered couches in the daytime.

Earle installed the heater which kept the cabin warm and before Christmas he made a rustic armchair with leather cushions. Opposite the window was a desk with a bookcase, flanked by corner closets for our clothes. The window was the masterpiece.

Earle made the two former windows into one large one which looked down-valley over the meadow and woods. He had bought a roll of plastic film to use instead of glass — something new, and we wondered why everyone wasn't using it. Stretching it tightly across the opening, he divided the space into smaller panes by using wooden strips. The effect was charming and we congratulated ourselves on inventing this easier and less expensive method of making windows. Everyone should be told about it! The plastic was thin enough so the view was almost as clear as through glass.

Just before Christmas the temperature

plummeted one night, and in the morning Earle built a roaring fire in the heater to warm things up. With the sound of a loud rifle shot, the plastic popped and literally blew itself to pieces; the sudden change in temperature was more than it could take. So we had to buy glass after all and were fortunate to get it installed in time for Christmas.

The cold weather brought a magnificent display of northern lights. The night sky over the mountains on the north side of the valley glowed as though a full moon was shining beyond the horizon. Then this diffused glow changed to ribbons of light like giant searchlights playing across the arc of the sky from separate places on the north side of the valley, disappearing beyond the rim of the mountains on the south. They moved constantly and sometimes were tinged with faint rainbow colors, but mostly they were the color of moonlight. They were awesome and we bundled up against the cold and stood in the snow to watch them. They appeared several times during the winter, usually as the forerunner of clear, cold weather.

Christmas was festive. We invited

Maxie and a friend who was staying with him, as well as B.C., our nearest neighbor to the west, a bachelor who had a farm about six miles down the trail. He had been in the Klondike gold rush and talked with a nasal twang about his experiences. Almost always he preceded each conversation with. "My father was a lawyer; afterwards got to be judge." He was a gaunt man with an odd look in his eye and somewhat eccentric behavior which frightened women. He had spent some time in a mental institution but seemed harmless and was a hard worker.

After our Christmas dinner was over and the men were sitting around the heater with their pipes, I decided to go out into the kitchen to put things away and was dismayed to find the old chap had followed me out and intended to kiss me. I backed into a corner and still don't know how I managed to escape, but it was frightening and made me realize how important it was to be friendly but reserved with such lonely bachelors.

Maxie was different and in all the years we were neighbors he treated me with an old-world courtesy and never once came onto our premises while Earle was away unless I asked him, although I was free to visit him when I wanted someone to talk to.

Christmas was a time of burying the hatchet and forgetting grudges between these bachelors. Without a woman to cook the yuletide meal for them it is doubtful if they would have bothered to have one or patch up old differences. I missed the conviviality of my family and felt no special joy in being a good cook and hard worker, although these were considered admirable traits in a frontier woman.

In the New Year we made one other trip with the horses; this time to the old Edwards' place at Mosher Creek, almost ten miles down the trail to the west. This was the place Earle and Ralph had bought from Mosher when Ralph took over the job of telegraph operator and lineman. He and Earle had lived there together with their mother and younger brother for a time but Ralph was restless to get started on his own preemption and he turned the telegraph

167

job and the place over to Earle when he went up to Lonesome Lake to stay. Earle remained on at Mosher Creek for several years until it was time for Bruce to get more schooling and they moved to Bella Coola where Mrs. Edwards and Bruce lived while Earle was in the army.

During the war Ralph left Lonesome Lake and joined the American army because he wanted to fly and the Canadian Air Force thought twenty-six was too old to learn to be a pilot. But in the American army he still couldn't fly because they considered him more useful as a telegrapher. It wasn't until he was sixty-two that he finally took his pilot's training and flew his own plane.

With Ralph and Earle both in the army, the cabin at Mosher Creek had been left locked, with many of their possessions still inside. Earle continued to own the place but it had been years since anyone had lived on it. Packtrains often spent the night since the fences were still intact and there was horse feed, but nearly everything of value was gone. However, Earle thought we would go down with the horses and see if there was anything left that we could salvage.

There was a useful table that could be taken apart and the boards packed on a horse, some stove pipe and a couple of hand-made chairs as well as other odds and ends.

We put the bulkiest pack on the quiet old horse, with a top pack of the long table boards and the lengths of stove pipe on top of that. The sling rope didn't quite reach over the bulky load so Earle looked around for a piece of rope to add to the end of it. He found just the thing and as he was pulling back to tighten the sling, the added section broke and the startled horse took a jump forward. As he jumped, the boards slapped his rump and his next jump went farther. He was still jumping as he went out of sight, with the pack scattering for a mile up the snowy trail.

It was getting dark by the time we caught the horse and picked up all the pieces. Earle rearranged the pack so we could manage with the sound rope but he thought we might need a light before we reached home. We hunted around in the cabin for a pack rat's nest where there might be a piece of candle to make a bug.

A bug is an emergency lantern made from taking the top off of a tomato or milk tin, making an X in the center of the side and pushing a candle through it. Then, holding the tin horizontally so the candle is out of a draft, the light is reflected by the shiny interior of the tin. If a wire handle can be attached to the top, so much the better, otherwise it can be carried by the protruding base of the candle.

We found a pack rat's nest with two pieces of candle in it which lasted until we reached home, the melted end of the last one dripping down through the X in the tin as we came in sight of our cabin.

9

Cutting Wood

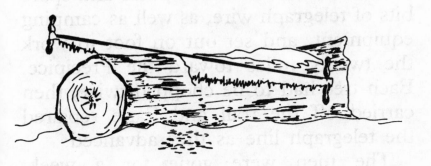

THE weather remained cold over the New Year, but the January thaw came in the form of heavy, wet snow which bent the young birches and alders down over the trail, making an impassable tunnel through which only a rabbit could run.

The trees pulled the telegraph line down with them, all the way from the end of the road to Anahim; then a sudden drop in temperature froze their tops solidly into the snow. Even if the trail had been open, the snow was covered with an icy crust which would have cut the legs of horses, so no one could get up from below until the trail was cleared and the crust thawed or broke.

Frank happened to be down with us on a mail trip when this happened and he and Earle took axes and pliers and spare bits of telegraph wire, as well as camping equipment, and set out on foot to work the twenty miles toward the Precipice. Each tree had to be chopped twice, then carried off the trail and Earle repaired the telegraph line as they advanced.

The men were gone for a week, repairing the line as they went, for until the line was connected all the way through, no messages could be sent from either end.

It wasn't until Earle returned and tested the line with the telephone at Maxie's that he learned it was open and there were two telegrams waiting for me from my parents in Victoria, sent two days apart.

The first was that my sister was gravely ill and the second carried the grim news that she had died. I was stunned. Only a few months before we had all been together at Anahim and she had been well and happy then. Grief-stricken, I felt cut off from my family and was oppressed for a long time by a sense of isolation.

For a time I even suffered a feeling of resentment over being cut off from contact with my family, although I had made the choice freely to live in this isolated country. Many pioneer women must have felt thus at times and resented the very devotion that willed them to follow their husbands into a life of loneliness. But the feeling soon passed, although my parents now became aware of the inaccessibility of Atnarko and wrote begging us to change our minds about living there. This added to my own feeling of insecurity and for a time took much of the joy out of being in Atnarko.

Time heals and I learned to write comforting letters. But no matter how much I tempered the truth with fiction, my mother could never be persuaded not to refer to our cabin as a hut, or animals, other than domestic ones, as anything but wild beasts. She was convinced that someday they would eat us alive or else we would be frozen to death in a blizzard. I couldn't tell her that a worse fate could be loneliness and winter isolation.

But we kept busy. There were so many improvements to make on the cabin and we wanted to build a woodshed and a small barn as soon as the cold moderated and the days lengthened toward spring. The snow had settled to about three feet and I helped Earle cut down a big fir tree for firewood, some distance from the cabin. By now he had taught me the art of cutting wood with a six-foot. cross-cut saw.

On each end of these saws was an eight-inch removable wooden handle and my job was to pull on my handle with the correct verve and sweep, neither jerking nor digging in nor pulling the saw out of the cut, while Earle pulled smoothly on his. This is remarkably difficult to achieve and the day I learned to do it smoothly was a proud one for me.

Earle was always careful to keep the teeth of the saw sharp and the rakers the correct length so the ribbons of wood that emerged from the cut were neither

174

too thick nor too thin. Dull teeth would tire the operator and short rakers would take out too little wood.

The best time to cut firewood was in the winter when the sap was down. It split easier then and was lighter to handle, and if it needed to be burned right away, it made a hotter fire than wood filled with sap, with less creosote forming in the chimney.

I never ceased to marvel at Earle's ability to fell a tree in exactly the direction he wanted. First, he would walk around and size it up, determining the degree of tilt in one direction or another. If there was any question, he would hold his double-bitted axe by the end of the handle, between his thumb and middle finger, letting it hang like a plumb bob so he could sight past the handle to the tree, determining which way it was leaning. Then a wedge-shaped undercut would be made with the saw and axe on the side toward which the tree was to fall. Earle would check the accuracy of this by placing the top edge of the blade of the double-bitted axe in the notch of the undercut, with the handle pointing directly toward the spot where he wanted the tree to go. Then the long, tiring cut on the opposite side of the tree would begin. Getting the cut started was a science. I was inclined to jab the points of the teeth into the bark, only to have the saw stick and have to pull it out and start over again. A long, smooth swing of the arms was what did it.

When the cut was almost finished and the top of the tree was beginning to show some movement, Earle could still control the direction of the fall by cutting a little more on one side and withholding the cutting on the other. Sometimes he would also have to use wedges to force the tree to go in the direction he wanted. This is when we started to watch the top of the tree between each stroke, and when at last it began to move slowly in the right direction. Earle would call, "Timber!" If the wedges were in the cut in front of the saw he would remove one handle and pull the saw out of the cut and take it quickly to where it would be out of harm's way; then we would move swiftly to a spot behind some other tree where we would be safe from flying branches.

There was always an element of risk at this stage and my heart beat fast, not only from fear but from the distress of hearing the sound the tree made when it tore loose from its final shreds of contact with the stump. It seemed like a cry of anguish and I have often wondered if trees have feelings.

Once down, Earle would limb the tree with the axe while I measured the cuts with a measuring stick and marked them with a hand axe, making little nicks in the bark.

The first saw-cut, near the base of the trunk, was always the hard one. This was where the muscles of the tree had toughened with constant movement in the wind. Sometimes in a fir there would be pockets of pitch which gummed the saw and we had to pour kerosene into the cut to lubricate it.

In cutting off blocks when the tree was down, the saw was held in a vertical position and the body had to move with a rhythmic, swinging movement, smoothly, without jerking. It seemed to take me years before I learned to do this well and Earle would call to me jokingly, "Take the caulks out of your boots!" This meant that if he had to drag me back and forth on the end of the saw, I could at least make it easier for him by not digging in my feet. These remarks always infuriated me, although I knew they were standard backwoods jests.

Sometimes when the tree was on a higher piece of ground than the house, we would pack down a trail in the snow with a sled and try to roll the blocks as far as we could, then load them and drag them the rest of the way. Most of the time we would load a couple of the huge blocks on the sled, some of them weighing as much as two hundred pounds each. The load was heavy and would constantly steer off course or tip over into the deep, soft snow and have to be re-loaded again. This was hard work as some of the blocks were three or four feet in diameter, and I never enjoyed it. Perhaps it was because we always did it at the end of several hours work, when I was tired and my feet were cold. I can never remember cutting wood in the winter when my feet weren't cold.

Modern winter apparel, designed for low temperatures, has made winter much more enjoyable than it was in those days and what I had was superior to what the early settlers wore. Looking at faded photographs, I have wondered how women kept dry and warm out in the snow with long skirts and leather shoes.

10

Spring in Atnarko

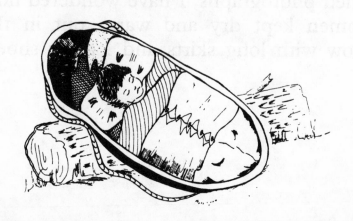

TOWARD the end of January the days grew longer and the sun returned over the mountain after an absence of more than two months. Day after day it crept slowly down the hillside behind us until it finally came through the window of the house at noon on January twenty-six. I let out a joyous whoop and we paid homage by sticking the discarded Christmas tree in the snow and lighting it.

There was a southwest wind blowing

and the temperature went up to 34°F. I celebrated by washing clothes and drying them outside for the first time that winter. This event seemed as exciting to me as the winter solstice; the clothes smelled sweet and there was no feathery coating of hoar frost to scrape off before bringing them in off the line. However, washing clothes was never a festive occasion, it was plain hard work.

All the water had to be carried from the river where Earle had built a ramp down onto a raft which moved up and down with the water level. In the winter it was low and the snow-covered ramp was steep, but Earle had attached a sturdy handrail. Most of the time we had to dip water through a hole chopped in the thick river ice.

Back at the house it had to be lifted up into a boiler on the stove, then when heated it had to be lifted from there into the washtub which stood on a bench. I used yellow bar soap and a scrubbing board, wringing the garments by hand. They had to be rinsed in two separate waters which also had been heated. The whole process entailed the carrying of innumerable buckets of water from the river, one in each hand, and then when the washing was finished it had to be taken outside again.

Usually I chose a day to do all this when Earle was away elsewhere. I don't know whether it mortified him to see me do such tiring work but it bothered me to have him witness it. However, it was considered a woman's job.

With washing clothes such an arduous chore it was no wonder bachelors wore their garments until they were stiff with grime. Earle told me of the time when he was living alone and he tried boiling his woolen underwear, with disastrous results. Another time he hung it in the river, hoping the gentle movement of the current would wash it clean, only to find the knitted wool full of silt and like sandpaper when he pulled it out of the water.

I used to dream of water running from a tap and a handcranked, wooden washing machine like the one advertised in the T. Eaton mail order catalogue. It had a wooden tub with corrugated interior walls and bottom and a round, hinged lid with pegs attached to the underside which gyrated the clothes against the rough surface of the tub. The gears on the top of the lid were set in motion by the handle which stood at the side of the tub and was cranked back and forth by the operator.

This, I thought, would take all the back-break out of washing and I yearned to have one, but it was years before we could afford this luxury. Instead, Earle bought me a new washboard for Christmas. My old one had a corrugated metal scrubbing surface which was getting dented and cracked but the elegant new one had ridges of roughened glass. It was beautiful, but coming up the trail on the packhorse, a small sliver of it had been broken out just inside the wooden frame and I lived in mortal fear of losing my little finger through the hole while I was scrubbing.

Years later when finally we were able to buy the washing machine, I found it to be almost as tiring as a scrubboard and so much more boring, standing cranking a lever back and forth with monotonous regularity. But the covered wooden tub did keep the water warm longer and there was a removable wooden bung at the base of the tub which enabled one to drain the water into a bucket.

The really attractive feature was the hand-operated wringer attached to the tub. The rubber rollers were hard and popped off nearly all the buttons from the clothes but they squeezed most of the wash water from the garments and it was less tiring for the hands than twisting out the water.

Later, we dug a well close to the house, not so much for its convenience but because an extraordinary large run of spawning salmon had filled the river with floating bits of decayed fish. Even boiled, the water still smelled of it.

I had really enjoyed going out to the raft and standing quietly, watching the wild life. One day I saw a fish hawk dive from a tall cottonwood tree just beyond where I stood on the raft. He caught a fair-sized fish and started to fly away with it when a Bald Eagle took off from his perch across the river and pursued him. They were still in the air over the field when the eagle caught up with the hawk which let go of the fish. I put down my buckets and started running, reaching the fish before the eagle got there. It was a Dolly Varden, undamaged, and we had it for lunch.

With the returning sun, cedar waxwings and junkoes joined the chickadees and in the open water of the river the mergansers were thinking of courting. Four swans landed in the river in front of the cabin but were restless and left when a couple of coyotes started barking. We heard crows cawing, and eagles screaming; these appeared now that steelheads were in the river and the ice was going out.

It almost felt like spring. Winter had been an absence of sound and smell. Even color was frozen and the evergreens were black and lifeless, but with the returning sun they came to life again. Under the fir trees on the ridge where the ground was bare and the squirrels were chasing each other, the sweet scent of the sun on the fallen needles reminded me of ripe strawberries.

Every fine day was spent outdoors and we were glad to rest in the evenings. There was no radio and there was time for reading. Sometimes I read aloud and I marvel now at my ability in those days to keep going for hours without fatigue, reading to Earle by the light from a coal-oil lamp.

We had brought in from Portland a dozen or more leatherbound complete works of classics. Every two weeks the mail came with fresh reading material. including books from the provincial lending library in Victoria. This was a service provided by the government for people like ourselves who had no access to a library. It was free with return postage provided by a self-addressed sticker from the library. We could keep the books for any reasonable length of time but usually they requested a quick return of the newer ones.

There were lists of books in almost any category from which one could make a selection and if these books were not available, a substitute would be supplied. Most of the time we described the sort of book we wanted and were pleased with their selection.

One evening Earle was reading a library book we had just received on the history of the Cariboo. In it was an account of the Chilcotin massacre of white men by the oppressed Indians, followed by the story of Indian Chief Sorrence's escape from the Chilcotin in 1863 with a party of eight men, three women and six children. They planned to go to the rugged, uninhabited country south of the Bella Coola River, where they would be safe from pursuit.

Leaving stealthily they made swift progress from the interior plateau country, down into a valley (the Atnarko) at the head of a long lake. (This must have been Lonesome Lake and the trail they used to get there was probably the one Earle used when he packed our things over Mount Kappan from Charlotte Lake.) Crossing the valley at the head of the long lake, they climbed the steep mountainside (Earle's trapping trail) up onto gently rolling country, then westward to a chain of lakes (the Turner Lake string) and beyond that to a river, gray with pulverized rock, flowing through a deep canyon (the Whitewater). With great difficulty they managed to cross this and then made the arduous and almost insurmountable ascent over the glacier, to a valley that was rich with trees and wild game where they could make their home. (The Noeick River which empties into the head of South Bentinck Arm.) Somewhere on the height of land over which they passed, they found gold nuggets.

When he had finished reading this portion of the book, Earle put it down and seemed lost in thought for a long time. Then he told me a fascinating story of how he almost learned the location of this now mythical gold.

During the beginning of the First World War when Ralph left Lonesome Lake to join the army, he asked Earle to trap his line, until Earle himself joined the Canadian army. On one of the trips to the upper end of the trapline, Earle was spending the night in the small trapping cabin, enjoying the warmth of the fire while he waited for his supper to cook. He heard a knock on the door. It didn't seem possible there could be anyone within thirty miles of the cabin but he called, "Come in." Quietly the door opened and in walked an Indian. He was about forty and spoke with dignity in broken English, telling Earle his name was Hunlen and that he was "broke grub." He said he had just walked over Mount Kappan and that "one more he stop". Earle didn't quite understand him but the Indian repeated what he had said and Earle realized that the man had a companion outside. Earle asked Hunlen to bring him in, there was plenty of food for everyone. Hunlen explained that his companion's feet had been frozen coming over the mountain, then he went out to bring this person in. Earle was startled to see the companion was a girl whom Hunlen introduced as Zodie, "all the same boy."

They had supper together and Earle did what he could to dress the girl's feet, and then it was time to go to bed. This posed a bit of a problem as the cabin was small. The bunk was wide enough for two, but Earle didn't want to sleep on the floor although it was covered with clean, dry slough-grass. Finally he made a bed of Hudson Bay blankets there for Zodie and he and Hunlen shared the bunk.

In the morning Hunlen reiterated that

he was broke grub and wanted to go south to the Kleena Kleene to trap. Earle decided to take him back to the home cabin for supplies, leaving Zodie to rest where she was.

Back at The Birches, Earle loaded Hunlen's packsack with venison, flour. baking powder, salt, tea, rice and beans. Enough to take them to where there was plenty of game. He was anxious to get Hunlen and Zodie as far away from his own trapline as possible.

After giving Hunlen the supplies, he cooked a big meal of venison steaks, fried potatoes and sourdough biscuits, topped off with stewed fruit and coffee. Hunlen filled his stomach and after the meal he was relaxed and expansive. He seemed to be wanting to tell Earle something. It turned out to be the story of the gold.

His mama had been one of the children in Sorrence's party that had fled the Chilcotin and escaped to the uninhabited wilds south of the Bella Coola River. In gratitude for Earle's hospitality he was about to tell him the location of the gold, as his mother had told him, but at the last moment decided against it. "Suppose

I tell white man, then white man get gold. Indian nothing." Earle agreed with him.

It wasn't until Earle read the library book, twenty years after Hunlen's visit, that he associated the date of the exodus from the Chilcotin with the age of Hunlen's mother. The date of Hunlen's visit to the cabin was 1915; the date of the journey over the glacier was 1863, and Hunlen's mother was a young girl of about twelve then, which would make her about sixty-four, as Hunlen was probably about forty. It all added up.

Hunlen must have been relieved that he had not revealed the source of the gold, but he had one other gift he wanted to give Earle — Zodie.

On this trial run over the mountains on snowshoes, she had proved a liability by freezing her feet, so the gift wasn't too painful to offer.

Earle thanked him and explained as best he could that he wouldn't be able to keep her. The next morning they parted amicably, Hunlen to pick up Zodie at the trapping cabin, leaving Earle to wash dishes, wondering if perhaps he shouldn't have kept her after all.

With a wistful expression on his face, Earle resumed reading about the Chilcotin.

Not all our evenings were spent reading. Earle made me a spinning wheel. So much hiking was hard on socks and we decided to make our own from virgin wool.

We had sent away for a diagram and directions for making the entire spinning wheel and while waiting for them Earle cut some wet, unseasoned vine maple. As it dried it warped and twisted out of shape but by standing the wood near the heater and turning it from side to side occasionally, he finally managed to dry it so it stayed in place.

He had no tools other than an axe, a handsaw, brace and bit, a small plane and a pocket knife, but when the spinning wheel was finished it looked beautiful. It worked too, but I didn't know how to use it.

We asked Maxie and he didn't know either. Then a friend stayed over with us one mail day who knew all about it — his grandmother had one. This huge man sat down at the wheel, his feet completely covering the treadle and his enormous hands fumbling with a carded batt. Something like a hawser came out of the spindle and in my distress I managed to get him away from my lovely spinning wheel before he damaged it. But, I did get the idea and with practice managed to spin useable yarn.

Earle had traded a packsaddle to a rancher in the interior for some sacks of raw wool, some of it natural dark brown and black which I mixed with white when I carded it, making a heather mixture for sweaters. We bought a pair of carders from the mail order catalog and Earle made a place for them on the edge of his workbench in one end of the long kitchen, the bottom carder being nailed firmly to the bench.

After washing the wool carefully so as not to mat it, it was dried and then teased by hand into a fluff. This fluff was then carded into a smooth batt which was removed from the carders in a roll. Expert carders do this with a graceful manipulation of their hands, but I never achieved this skill and managed quite well with the bottom carder attached to the bench.

With a box full of rolls, I was ready to spin. This was a delicate coordination of hand, eye and foot. I had to maintain constant, steady speed with my feet, while my fingers fed the wool in a uniform amount, a few threads at a time without a break. No breaks, no lumps. This was extraordinarily difficult to do and I grew so tense in my concentration, my shoulders ached and I constantly wondered how mothers could find it relaxing to sit down for an evening at the spinning wheel after taking care of a big family all day.

The first yarn I spun was a bit coarse but Earle made me several sets of knitting needles of different sizes, from the same tough vine maple such as he used to make the spinning wheel.

Before long, I had knitted heavy socks to wear inside our gumboots. It was incredible how much better they wore than the manufactured ones and how much warmer and more comfortable they were. From socks, I graduated to a sweater for Earle, a pullover that withstood heavy duty for years, wearing at last to a silky thread.

Several of our bachelor friends asked me to make socks for them too. I was secretly proud of my achievement, but after making several pairs, found it to be not very profitable. The most careful calculations showed I was making two cents an hour for my labor.

Winter hung on. Sometimes there would be a few days of spring-like weather then it turned cold and stormy again, with more snow. It was during one of these storms that we shared in a distressing experience.

The telegraph line had broken several miles farther up the valley and late one afternoon we had seen a young, temporary lineman ride past, probably to stop at Maxie's for the night before going on to the break the next morning.

Just before noon the following day we heard a loud call for help from the trail and ran out to find the young lineman, too weak to dismount from his horse, with blood dripping from one boot onto the snow.

We led his horse to the cabin and

between us managed to get him off and into the living room where we placed him on a cot. Earle removed his boot and sock to find he had chopped the top of his foot deeply with an axe. It was a large, gaping wound and even bound tightly, it kept bleeding and dripping.

Earle tied a tourniquet, but this stopped the flow only temporarily, so he decided to try to stitch the gash. We had disinfectant and Earle could inject analgesic into the site of the wound, but what he didn't have was a curved surgical needle; so he made one.

Heating one of my sewing needles in the fire, Earle held one end of the bench vise, and took the other end in his pliers and bent it to the desired curve. Then he sharpened the point with meticulous care on his hone and boiled the needle along with some silk thread of the right thickness and strength.

The stitching was a complete success, and after a couple of day's rest in bed, the young chap was able to ride to the end of the road on a horse when his brother came up after him. At the hospital, the doctor was satisfied to leave

Earle's stitching as it was.

Earle was teaching me to prevent accidents; to think first about what I did and to watch where I placed my feet. I was learning that his knives and axes were always sharp and a gun always loaded. There were other things that could be just as lethal, a slippery stick in the woods, or thin ice.

One incident we weren't expecting was a hole in one of Earle's teeth. There was no dentist in Bella Coola and most people let their teeth go until they were so bad the doctor had to pull them.

This tooth was an upper bicuspid and the hole wasn't too large but Earle was beginning to be aware of it, so we decided to fill it. We had some copper cement in our first aid kit and Earle fashioned a scraper from the tip of a file. We had an exceptionally fine dentist in Portland, and remembering his tools and technique, it seemed just a matter of thoroughly scraping away the decayed portion of the tooth, shaping it to hold the filling, cleaning it out, disinfecting it, then drying it thoroughly and putting in the cement. Earle had steady nerves and let me do this for him. The result was satisfactory and lasted for years.

We administered first aid once more that winter. This time to Maxie's injured feelings. He stopped in late one afternoon on his way home from a long day's trapping trip up the Bunch Grass sidehill. He told us that after eating his lunch at the top of the hill in the sunshine he tried in vain to light his pipe with a lighter that looked like his old reliable one, but wasn't. A packtrain from Anahim had stayed at his place the night before and one of the men had surreptitiously swapped a broken-down Bullet lighter for Maxie's good one.

Max had been seething all afternoon, and as he lit his pipe with the matches which Earle produced in a hurry, he kept fuming, "Them slough-grass ranchers!"

Maxie liked trapping. It was not so much the catching of furs, but the purposeful exercise out in the woods which he enjoyed, and the day he stopped in to tell us about the lighter had been bright and sunny. It must have been almost spring-like up on the hillside facing the sun; but the following day we were thrown back into winter with snow and zero temperatures.

The cold weather lasted a couple of weeks but on Valentine's Day there was a thaw that started the roof dripping. The snow settled and the cold at night formed a hard crust on the surface so we could walk anywhere on it.

Our fields were criss-crossed with the tracks of coyotes that were looking for mice. The rodents lived off clover in their burrows beneath the snow. There was never a night when the coyotes didn't entertain us with a chorus and the wolves howled frequently from the hillside or the game trail on the other side of the river. I grew accustomed to the sound of the coyotes but there was something electrifying about the vibrant howl of the wolves and I always stopped what I was doing to listen; it was beautiful but frightening. We had no dog to be concerned about, but there were many tales of dogs being lured to their death by seemingly playful wolves in February, the mating month.

With the milder weather, Earle was restless to get started on the construction of the woodshed and barn. Having the hard surface of the snow to travel on, he decided to search for a shake tree so we could cut the shake bolts and drag them in on a sled before the weather warmed in March.

In selecting a shake tree, he started by looking in a sheltered spot where the tree would grow straight and tall, unbuffeted by winds. Then he would find one whose bark grew in straight, vertical lines, without a spiral twist, also without limbs on the lower portion of the trunk. He cut a sample by making two notches, one above the other about a foot apart, so he could split out a slab about three inches thick. From this, a miniature shake was split, slicing across from the bark toward the heart and examined for twist and waviness.

After the tree was down, the cutting of the shake bolts would start beyond the swelling butt, and the tree would be marked in precise thirty-inch lengths. Cedar was much easier to saw than fir.

When we bucked off the blocks with the cross-cut saw, Earle split them into bolts with a sledge-hammer and wedge, and I had the job of standing them on edge and removing the bark with an axe. With the sap up in the tree the bark came off easily.

Splitting the shakes was something I couldn't do, as wielding the heavy wooden mallet and striking the froe with sufficient force to split the shake was a bit too much for me. The shakes we made were thirty inches long and about six to ten inches wide, with a uniform thickness of three-eighths of an inch, the size used for sheds and barns. Shakes for cabins were sometimes shorter.

The Norwegian settlers farther down the valley were expert craftsmen and built beautiful homes. They had a seemingly inexhaustible supply of knot-free cedar for house logs and shakes. The logs for the houses, some of them three feet wide, were hewn on all four sides with a broad axe and looked as if they had been planed, as indeed some of them were on the inside. The planes used for this job were wooden ones, three feet long with a steel blade nearly four inches wide. These planes were much too heavy for one man to use alone so they were made with a handle on each end, allowing two men to operate it facing each other. One man pulled while the other pushed.

Some of the logs were hewn with a rounded top which fitted into a corresponding concave contour on the bottom of the log above. They required little caulking, and easily shed the rain. Some of the builders pinned their logs together with dowel pins and all were meticulously dovetailed at the corners.

Roof shakes for the houses were tapered on the upper half of one side to make a better fit. Somewhere in the backyard of most of the settlers was an odd-looking contraption that looked like a wooden horse for children to play on. It was a shaving horse; a six-foot log set up on four legs. Near one end was a comfortable place to sit and not far from the other end was an arm which came up through an opening in the log, swinging back and forth on an axle driven from side to side through the log.

Through the base of this arm was a rod which supported the feet of the operator, one on each side, and as he pushed the rod away from him with his feet, the top of the arm swung toward him, pressing down on a shake which had been placed on a sloping surface in front of him. Teeth, made by spikes driven through the head of the arm, clamped the shake in place and held it immovable. It was then possible to taper one side of one end of the shake with a drawknife, making it a slim wedge shape. Shakes trimmed this way were placed smooth side down on the roof, to give a watertight, wind proof fit.

Shakes for barns and sheds weren't usually planed, so before long we had enough split and stacked to do the woodshed and little barn we were going to put up.

By the time the shakes were made, the sap was well up in the trees and Earle was ready to cut the cedar posts for the two buildings. Max hauled in the logs with the team while there was still a little snow left; not enough to make it difficult for the horses, but enough to keep the logs clean and free from dirt. With the sap up when they were cut, they peeled easily. This was my job and I enjoyed peeling off long strips of bark without a break. It made me feel stalwart and helpful.

Putting up the frame of the woodshed was considered a bit hazardous for a woman, so I kept out of the way while Earle did it alone, but I peeled the jack pine poles to which the shakes were nailed when the roof went on. I passed the poles up to Earle and then fastened bundles of shakes together for him to haul up onto the roof with a rope. When the shed was finished we were going to have a dry place to store our next winter's wood.

After the woodshed, the next project was the little barn for the cow we hoped to bring back with us from Bella Coola in the fall. Earle had decided to go fishing in the summer and Max had agreed to get some Indians to help put up our hay while we were away.

I was beginning to learn that spring was not a specific date on the calendar, but a gradual relinquishing of the bonds of winter. One of the last to go was the deceptively dry-looking little piles of horse manure that dotted the meadow at Maxie's, where the horses had stood during the fall before the deep snow came. Well-insulated, the cores of these little mounds remained frozen long after the surrounding field was bare of snow.

Walking up the field, Max found these little hummocks irresistible. It was almost a rite of spring that he scatter them with a vigorous kick, his long leg swinging like a pendulum. No matter how many times he struck a still-frozen one, he continued to kick the hummocks and limped about a good deal of the time. I have often wondered if this might not be Maxie's release from the tensions of winter.

With the warm sun drawing frost from the ground, little green shoots of grass began to appear and it was time for land-clearing. There was a lot of it for us to do around the margins of the fields where the willows and alders had encroached on the former clearings.

Day after day we were out sawing and chopping and digging roots with a grub-hoe. Even though it was tiring, there was an exhilaration in this that drew us out of the cabin early in the morning and brought us in, smoke-begrimed and covered with dirt at suppertime. We kept fires burning whenever the wood was dead and dry enough. The fragrance of woodsmoke filled the air, not only from our place but from Maxie's. Years later, even after there was machinery to do the work, we still felt compelled to go out in the spring and clear the land by hand. There was a springtime resurgence of life in the body as well as in the soil.

Before long, it was time to plough the garden spot and get it ready for planting. Maxie brought the horses down to plough and disc it for us, dragging the machinery on a stoneboat, a sort of low, heavy-duty sled. My job was to rake the rich soil, removing roots and sticks and lumps of sod that came to the surface.

The time of planting was anywhere between the first and fifteenth of May, according to the weather, Maxie advised us. Some years it was necessary to wait until the twenty-fourth of May, when the frosts were over, before putting the seeds in the ground. This was the day marked on the calendar as a legal holiday to celebrate Queen Victoria's birthday. But, come frost or hail, that was the day Maxie went spring salmon fishing. It was a ritual.

Carrying a spear, he strode by with a buoyant step in the morning to his favorite spot at the head of the Swiftwater a few miles down the trail. The water was shallow and the fish tired by their passage up through the swift, turbulent stretch, swam slowly in the quiet channels among the boulders near the shore. Max stood for hours on end in the shadows under the over-hanging alders and willows, spear in hand, waiting. Almost always he came home with a big spring strapped to his packsack.

The spear he used was one he made himself from a slim cedar pole and the head of a three-pronged pitchfork. The two outer tines had been heated and then bent inward in the shape of hooks, with the center tine cut shorter and sharpened into a spear. The shaft of the pitchfork was fitted into a hole in the end of the cedar pole which was bound with cord. The pole and the spear were attached to each other by a length of braided, stout linen cord so that when the fish was speared, preferably just back of the head, the two outer tines held it from escaping, then the head of the spear came loose from the long pole handle, allowing a little play while the fish was d ragged out onto shore. Some of the spring salmon weighed fifty pounds or more.

Maxie always brought us some of the salmon he caught. It tasted wonderful and we were pleased to have it as neither Earle nor I had the patience to stand for hours on the riverbank with a spear. Trout were easier to catch.

The Bella Coola and its tributaries, particularly the Atnarko, were one of the great salmon spawning areas on the Pacific Coast and there was a constant supply of fish, as one species followed another up the river to spawn. This sustained first, the large Indian population before the white man came; then the Norwegian settlers when they arrived to homestead and fish commercially in the inlet.

There were two canneries near the head of Burke Channel — B.C. Packers on the south, and the Tallheo Cannery operated by the New England Packers on the north side. Earle had fished for them for three seasons after the First World War and had done very well. Since there was no way for us to earn a living in Atnarko, he planned to try fishing again, taking me with him, but this time it would be for the B.C. Packers.

When Earle had asked me if I would like to spend the summer in a sailboat, I had visions of a graceful white hull with white sails, gliding down the inlet. But when he explained that he was thinking of applying for a fishing permit and a boat from the B.C. Packers, I reminded him of how seasick I became in small boats.

"You'll get used to it," he rejoined, "And before long you'll grow to love the motion of the waves."

I was going to have an opportunity to find out.

About the first of June Earle left with the mail carrier on the return trip to Bella Coola to see about getting a boat and gear ready at the cannery. He would be gone for two weeks and then would return with the mail on the next trip to

Atnarko, taking me back with him the following day.

We were going to be gone for the summer and I was busy preparing our clothes and getting the cabin ready to leave unoccupied for three months or more. Ralph would be coming down to sleep in it on mail nights so he could stay up late answering letters without disturbing Maxie.

The garden also had to be put in order before we left. I loved hoeing and weeding but the mosquitoes were troublesome in June and took away much of the pleasure in being outdoors. Patented insect repellents were not available so we used a highly pungent, but effective mixture of citronella oil and pine-tar. It was oily and black and stained everything it came in contact with, but the mosquitoes couldn't stand it. The aroma was reminiscent of someone who had been on a long camping trip and spent much of their time over a smoky campfire, without changing clothes or washing.

It was lonely without Earle and sometimes on hot afternoons I would take the rifle and walk up the trail to Maxie's. We sat in the shade of the cabin with a smudge keeping the mosquitoes at bay while we watched the deer browsing on the hillside, and Maxie spun yarns.

There were no newspapers, no radio, no news of the outside world to disturb the tranquillity, but Maxie did have a telephone. It was an old gooseneck, hand-cranking one the Yukon Telegraph kept there for testing the line. Maxie loved to listen on it. He was "rubbering" on it one day when I arrived unexpectedly.

There were certain amenities to be observed in rubbernecking, or "rubbering." One listened with the receiver in one hand and covered the mouthpiece with the other so sounds would not disturb the conversation. Maxie used the leather-sheathed stub of his left arm to plug the mouthpiece and on this occasion, when I knocked at his door, Rex was lying sleeping at his feet. Startled, the dog set up a loud barking which confused Maxie. He removed his stub from the telephone and shouted into the mouthpiece, "Shut-up." It was the only time I saw him embarrassed.

There was always a sense of guilt associated with rubbering which probably added to the enjoyment; but everyone did it. The Yukon Telegraph and Telephone with its branch lines was a lifeline in more than one sense — it kept people in remote places from losing their minds with loneliness.

11

Going to Bella Coola

EARLE returned with the mail carrier at the end of two weeks and I was ready to go with him on the return trip the next morning. We walked the fifteen miles to Belarko at the end of the road, where the carrier's horses were returned to the farm they came from. There, we transferred our things to the truck which took us down the forty miles of narrow dirt road to Bella Coola. The genial mail carrier, Ole Nygaard, brought Earle up to date on all the changes in the valley that had taken place since he went away several years before. It seemed strange to be in a vehicle again, everything went by so swiftly.

What seemed even stranger to me was to find the townsite of Bella Coola on the south side of the river situated on what used to be the Clayton farm. Since I had visited my sister during school holidays, there had been a disastrous flood in the old townsite on the north side of the valley and the government had bought land from the Claytons and moved everyone to the present site. The new, more crowded townsite had a magnificent view but lacked the nostalgic charm for us of the former sunny location, and it was a long time before we adjusted to the change.

Earle and I had arranged to spend our weekends in the rambling old Clayton house which still stood on the riverbank. It was just as my sister and her husband had left it and no one had been living in it. Vincent never returned after my sister's death in Victoria, and the house was empty and smelled musty after a winter without fires.

We spent most of our time in the book-lined library which was comfortable with a huge fireplace and bear rugs. Indian masks and muskets mingled with leather-bound books, and standing in one corner was a large brass-bound cedar chest with a heavy lock that had been used for storing furs.

The room was filled with memories of the past.

The windows in the thick log walls looked out across the flowing river to the snow-capped mountains beyond. In times past one could have looked out to see Indian dugouts bringing supplies up the river from the sidewheeler anchored out in the inlet, or canoeloads of furs from the interior floating down to land on the gravel beach at the edge of the water, to be traded for muskets or Hudson Bay blankets and tea and sugar.

The house was part of the former Hudson Bay Post which John Clayton had purchased from the company and it was here that he brought his bride, Elizabeth, in 1890.

There were four children born to them,

Vincent and Davenport, Margery and Dorothy. It was Vincent who brought my sister, Florence, to this house to live after their wedding in Victoria.

Nothing in her earlier life in gentle Sussex, England, or later in Victoria, British Columbia, could have prepared her for the magnificent isolation of the Bella Coola Valley, but in time she grew to love the comfortable way of life in the charming old house where "Granny" Clayton continued to live with them when their own two children were born.

When my sister came, the townsite of Bella Coola was on the north side of the valley, about a mile from the waterfront. Only the Indian Village and the Clayton property were on the south.

There was a wooden Howe Truss bridge spanning the river not far from the Clayton house and one could hear the sound of horses' hooves as they crossed it. A narrow dirt road through the woods joined the bridge to the townsite on the north side of the valley.

Where the Bella Coola River empties into the head of the inlet, sixty miles inland from the Pacific Ocean, the valley

216

is about three miles wide, with towering mountains rising abruptly on either side. The peaks on the south are jagged and snow-capped the year round while those on the north are rounded, ground smooth by glacial action in eons past.

The main road up the valley began at the townsite and crossed the river on another bridge about four miles farther east. Winding its way through heavy timber, it passed over several mountain streams with smaller bridges, between which were isolated farm clearings.

About twelve miles from Bella Coola the road came to Hagensborg, a picturesque Norwegian settlement of small farms, a Lutheran church, general store, post office and a school. From there the road continued on up the valley until it reached Canoe Crossing where there was a cable ferry crossing to the north side of the valley.

Thereafter the road remained on the north, reaching at last the Seventh Day Adventist settlement of Firvale, about thirty miles from the townsite. At the time of my sister's arrival as a bride, only a rough wagon road existed for a short distance beyond this point. Each year the road was extended eastward up the packhorse trail that climbed the mountain out of the valley, almost seventy miles from the inlet, up into the interior jack pine country of Anahim Lake. It wasn't until 1952 that work on a road was begun that would link the valley with the rest of British Columbia, ending its splendid isolation.

In those early days the Valley seemed roughly divided into areas. There was an Indian Reserve which was a large tract of land with a village of ancient Indian dwellings and totem poles, as well as a growing number of newer, lumber houses, all of them close to the river. The townsite of Bella Coola was a white community of government employees, an Indian agent, a police officer but no jail, two stores, a post office and a telegraph office, a branch of the Bank of Montreal, a newspaper called *The Courier*, a combination church-community hall, a small hospital, a hotel and a boarding house. Farther east, the main body of the valley was settled by the Norwegian colonists who had drawn lots for the surveyed land when they first arrived from Minnesota in October of 1894.

They cleared land in the heavily-timbered forest and built beautiful log houses, hewn with expert craftsmanship. Every Norwegian homestead was neat and orderly, with well-kept fences and a full woodshed. They planted orchards and cleared land for hay to feed a milk cow, had a pig and chickens as well as a garden, and the men fished commercially for salmon in the inlet during the summer.

The latecomers, most of them non-Norwegians from the United States, took up their preemptions beyond where the land had first been surveyed and allotted to the Norwegian colonists.

The farther up the valley one went, the greater the distances became between the clearings until beyond the Seventh Day Adventist settlement at Firvale, thirty miles from Bella Coola, there were no longer women and families, but only bachelors in the cruder log cabins.

Now, after sixty years, most of the bachelors have gone and the life of freedom and independence has been circumscribed by regulations. Many of the cabins have fallen into disuse and decay and the forest has reclaimed some of the clearings. In this rugged frontier the pioneer spirit has given way to the comfortable amenities of life and something colorful has gone from the land.

12

Salmon Industry

SOCKEYE fishing began at six o'clock in the evening of the last Sunday in June.

For two weeks before it started, the cannery was alive with activity. The fishermen were painting their boats and getting their gear ready. They stripped the cork and lead lines from old nets and attached them to new ones, making everything ready to start fishing sockeye.

The cannery crew had arrived to get the machinery in order, and the mess house had opened up.

Most of the women who worked in the cannery filling the tins with fish were from the Village or from farms farther up the valley. The ones from the Village went home every night but those from up the valley lived in a row of small cabins on the hillside adjacent to the cannery. Each one was large enough for two women and was heated with a small coal-burning cast-iron stove on which they did their cooking.

The Chinese men whose chief job was to remove the head, tail, fins and entrails of the fish with their sharp knives, "gutting" it was called, lived a life of their own in a large communal building on pilings over the water. They spoke little English and most of them wore their hair in a braided cue and smoked opium. Their tiny, empty opium bottles are still found by glass collectors in the old garbage dumps near the cannery. The Chinamen were fond of flounders and spent their leisure hours fishing from the cannery dock, hanging the fish to dry in the sun on clothes lines or on the railings.

Every spring a freighter came in with the Chinese crew and materials needed in the cannery for the entire season; nails and lumber and pre-cut box material for making the shipping crates for the canned salmon. The tins came flattened, without bottoms or lids. There was a machine at the cannery that opened the flattened tin and shaped it, then attached a round bottom to one end.

The Indian women cleaned the trimmed fish with constantly running water piped in from the hillside, scrubbing them with a stiff brush. Once cleaned, they were placed on a conveyor belt to be cut by machine and distributed by the Chinamen to the fillers. A tray of tins was brought to each of the women and a precise amount of salt was placed in the bottom of every tin before it was filled, expertly and completely, with the sliced fish.

After the fish was packed, the rims were cleaned and the lids put on loosely. Then the filled tins were taken on a conveyor belt through a steam chamber. With the air exhausted, they were sealed and cooked in a huge pressure chamber.

After they were cooled, a Chinaman tapped each one with a light wooden mallet to test the seal by listening to the sound it made; very much like a housewife tapping the metal top of a preserving jar with her fingernail to listen for the high-pitched ping which indicates a perfect seal. After this the tins of fish were labeled and put in wooden cases which had been nailed together by the men. Then the boxes of canned fish were stored in a warehouse to await the freighter which came when fishing was over.

The British Columbia coast was dotted with canneries of a dozen different companies — Goss Millard, New England, Canada Packers, McTavish, B.C. Packers. Each cannery had its own colors and flag which the fishermen flew from the mast, identifying them to the collection boat from their own cannery which picked up their catch each morning.

The gas boat was being introduced for fishing in Bella Coola, but so far there were only a few in use. Most of the boats were sail boats provided by the cannery for the fishermen.

The cannery fishing boats were open ones, twenty-eight feet long, with a seven-and-a-half foot beam. The cockpit in the stern, where the net was piled, occupied about seven feet of the boat. Forward of that were the fishboxes, covered with boards to within three inches of the gunwale. Between the rows of fishboxes was the centerboard which was pulled up or let down by a folding metal rod handle. There were two long oars for rowing the boat when there was no wind. These were kept fastened to the gunwales.

The living quarters extended for about eight feet, between the stem and the fish boxes. This was covered by a hinged lid which was flat when down and sloping toward the bow when open. It was made tight with a painted canvas to keep out the rain or sea, and canvas extended down the sides and was fastened to the gunwale of the boat, somewhat like the hood of a baby carriage. There were also canvas curtains that rolled down to the deck, making it snug within.

This was the fisherman's living quarters, commonly called the "dog house." The lid was held up by a stick which was removed to let it down when the boat was traveling. The livable part of the cubby hole began just aft of the mast where the boat was four feet wide. On one side there was a single bunk which narrowed and extended past the mast almost to the stem. On the other side was a shelf for supplies, and on the floor was the gasoline campstove or a kerosene primus.

These cramped, uncomfortable quarters were not designed for leisure and certainly they weren't made to accommodate two people but Earle wanted me to go with him.

The boats were pointed on both ends, with a rudder fastened to the stern post by metal hooks so it could be removed while casting out the net. The tiller was also removable from the rudder.

Most fishermen had at least three nets, one each for spring salmon, sockeye and coho. Old sockeye nets could be used for fishing humpbacks, or pinks, as they are now called. They are a softer fish with less fight than the others and a weaker net would hold them. The coho nets were also used for dog salmon, or chums.

These nets were designed to allow the fish to penetrate the mesh a quarter of the way along its body so the strand of linen would catch behind the gills and pectoral fins. The nets were also of different shades of green and density of fiber, according to the size of the fish and the color of the water in the inlet. During hot weather when the glaciers were melting, the water was sometimes a light gray as far out as ten miles down the inlet.

The nets were twelve hundred feet long and forty meshes deep and were hung from cork lines. Corks were oval-shaped cedar floats, tarred and strung on three-eighths inch cotton rope. The lead line was one-quarter inch cotton with lead weights every eighteen inches, which had been fastened to the line by drawing it through a closed metal mould into which a controlled amount of melted lead was poured through a hole, making the lead weights uniform in size and smooth in contour. The lead line was twenty or thirty feet longer than the cork line which made the net hang more loosely, enabling it to catch more fish.

Attached by a rope about twenty feet long to the far end of the net was a wooden float which held a red kerosene lantern with a clear glass globe. This indicated the position of the net at night in relation to the boat, which also kept a lantern burning. The float was stable enough not to tip over in a storm.

A gallon tin of coal-oil was part of the weekly supplies bought at the cannery store and paid for in cannery script. Script books were supplied in five or ten dollar books. Each book had a number and these were charged against the fisherman's account which was settled at the end of the fishing season. It was a good year when a man took home more than a thousand dollars. A really good year might be two thousand. A poor year might leave a fisherman owing the cannery.

Besides coal-oil and food, the store also carried underwear and socks, pants and shirts, waterproof aprons and cotton gloves, waterproof pants, coats, sou'westers and cotton hats. The weekly steamer from Vancouver also brought fresh fruit and a few vegetables, as well as a case of mouldy bread. It took the boat several days to get to the Bella Coola cannery since it stopped in at every cannery and logging camp along the coast. Unwrapped bread that was warm and fresh when loaded in Vancouver was often a solid mass of green mould in the closed wooden case when it arrived in Bella Coola.

The first fishing of the season began with spring salmon in May, but not many of the men went out because of the high winds and unsettled weather and the numerous seals; also, because of the scarcity of spring salmon and the low price paid for them. All salmon were paid for by the piece and a spring salmon, whether it weighed ten or fifty pounds, brought fifty cents. Sockeye were twenty, humpbacks three, dog salmon five and coho fifteen cents.

Fishing usually ended on the fifteenth of September since the equinoctial gales were considered too treacherous for open boats. During the last weeks of fishing, the cannery manager spent many anxious hours peering out the office window or walking up and down the dock in a gale, watching for a boat that had yet to come in.

At the end of the season the boats were hauled up on the rocky shore at the cannery, and the drainage bung removed. Everything removable, including the dog house roof, was stored inside the cannery.

13

Fishing in a Sailboat

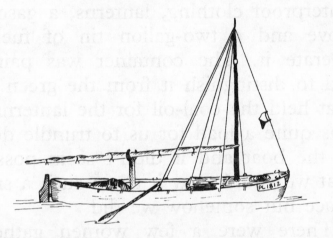

AFTER arriving in Bella Coola to go fishing, Earle had a few days in which to get organized and make final adjustments to the boat while I caught mice and aired out the old Clayton house.

On Sunday we took our packs of bedding and clothing as well as a week's supply of prepared food, and hiked to the cannery.

Earle's boat was tied to the float and after opening up the dog house we put the things inside and walked back on the long boardwalk to the cannery store. It was full of fishermen stocking up for the week. I was the only woman.

When it was our turn to be served we had a long list to be filled: groceries, waterproof clothing, lanterns, a gasoline stove and a two-gallon tin of fuel to operate it. The container was painted red to distinguish it from the green one that held the coal-oil for the lanterns. It was quite a load for us to trundle down to the boat and it didn't seem possible that we could stow it all in such a small space but somehow we did.

There were a few women gathered together talking to each other on the dock. They were wearing starched summer dresses but none was in fishing garb and I asked Earle, "Where are all the other women who go out with their husbands?"

"I guess there aren't any," he admitted.

It wouldn't be long before I found out why.

At five o'clock the packer was ready to tow the fishing boats down the inlet to their desired locations.

There was a long, sturdy towline from the packer, with short lengths of rope spliced into it at suitable intervals, spaced to tow up to fifty boats. Each piece of rope had a honda in the end through which the fisherman slipped the painter of his boat. The honda enabled the rope to slide freely when one end was released from the cleat on the bow of the sailboat. Leaving the towline required some skill, the boat being steered away from the line as quickly as possible to avoid being hit by the boat behind.

Usually the afternoon wind kicked up quite a swell by five o'clock and started tossing the boats soon after they left the cannery and rounded Dead Man's Point. Fortunately my first Sunday out was a fairly quiet one, but still I felt squeamish from the movement of the boat and much of the excitement of the tow was lost to me. However, I did enjoy the swish and slap of the bow against the waves and the absence of any motor noise.

Earle decided to spend the first night in a large bay where we would be relatively free from wind, and when it was time for us to drop off the towline, he put the rudder in place and inserted the tiller, then went forward and untied the end of the painter. Still holding the rope, he returned to the stern and swung the rudder hard over to clear the boat from the ones behind. I thought he did it in a masterful way. As soon as we were clear of the tow he rowed closer to the shore where the fish liked to swim, and prepared to set his net across channel.

By six o'clock nearly every boat was in place, waiting for the bomb at the boundary which signaled the beginning of fishing for the week. With the dull boom, the inlet burst into activity. Earle's sail went up to give the boat a bit of speed, then it was released to flap about in the wind while the rudder was removed and the lighted lantern put overboard on its float. With a section of cork line in one hand and the lead line in the other, Earle cast the net over the stern of the boat, trying to prevent the two lines from tangling as he threw swiftly to keep up with the speed of the boat.

Happily, the first night was calm but I was glad when the net was all out and

234

the twenty-foot extension of cork line was made fast to the stern of the boat. This way, we could sit in the shelter of the dog house and watch the corks.

We sat watching the net for some time, seeing one cork and then another bobbing, which indicated fish in the net. Then the net seemed to be getting shorter, "bunching" Earle called it, and this required putting the boat in a bridle which placed a strain on the net and pulled it out to its full length again.

It seemed terribly cramped in the dog house. The bunk on which we sat was so low we were sitting with our chins on our knees. But it was snug and we had a snack before lying down. Earle kept on all his clothes in case he had to get up in a hurry during the night to tend the net.

At this latitude there is scarcely any darkness at night during the summer months, but once I woke from my sleep and looked out through the curtains to see lights of the boats dotted all over the inlet in the quiet water. They could have been fireflies they seemed so small.

Without any night wind, the net was

twisted and bunched in the morning, but a large number of corks were down and Earle was hopeful he had made a good catch.

We were up early and after a cup of coffee, Earle donned an oilskin apron and cotton gloves, and started pulling the net. There seemed more sticks and branches than fish, and these took a lot of time to extricate from the linen mesh, as every twig had to be removed and the knot it created shaken free before the net was pulled on in and piled neatly with the corks on one side and the lead line on the other. The fish went into the fishbox below the deck.

Disentangling the fish from the net was often a slow process. The smaller ones pulled right through the mesh with little effort but the larger ones had to be pulled out backwards, the net eased over the pectoral fins and gills. Some of them had twisted the net into knots and in their struggle became entangled in another section of the net as well. Jellyfish were often a problem. Any exposed skin burned for hours if even a tiny particle splashed onto it, and to rub one's eyes after touching jellyfish was painfully blinding.

It seemed to take forever before the net was finally in, the lantern hauled aboard and the light blown out. The globe was quite smoky and had to be cleaned before being used again. This was my job.

We were near the shore and I climbed out onto a tiny beach in search of a tree. There were no bathroom facilities on board any of the boats and the call of nature was answered over the gunwale. Earle made me remain in the dog house until this period of the morning was over with on the other boats, and I began to understand why respectable women rarely went fishing with their husbands.

Before long the collection boat had gone out to the farthest of the fishermen and was working its way back toward the cannery. It reached us before Earle had set the net again and the skipper brought his boat alongside in a skillful maneuver, not bumping or jarring our boat. He handed Earle a fish pick for tossing up the fish onto the deck of the collection boat and Earle handed the skipper his tally book in which were noted the date and the number and species of fish Earle had caught. Most of ours were sockeye but there were still a few springs and steelhead among them, or so the book recorded. It was a long time before I could tell one from another.

Sometimes the fishermen gathered in a group to wait for the collection boat. This gave them a chance to have a "mug-up" and an opportunity to compare catches. Hearing of a good catch in a certain location, a fisherman could estimate where that school of fish might be by the time he was ready to set his net again and go there to intercept the remainder. Everyone was interested to find out who was high boat for the day and where he had caught his fish. The boats were constantly moving about on the inlet, drifting with the currents or the tide, or sailing, or being rowed. After a blow, it was amazing how far a boat would travel with the surface current. This wasn't always good for fishing since a strong wind could set up a current that would carry the boat and the top of the net faster than the bottom of it, so the mesh would hang in the water at an angle, reducing its capacity for catching fish.

In the morning, with the water of the inlet glassy and still, Earle had to row the heavy boat to get out the net. He stood up to do this, sometimes letting go of the oars to straighten out the lines as the corks dragged slowly across the gunwale. With the fish delivered and the net out again, it was time for breakfast. I sat hunched over the camp stove and cooked bacon and eggs for Earle. My own stomach wasn't interested in food yet.

After breakfast Earle was ready for a sleep while I sat knitting and watching the net. Morning was the best time; the inlet quiet and peaceful before the first ripple from the wind arrived about ten o'clock. The fragrance of the evergreens from the shore mingled with the aroma of seaweed on the rocks and there was a faint tang of salt water in the air; the powerful smell of the sea rarely penetrated this far inland. We were sixty miles from the ocean and the salt water that filled the inlet was diluted for ten miles out by the fresh water of the

Bella Coola River which was in full flow from the glacial run-off during July and August. Not only did it dilute the salt water but it turned it gray with glacial silt.

By afternoon the regular westerly had started up again and my queasy stomach rebelled; but Earle slept on, the boat rocking like a cradle. At five o'clock it was time to prepare something for him to eat before pulling in the net and getting ready for the night.

There seemed so little I could do. Earle was afraid I would get hurt in the rolling boat or fall overboard and get caught in the net. It was several days before I really cared whether I did anything or not, but the nausea gradually wore off and I began to get my sea legs. It was a relief when Friday afternoon finally came and we could go in for the weekend.

Before we left the boat the net had to be put in a bluestone tank for the weekend. The bluestone tanks stood along the edge of the cannery dock, filled with water and enough bluestone and salt to destroy the bacteria that would damage the damp linen mesh if it were left in the warm sun. Earle stood on the raised platform beside the tank and pulled his net like a rope up to the edge of the tank from the boat in the water below, coiling it within the tank until it was all in. Then placing a heavy wooden lid on the net, he pressed it down with a wooden lever to keep the net immersed. Then we were ready to leave.

The sturdy cannery dock seemed to undulate as I staggered along it, and all weekend the scenery moved past our windows. We slept for nearly forty-eight hours and on Sunday afternoon we were back at the cannery again, buying supplies, taking the net out of the tank, then getting in place on the towline once more.

There seemed such an absence of ceremony attached to this departure into the elements. I felt there should be a band playing and flags flying as the packer pulled out with its tow, but there wasn't even a minister of the gospel on hand to bless them.

After a week of confinement in the tiny dog house, I had begun to feel that fishing wasn't my forte and before we left to go out in the boat again, I asked the cannery foreman if there was any sort of job in the cannery for an inexperienced woman. He thought there might be.

The second week began very much like the first, except that the sea-sickness had almost disappeared and I was beginning to take an interest in how to do things. This lasted until I smashed my thumb on the rudder iron when the boat gave a lurch while I was trying to fix the heavy rudder in place.

I did learn the names of the landmarks in the first ten miles of the inlet where we fished: Dead Man's Point, Clayton Falls, Whiskey Bay, Tallheo Point, South Bentinck Arm, Green Bay, Big Bay, Tallheo Cannery and the old wharf on the north side of the inlet. Westward, beyond these landmarks the inlet was windier and rougher, with less shelter from storms, until one reached the comparative quiet of Labouchere Channel around the point from Masachiti Nose, the wildest and most treacherous place on the inlet.

The second night out we had a fascinating experience. Earle had put out the net near the boundary where the current carried the boat and net eastward over the boundary faster than anywhere in the fishing grounds. After dark we heard the chug of a gas boat which seemed to be operated by two men with very English voices. Apparently they were amateur fishermen and were puzzled about where to put out the net.

After a time a lantern appeared and then corks started banging on the gunwale, with the engine starting and stopping. Then there was a magnificent string of oaths — they had fouled the propeller in the net. This stopped the engine and they were drifting toward the boundary.

In the dark they were helpless and from the sound of things there seemed nothing for it but to go overboard with a knife and cut the net free. I only hoped the one who went into the frigid water had nothing on his clothes that would catch in the net, but at this point Earle made me stay inside the dog house. I hadn't had many opportunities to hear colorful profanity but what I heard that night held me enthralled. I think Earle would have liked to have gone over to help but it would have embarrassed them to know there was a woman on board.

With an incoming tide and the swift current flowing in over the boundary on the south side of the inlet, it required constant vigilance if a fisherman set his net there. Good catches were made here too, so it was a temptation to take a chance. There was a single triangular boundary marker on each side of the inlet and at night there was a single light at each marker, so that even an experienced fisherman in the center of the inlet found it impossible to line himself up or know whether he was over the boundary or not. It was left to the discretion of the patrolman to decide whether or not the boundary had been crossed. An arrest meant appearing in court immediately, to be tried and sentenced by the Fishery Officer, with the patrolman as the only witness.

Later in the week Earle had occasion to experience this judicial system. With an outgoing tide and no strong surface current, the fish sometimes came back out across the boundary line from where they had been milling before going up river. Earle set the net near the center of the inlet where he thought it would be safe from drifting too fast and decided to have a nap while I promised to keep an eye on the net.

I watched the single boundary marker carefully, feeling helpful at last, until I looked over my shoulder to see the patrol boat chugging toward us from the far side of the inlet. Earle awoke in time to be arrested for fishing across the boundary and was ordered to appear in court that afternoon. I didn't know whether this meant he was going to have to go to jail or what would happen to him but I was sick with remorse.

Earle picked up the net, then we went to the cannery dock and tied up. I walked in silence with him to the townsite where the court hearing was held, comforted by the sight of other fishermen in the same plight as ourselves.

It seemed an eternity before he came back out again and told me about the court proceedings. The other fishermen were all charged with fishing inside the boundary and fined ten dollars each. When it came to Earle's turn, the Fishery

Officer asked him if he pleaded guilty to the charge of fishing inside the boundary.

He replied, "I really don't know. It was impossible to tell where the boundary lay from where I was in the middle of the inlet. The patrol officer probably could see from where he was over the north side of the inlet beside the marker, but if he had tried to steer straight across he might have been off the line too."

The Fishery Officer thought for a few moments and then said, "Well, you might just as well be tarred with the same brush. Ten dollars." That was a lot of money in those days, but I was relieved that he didn't have to go to jail. However, not long afterwards, an additional marker was set up on both sides of the inlet so they could be lined up from anywhere on the boundary.

This was an eventful week, but Friday cured me of ever wanting to go fishing in an open sailboat again.

There was an ominous feeling in the air that morning. It was hard to define and without a barometer we had no way of knowing we were in for one of the worst blows the inlet had ever experienced.

On Fridays it was customary for the men to throw their nets in close so they would have a short run to the cannery when the week's fishing closed at six o'clock. There were about seventy-five boats within four miles of the cannery and we were among the outside ones. The net lay across the inlet on the side farthest away from the cannery and an experienced fisherman who claimed to have fished all over the world had thrown his net parallel to ours, a net-length farther out the inlet.

The blow came suddenly in mid-afternoon and grew rapidly in intensity until there were gusts of wind up to eighty miles an hour. The waves were steep and curling, and spray flew in the wind.

Our neighbor's boat soon drifted toward ours and his net started bunching. He was in danger of being entangled in his own net as well as ours, so he cast off and tried to steer toward the cannery. As he passed us he shouted, "Make a run for it!" Alas, his own run ended in disaster. Without any sail he was unable to control the boat and was blown up onto the tide flats, punching a hole through the hull of his boat on a snag. Fortunately he was able to swim and wade to safety but his net also drifted up onto the flats and was a total loss, torn by old tree stumps and snags lodged in the mud.

Before long the spray from the waves was coming right over our boat and we were having to pump the bilge. Nearly all the other fishermen had gone in, some leaving their nets; and finally Earle decided to pull ours.

Hauling the net by himself was too much for him as the abandoned net was in bunches and lying against ours, so I helped. Standing on the fishboxes in the center of the tossing boat, I pulled with all my strength, piling the net about me to keep the weight out of the stern of the boat, giving it more freeboard.

It was exhausting work and having to separate the two nets made it even more difficult. Some of the fish had even gilled themselves in both nets, tying them together. I have no doubt adrenalin helped speed things, but it seemed to take forever to get the net all in.

Earle put up about five feet of the sail and steered for the cannery. By this time the seas were very heavy and I had to pump as we were shipping water over the stern from the curling waves. We were drenched and I was frightened but Earle was exhilarated, challenged by the elements.

It didn't take long to get in as we were flying past the scenery at a terrific speed. The most harrowing part of the trip was coming about at full tilt around the end of the huge breakwater log anchored to the cannery to create a shelter for the boats. There was quite an audience in the lee of the building, watching to see if we would make it. I don't know what would have happened if we had swamped, but there was a packer that would have come to our rescue if we had signaled for help. It did go out and bring in one boat that was drifting helplessly toward the tideflats, maneuvering so the fishboat was in the lee of the packer, giving it a bit of quiet water while the painter was being tied to a towline. Only just in time, as the boat was almost swamped. Also, the water was shallow there, and a little farther in the packer would have been aground.

It was a dramatic ending to my short, open-boat fishing career but I had no regrets except being parted from Earle during the week. So I was delighted when I found the cannery had a job for me beginning Monday morning. It was really quite a posh one, oiling the moving parts of the machinery, but at least I wouldn't have to handle fish and no one ever oiled bolts and nuts more assiduously. I didn't miss a thing.

There was a hustle and bustle about the activity of a cannery in operation that was exciting and I enjoyed it. It took some time to grow accustomed to the effluvia that enveloped all canneries in warm weather, in spite of the constant scrubbing and hosing by the Chinamen and the disposing of offal directly into the "salt-chuck."

The women wore white uniforms and caps trimmed with green, and always looked clean and fresh at the beginning of each day. It was tiring for them standing for hours without relief at the benches where they filled the tins, but they were anxious to have the jobs as this was the only opportunity valley women had to earn money.

The older women from the Village mended nets and charged the fishermen by the hour, so they were free to work as many hours as they wanted. Each week I added up the money I was earning with my oiling job and it looked as if there would be enough at the end of the season to buy a cow.

14

Modesta

NEITHER of us had ever had any experience with a cow but she seemed to us a symbol of the kind of life we wanted to have, and furthermore, we needed the milk. "The Mother of Prosperity" was what she was referred to in the government bulletin on the care of cows. We sent away for booklets on how to feed cows and how to teach a calf to drink from a bucket, how to do everything except milk a cow; and neither of us knew how to do that.

All during the summer Earle had been enquiring of the fishermen during mug-up times if any of them knew of a cow for sale. Several times he made a sortie up to Hagensborg where most of the farms were, to inspect some cow that was reported to be for sale, but always came back disappointed. This was going to be a sort of surprise for me so I stayed behind on these trips, but I was going to go with him when he finally found the perfect animal.

Fishing was drawing to a close and we still hadn't found a cow. It began to look as if we were going to have to settle for whatever we could get. Then Earle returned from his final trip up the valley looking triumphant. He had found a beautiful Jersey heifer. Without my seeing her he knew she was exactly what we wanted and had bought and paid for her on the spot, so we were going to pick her up the following weekend and take her home.

She was at Hagensborg, about ten miles up the valley from Bella Coola, and we decided to walk to Atnarko from there. Leading a cow, it would take us four or five days and we could stay overnight with friends along the way. Anyway, it would be pleasant to be walking again after being confined to the cannery and fishboat for three months. What we didn't know was that a little Jersey heifer can put up a lot of resistance when being taken away from home.

Arriving at the Hagensborg homestead on Sunday morning, we were taken to the barn and there she was! It was love at first sight. I had never seen anything more beautiful and we decided to call her Modesta.

Earle was beaming as we attached a lead rope to her halter and started toward the gate. But she didn't want to go. She did everything but roll on the ground, and then the bull started to bellow. We could still hear him bellowing when we got to the church a mile up the road, and Modesta was answering back, her eyes rolling and her tongue hanging out between bellows. Church services were almost ready to begin as we dragged the bawling heifer up the road, and it seemed to me that most of the congregation must have come back outside to watch the spectacle.

Earle pulled and I pushed. Then we would change ends. We cajoled and pleaded, then threatened, and still she dug into the dirt road with all four feet, ending with a swing across the road on the end of her rope, like a pendulum. Then about ten miles up the road, when we were all exhausted and I was in tears, beseeching Earle to get a truck before she lost the calf she was carrying, she suddenly stopped resisting and started walking briskly. We couldn't believe it. Perhaps she knew she had a couple of greenhorns on the other end of the rope and had wanted to test them out, or perhaps she began to pick up the scent of another farm and more animals up the road. Whatever it was, her behavior changed completely and there was no more trouble all the way home.

It took us four days to get there and we had to watch her carefully when we got home as she must have been lonesome by herself and would be looking for a way to escape. But it wouldn't be for long; she was due to have her calf in the middle of October. The feed was lush so we kept her on a tether during the day, and at night cut clover for her to eat in the snug little barn. We were beginning to be farmers. It was wonderful to be back.

Haying was over for the year at Anahim and packtrains were beginning to move over the trail, packing in vegetables and supplies for the winter. We had frequent visitors and of each one we asked the same question, "How do you milk a cow?"

The replies were all the same, "Just squeeze it into a bucket." It must be simple, we thought, they all say the same thing.

On the fourteenth of October, my birthday, it became obvious that Modesta was going to have a calf during the night, so we gave her a big nest of fluffy hay in which to lay her little egg.

We were out the first thing in the morning, and there in the middle of the hay was a tiny doe-eyed calf, an exquisite replica of her mother. We named her Bonnie.

In absolute awe we watched as the calf

nursed her mother, but it soon became obvious that Modesta had more milk than the little calf could handle. This was where we were going to have to do some of that squeezing they talked about.

Getting a bucket, I sat down beside her and squeezed. Nothing happened, then I tried again. The milk must have gone the wrong way because Modesta flinched. On the third try, she kicked. A wholesome, full-bodied kick that sent me and the stool and bucket flying. It didn't seem possible that such a delicate little animal could have so much vigor.

Someone had told us how to tie a figure eight on the hind legs of a cow to prevent her from kicking, so we found a rope and did this. Then we boosted the calf up to nurse on one side, hoping I could get milk from the other, but the calf wasn't interested. It had already had its lunch. We kept trying, and after a while some milk did dribble into the bucket. Observing the movement of my fingers that produced this miracle, I was able to do it again, and before long milk began to cover the bottom of the bucket and creep up the sides. We were in business. My arms ached so badly, I had to keep resting, but we took what milk the book said we should at first, leaving enough for the calf.

The book also said to remove the calf after the first few days when there was no more of the stimulating colostrum in the milk and it was fit for human consumption. It would mean separating the calf from Modesta and feeding it with a bucket. This seemed unnecessary work, but like the proverbial man who couldn't serve two masters, a cow does not like to share her milk with someone other than her own calf. It can be done, but the book recommended separating the two after three days.

Teaching a calf to drink from a bucket was going to be easy because the book described it in detail and even gave illustrations of a large man with a small calf backed into a corner and happily drinking milk from a bucket. The instructions in the book said the operator has the required amount of warm milk in a bucket, then backs the calf into a corner, straddles its neck, holds the bucket with one hand and the calf's nose with the other, inserting a finger in the mouth, at the same time pushing the head down toward the milk. The book doesn't mention the calf walking all over one's toes with its sharp little hooves, or giving the bucket a bunt that sends the whole thing flying so the entire procedure has to be started from the beginning again. I was drenched in milk and exhausted at the end of the first session and I don't think the calf got more than a few drops. However, hunger must have made her more cooperative because on the second attempt she started drinking, and from then on there was no problem.

We scarcely knew what to do with so much milk but as the calf grew, she drank more. I learned to make butter and cheese and Maxie was able to take buttermilk home to his chickens and guinea fowl.

Modesta survived our ignorance and a great rapport grew between us. Over the years there have been other cows but never have I felt the same affection I had for her.

When the calf was six weeks old there

came a day when Modesta knew better than we that it was time for us to have a herd sire. She mooed all day and we kept wondering what was wrong until we referred to the book. Here we were, twenty-five miles from the nearest cattle where a bull might be available, but if we were going to have milk next year it looked as though we had better get one. Earle made some inquiries, then started out with Maryanka to find one.

He was gone for five days and I kept watching and listening for his return. Late in the afternoon I heard them coming. There was a high-pitched call from a bull down the trail and Modesta answered. I ran to open the gate and Earle rode in on Maryanka, leading the smallest, skinniest, most undernourished bull calf I could have imagined. I looked past them to see if something more was coming, but no, this was it.

Earle explained sheepishly that this was all he could get, "But he is old enough," he assured me. "We'll just have to dig a hole for Modesta to stand in."

I thought I detected a somewhat haughty look from Modesta to begin with

260

when she met the bull, but her delight in bovine company overcame her reserve and she overlooked any difference there might be in social status, just as a little spade work at the right time overcame the difference in their height. We were blessed with a calf in due time. True, it wasn't the little aristocrat Bonnie had been, but it was a calf and we had milk.

Since coming home from fishing, we had built a root cellar, harvested the garden, established a herd, and now it was time to do the winter packing-in of our yearly supplies; everything had to be brought in by packhorse, once a year.

Ordering had to be done carefully and in bulk, so as not to run out of anything before the year was up. We had started making out the order for supplies while we were still out in the boat, considering each item and discussing its merits, making sure the list was clear and understandable to the suppliers in Vancouver.

Nothing could be more frustrating than to travel to the end of the road with horses and find only half the order had arrived, along with a notice saying they were shipping the rest of the things later.

Another distressing experience Ralph had was finding a substitution in his order. Instead of the tins of shortening he had sent for, he once received some large wooden boxes of raw beef suet, green with mold.

Mistakes like these were hard to understand. However, we had been particularly careful in making out our order and felt that nothing could go wrong. But we had slipped up on one item; we had forgotten to specify a screw-on lid for the fifty-pound tin of roasted coffee beans.

Jack Weldon was packing up our supplies again and he used the square tin of coffee beans as a top pack, placing it upside down on the top of the load without noticing that the lid was not the screw-on type, but a clamp-down one that was easily removable.

Part way up the trail the lid came off. Like stinging wasps, the coffee beans trickled down between the saddle pads and the horse's back. He started to buck. Running and bucking, it started a chain reaction with the other horses, one of them smashing into a tree and turning its pack. Coffee beans were scattered for a quarter of a mile along the trail and for weeks each time a packtrain went over them the air was aromatic with the spicy fragrance of freshly ground coffee.

With the packing finished, it was not long until Christmas. Mail day didn't come until the twenty-seventh so we would have to wait until then for our letters and packages. But I decorated the house with evergreens and put a small tree on the little desk. There wouldn't be room for a large one with five bachelors in the living room.

Jack Weldon and his son came down from the Precipice to stay with us and Max and his companion walked down on Christmas Day, and B.C. rode up on his horse.

The cabin was redolent with the aroma of roast venison, and after the festive dinner we drank some of the black currant wine Earle had made from berries picked from the battered old bush near the house. The men relaxed and groaned a little, smoking their pipes in contentment.

The murmur of their voices drifted out to me as I put things away in the kitchen and I heard Max telling about a Christmas he and his brother, Lou, had spent in this cabin with George Young twenty-five years before. Frank and Walter Ratcliff were also there with them, down from the Stillwater. The Christmas cheer had flowed freely and George had reached the sentimental stage.

Maxie's voice went on, "'Boys,' George says, 'I'm tired of doing my own cooking. I'm going to get a wife.' He puts on his mackinaw and heads for the door. 'I'm going to Bella Coola and find one,' he says. It was the middle of the night and cold as charity outside. Musta been three feet of snow but old George puts on his snowshoes and started out. About half an hour later he was back. 'Get a wife, George?' 'Naw, steam ran down!'

"Got one after a while, though," Max went on. "One of them mail-order brides. Come from England. Never been outa London before, but George sent her the money to get here and married her when she come. Didn't last long. Said the summer was all right but the winter was too lonely. No wimmen-folk to talk to. Said the cabin was cold. Said it kept her busy 'pluggin' up all the 'oles with bits of piper.' Feller's a damn fool to get mixed up with them lonely hearts wimmen."

I wanted to laugh but something in the story of the lonely woman struck a sympathetic chord in my soul.

The frontier may have been conquered by stalwart men but it was the women who held the wilderness at bay by their loyalty to their husbands. They endured hardships and privation but there were some for whom the loneliness and absence of female companionship were too much to endure and they left, their husbands following. All through the frontier were log cabins that were falling in decay because there was no longer a woman in them and the men had abandoned their once-ambitious plans.

The moon was shining but there was a bitter wind blowing when Max and his friend and B.C. finally left. We were glad to close the door against the cold and Earle tucked a little rug over the crack under the door to keep out the draft;

then the Weldons climbed the ladder to the attic and went to bed.

During the night I woke to find the cabin full of smoke. I panicked and woke the men. Earle got the water bucket and dipper and Jack and Johnnie came down, but we couldn't find the fire. We even looked down into the old storage space under the floor. Then I discovered it; while he was tucking the rug over the crack under the door, Earle must have dropped a glowing ember from his pipe, and fanned by the draft, it had smouldered and smoked but not burst into flame. Christmas had been exciting after all.

The following day we counted up the number of fires that had occurred on farms between Atnarko and Hagensborg and there had been one on nearly every preemption. Dry cedar shakes were responsible for most of them. Cedar kindling made a quick, hot fire and most people used it for starting their fires, sending sparks flying up the chimney to land in the dry mossy cracks between the shakes and be fanned into flame by a breeze. Once a fire started, water was not readily available to put it out; a bucket from the well was too slow. Fear of fire often became an obsession with women in this country.

The Christmas mail arrived late in the afternoon of the twenty-seventh. It was pleasant having Christmas spread over several days; it made it last longer. The parcel of holly and the baubles someone sent seemed an anti-climax and the cards had somehow lost their flavor, but they were beautiful and we pinned them on the wall anyway.

What seemed real about this Christmas was the little cow and her calf out in the barn. Snug and warm in their log shelter, they were the symbol of all that was good in our lives. As I fed them and gave them extra bedding by lantern-light, I thought, "No wonder they chose the stable for the scene of the Christmas Story."

January grew colder with more snow. The river froze over, with only a few small open spaces in the middle where the current was swift, and we had to chop ice in the mornings on Modesta's water hole near the river's edge.

One day we forgot to chop it before

turning her out of the barn. Before we knew it she was out on the ice at the deepest part of the river, looking for a drink from the open spot in the middle. In another moment she would have reached it and the ice would have broken beneath her, but I saw her in time and called.

Banging on a bucket was a signal for a feed of grain, and calling and banging, I walked to the edge of the riverbank where she could see me.

Slowly she turned, taking forever to make up her mind which she wanted most, a drink or some more grain. Her tail was almost hanging over the edge of the open water which ended a short way downstream beyond her. From there, for a long way around the bend of the river, was solid ice and she would have been beneath it. There would have been no possible way for her to get out had she fallen in.

I wanted to look away. My throat was constricted and so dry I could scarcely call. She even took time to have a bowel movement; then slowly, because of the slippery ice, she started moving back toward the shore again and my knees turned to rubber. That afternoon we built a fence around her water hole.

During a mild spell in January, I almost had a watery grave myself. The temperature warmed to 20°F and Earle thought it might be a change to have some trout to eat, so we took our fishing gear and hiked down the trail about a mile to some good open holes. I ventured out a bit too far and the ice suddenly let go and I was in water up to my armpits. Earle was there in a moment. Lying down on the ice he took hold of my hands and managed to get me back to safety again. But the water was frigid and the air cold enough so that my clothes began to freeze and they were quite stiff by the time we reached home.

The warmth from the heater was painful as I stripped off and I had to pat gently with the towel since it hurt too much to rub vigorously. Both legs developed the most spectacular chilblains and I felt very sorry for myself for about a week. The circulation in them was impaired for years afterwards and every time they became chilled they started to ache.

In spite of the snow and cold we had a surprising number of visitors during the winter. Now that the ice of the lake was safe to travel on, Ralph was down again with mail and a load of furs to ship in time for the fur sales.

He sat up most of the night with his back to the kitchen stove, writing on the table by the light of a candle, answering letters he had just received. Writing vigorously, it still took him most of the night to reply to the important letters and catch up on the world news in his newsmagazine.

Probably he wouldn't have slept well, even if he had gone to bed. After living in isolation, it was always highly stimulating to be with other people again. Frank, who was completely alone at the Stillwater for two weeks between mail trips, talked endlessly when he first arrived. We had found we did the same thing when we were at the Stillwater; it was a compulsive need.

There were mail trips in January and February when the weather was so cold we had to help the mail carrier dismount. Ole Nygaard had been carrying the mail for a long time and was getting on in years. There were times during the winter when it was a bit too much for him and he would stay hunched within his heavy mackinaw for the entire trip, arriving stiff with cold and unable to dismount by himself. He was a big man and getting him off the horse was a job for the two of us. We brought him in and thawed him out before he resumed the trip to Maxie's.

Once, following a blizzard when the snow had drifted deeply on the trail at the foot of the rockslides, there was a thaw which soaked the top two inches of the snow. Then it froze hard, forming a thick crust of ice, sharp enough to cut a horse's legs. The day Ole was due with the mail, Maxie and Earle took metal bars and bashed on the drifts where it seemed to freeze more solidly in the cold drafts near the rockslides. Without this, the horses wouldn't have been able to come through.

The day following the arrival of the mail was usually our day of rest. Very often there was someone staying overnight with us, Ralph or Frank or Jack Weldon. This alone was stimulating and we stayed up late talking, but the added excitement of getting letters and fresh reading material kept us awake so that we were tired the next day and were glad to spend our time resting and reading.

Soon after Christmas the colorful and enticing seed catalogs began to arrive. January was the time for ordering garden seeds. We needed to send away early for the ones that had to be started indoors in flats, such as tomatoes and green peppers. The frost-free growing period in the garden was between the twenty-fourth of May and the middle of September. In the hot sun of Atnarko things grew well and Maxie always had ripe corn on the cob and ripe tomatoes before anyone down the valley. The seed catalogs were an antidote to winter and I had difficulty keeping Earle from ordering one of everything.

Winter was passing quickly with so much to do. I was still spinning wool and making socks and Earle was making packsaddles. There was a fair demand for them; however, he was occupied with another more important project.

A Bella Coola fisherman had asked him to build the hull of a power-driven fishboat in the spring. After he had completed this, Earle intended to build a boat for himself as well, hoping to finish it in time for the coming fishing season. He was busy carving models in cedar wood and his own was going to be an original and unique design.

Most of the fishermen still used the open cannery-owned sailboats, but the few gas boats that were designed for fishing and were in use in the inlet had much better catches, were easier to handle and more comfortable to live in.

They were built with a high pilot house which caught a lot of wind, both while traveling or when tied to the net. The tall, square cabin not only created a lot of wind resistance, but behind it there was a partial vacuum which also helped slow the boat. Earle wanted his to be streamlined, not only in the hull but in the superstructure.

There would be a slope to the front of the cabin and a longer one behind, allowing the air to flow unrestricted. The cabin had what Earle called a low profile, but there was adequate head room and the windows in it were to be somewhat like those of a car.

The spacious cabin would have two bunks, narrowing at the bow, with cabinets and drawers for clothes and food, and a pull-out table. Earle wanted to paint the boat two shades of soft gray, with white trim and I suggested he call it the *Stormy Petrel*.

Probably the most important part of a boat to a fisherman is the hull. Earle spent a lot of time thinking and carving on his model until he had one that would be seaworthy, wouldn't roll, had little or no drag and cut the water cleanly, leaving little wake. This sounded like a cross between a duck and a porpoise but the model was beautiful and had lovely lines. We tried it out many times in a quiet, open spot in the river, with a string tied to the bow.

Earle's boat would be thirty-one feet long, with a seven-and-a-half foot beam and there was to be a stout towing post attached to the keel, about a third of the way from the stern.

While we were fishing the previous summer, we had made a trip out to Labouchere Channel with the sailboat and climbed the dangerous bluffs of Masachiti Nose to get two yellow cedar crooks, one for the stem and the other for the stern of the new boat. The fir keel was being ordered from a mill in Vancouver.

Years before, after Earle had left the job as telegraph operator and lineman at Mosher Creek and had gone to live in Bella Coola, he had built a forty-five foot boat for himself, called the *Noohalk* which was the original name for the Bella Coola Valley. The boat had been leased by the Department of Fisheries and placed on patrol in the inlet. It was used in this service for years and in the fall when fishing was over, Earle made trips to the paper-mill town of Ocean Falls with boatloads of farm produce from the farmers of the valley. When he finally left Bella Coola for Portland, the boat was used for the same purpose by other people but eventually it came to an unfortunate end.

Now Earle was going to build another boat. We made arrangements for him to stay in the old Clayton house and use the barn for a boat-building shed. I wanted to go with him when he left to begin his project but there didn't seem any possible way to take the animals down with us and also have a garden in Atnarko, so I decided to stay alone on the farm for the summer.

Alone, in some of the best bear-hunting country in British Columbia, when a scant two and a half years ago I had been afraid of my shadow. We had no dog nor even a lock on the door and I had learned to shoot by closing my eyes and trying to stop the gyrating of the rifle barrel. But still I had no fear, and I don't know why. It seemed perfectly natural for me to stay and take care of my little Jerseys and tend the garden so we would have something to eat when Earle came back in the fall. He planned to go down about the middle of March, when the snow would be gone in Bella Coola.

There was a terrible emptiness when he left, and I could find no comfort from

Ralph and Earle

The Indian Village at Bella Coola *(Photo by Ivor Fougner)*

Isabel with Maxie
and his team. *(Top)*

Isabel with Modesta -
"the one animal I
loved unreservedly."

Isabel with Modesta
and Bonnie at
Atnarko. *(Bottom)*

Earle and Cliff Kopas at our
Atnarko cabin.

Isabel and her handmade
spinning wheel, Atnarko 1934.

Left to right: Walter Ratcliff,
Earle and Ralph.

Left to right: Trudy, Isabel
and Ethel, 1938 at The Birches.

Packing in the swan barley – Earle with Queenie, Isabel with Ginty, and Old Blue bringing up the rear, in 1933.

Every fall the trumpeter swans return to their winter feeding grounds at Lonesome Lake, and whenever the weather is extremely cold, Ralph - and now his daughter, Trudy - spreads grain for them.

Coast mountains - "breathtaking vistas".

The first bridge across the Fraser River to the Chilcotin.

Isabel.

the ache of loneliness except in hard work. There was plenty of that, getting the garden patch ready for ploughing and the pasture fences patched so the animals couldn't get out. Many of the fences were temporary brush fences which flattened under the weight of winter snow. They were a way of using the brush as we cleared the land but they required constant attention as the branches rotted and broke.

I thought I had every weak place patched, but Modesta and the bull found a way out.

Earle and I had arranged to talk to each other on the phone on Saturday afternoons at five, and I had taken the rifle and walked up to Maxie's to keep our appointment. The weather had turned warm and a few bears had been seen, mostly along the margins of sloughs and quiet streams where the bright yellow shoots of the skunk cabbage were showing. The immature leaves of the plant were folded like the heart of celery and had the pungency of cayenne pepper, probably what the bears needed after their winter hibernation.

Tiny spears of new grass were showing where there had been snow not long before and the rose-colored alder catkins were as exquisite as a Chinese painting as they hung over quiet water in the sunlight. The air was filled with the fragrance of cottonwood buds. There were birds everywhere; junkoes and chickadees, bluebirds and grosbeaks, robins and a large flock of pine siskins. The days were noisy with them. And then there were the mosquitoes.

The first ones were large and slow, giving one lots of time to swat them before they did any harm, but it was the second crop of small ones that were active and full of direction, darting in for the kill without warning.

All this activity must have stirred something in Modesta and the bull because they were nowhere to be found when I came back from talking to Earle. The calf was safe in her own pasture and I couldn't believe Modesta would go very far away from her. However, it was past time for milking and soon would be growing dusk.

Checking the pasture fence, I finally

278

found the weak place where they had broken out and was able to follow their track which led to the trail and down it. Not knowing how far they would go, I ran back to the cabin for a coal-oil lantern, the rifle and a rope.

The horse trail was simply a path through the woods, widened out sufficiently to keep horses from bumping their packs on the trees. Branches met overhead, and in the dusk it was eerie not knowing whether the black form at the turn of the trail ahead was a stump or a bear. It was more than six miles to B.C.'s place and my heart stood still several times before I arrived. His cabin was surrounded by trees and it was quite dark when I finally knocked on his door. I heard him muttering inside, then the door creaked open and he stood there in his longjohns.

"Sure I got your cow," he cackled in answer to my query. "Got 'em locked up in the corral. Got the cow, now I got the milkmaid!"

"I'm afraid I'll have to milk her," I gulped. "Do you have a bucket?"

He emptied something out of one and handed it to me, then went back into the other room of the cabin and put on his trousers and a coat.

Modesta seemed happy to see me and I tied her up before squatting down and starting to milk. There was a tiny spring creek flowing through the corral which made it a bit muddy underfoot, and halfway through the milking, the irregularity of the situation and my tension must have reached her for she lifted one foot and placed it squarely in the middle of the bucket. I was about to empty the mess and start over again, but B.C. wanted me to save it so I kept on with the milking until we were finished.

By now, I had reached the point of no return and sooner or later was going to have to ask B.C. where I was going to spend the night.

It was nearly midnight and not very sensible to think of walking back up the trail in the dark with two animals, especially with bears about. All the while I had been milking, I had been thinking of B.C.'s eccentricity and cogitating over what I should do. Borrow a horse and ride home, then come back in the morning? But I knew the horses were out in the pasture and B.C. wouldn't be pleased about having to get them. However, it was worth a try.

I held the bucket of milk and B.C. picked up the lantern and opened the gate. I stayed where I was and then stammered, "Er, do you think you could let me have a horse to get home with."

"Naw. There's a good bed at the cabin."

"Well, perhaps I could sleep in the hay."

"Naw. It's a good bed. Put fresh shavings on it not long ago."

Perhaps something would come to me. I untied Modesta and picked up the rifle and we walked back to the cabin in silence. B.C. opened the creaking door and ushered me in with a flourish. I handed him the bucket of milk with the black lumps floating in it.

Closing the door, he went over to the bed, pulled off piles of packsaddles and horse blankets and patted it admiringly. I had stopped thinking and was scarcely able to talk by this time, but we shook out some of the less sweaty horse blankets and then B.C. retired to the second room of the cabin, the other side of a sort of pantry.

I darted to the outer door and opened it wide enough to make a hasty exit, then sorted out the blankets and climbed in between them, sitting bolt upright with the rifle across my knees.

Toward daybreak I must have fallen asleep. Suddenly I was awakened by a sound at the pantry door, "Oh, God!" I thought, "This is it!"

The door opened slowly and through it squeezed an enormous tom cat. I scarcely heard his raucous meowing for the pounding in my ears.

But day came at last and I heard B.C. stirring and lighting the fire. After a while he called me and said breakfast was ready. I washed in the grimy basin and found a handkerchief in my pocket to wipe my hands. Then we had porridge and cream from which the larger pieces of corral had been lifted. I was so hungry, it tasted delicious.

In the bright light of day and in the face of this warm hospitality, I felt ashamed. However, from then on I kept a close watch on the fences.

15

Summer in Atnarko

EARLE phoned from Bella Coola every Saturday to tell me how the boat-building was getting on. I didn't mention my trip down the trail but I did tell him the garden was planted and that Maxie had caught his first spring salmon of the season, and that there was a traffic on the trail.

The Indian packtrains were coming down from the interior, loaded with camping equipment and all the family. Father always rode ahead, carrying his long fish spear, almost as though the rest of the packtrain didn't belong to him. It was up to the women to take care of the horses.

They wore bright kerchiefs and several layers of voluminous skirts, usually with a wide ruffle around the bottom, reaching almost to the ground, and the top one was the newest, made of gaily-flowered cotton print. These not only kept them warm but afforded a degree of modesty when riding a horse. They never wore overalls or slacks.

Their legs bulged above buckskin moccasins with several layers of woolen stockings, nearly always of different colors. That is, the hole in the black outer stocking revealed another beneath it of red, and the hole in that exposed a bit of green. Wearing several layers of stockings seemed sensible to me because it must have kept the mosquitoes from biting.

Nearly all the mature women carried babies, or papooses, swaddled and strapped like little mummies in baskets slung across their mother's backs. The baskets were beautifully woven of willow and lined with colorful printed fabric, with flaps attached to the sides of the basket, laced across the infant to hold it securely in place. There was usually a bit of netting to keep the mosquitoes out, but not always. The baby lay on a disposable pad of peat moss gathered from the interior meadows. Not only was this absorbent but fungicidal as well, preventing rash. A sturdy buckskin strap swung the basket safely from the mother's shoulder or from a tree, out of harm's way when they camped.

The younger children either rode behind an adult, or two of them rode together on a saddle pad secured to a gentle horse.

In May, the horses from the interior all looked as if they had been through a hard winter, and part of the reason for the visit to the verdant valley was to give them green feed. Spring didn't appear for another month in the harsh slough-grass country and most of the horses had been rustling in the snow for their feed all winter.

Another reason for the visit was to get a feed of spring salmon for themselves after a constant diet of moose meat and bannock, and they were ready to spend their hard-earned trapping money to buy whatever took their fancy in the general store in Bella Coola. "Just I eat good," was their explanation.

With the coming of warm weather, travel on the trail increased and I had an unexpected visitor from the Precipice one day. Jack Weldon came down on his way to go fishing for the summer and wondered if I would keep his dog Jerry, while he was gone.

Jerry was a shaggy-coated collie who had once been kicked in the head by a horse, leaving him with a sort of side-winding gait and a yodel. When he barked it sounded like a cross between a coyote and a wolf. It was weird.

Jack usually clipped Jerry in the summer, and as the weather had turned warm he thought the dog should have a haircut before he left. Armed with scissors, we both went to work on Jerry. He was a sorry mess when we finished but at least he would be comfortable and the hair would grow out again.

Jack was in a hurry to get away as someone was going to meet him at the end of the road with a car that afternoon. He asked me if I would mind going up to Maxie's to phone that he would be down. Jack had stayed there the night before, so when I arrived with Jerry, Max took a horrified look at the dog. His own dog had naturally short curly hair and didn't need clipping.

"Where did you get the dog?" Max enquired.

"Oh! That's Jerry. Jack and I gave him a haircut," I explained.

"Well, you sure done a hell of a job of it," growled Max.

Jerry's unique yodel attracted an answering howl from coyotes and wolves. The nighttime duets were nerve-wracking so I kept him in the cabin after dark, and then he snored. Anyone associated with Jerry since his accident was a loser. Taking him with me on the trail, he would dart into the brush after a bear, then bring it back to me. But, he was company.

One day I held on to his collar while we watched a mother black bear cross the rockslide by the trail. She was followed close behind by her cubs, three tiny black teddy bears, in tandem, serious and intent, getting the message from their mother that this was open and dangerous territory.

I worried about meeting bears on the rockslide trail between our place and Maxie's when I had Jerry with me. There was one stretch where there were no trees to climb, but it was too early for the wild berries along the trail to be ripe, so this lessened the hazard.

Although I always carried the rifle, I think it was more of a morale booster than a protection. Often, when I had been by myself and had seen a bear, I hid behind a tree or climbed one until the bear had wandered off. Once, when the wild raspberries were ripe, I startled a black bear below me as I walked. Running blindly up the rocks, it landed in the trail beside me and I slapped it in the face with my straw hat to turn it away. Bears have notoriously poor eyesight and this one was as scared as I was.

Perhaps the greatest fright I ever had was when I was walking along a part of the trail that wound through the trees and dense brush. Suddenly, I was startled by a commotion immediately behind me and fully expected to be attacked by a bear. Whirling around, I was amazed to see only a mother grouse fluttering along, dragging one wing and trying to lure me away from the twelve tiny balls of fluff that were darting in every direction to find shelter beneath the leaves. I laughed with relief but my knees had turned to putty.

The third week in May was the time of high water on the Atnarko. It was nearly always bank-full of brownish-looking water by then, the spring run-off from the slough-grass meadows of the interior plateau country. Oftentimes it overflowed its banks in Atnarko, but this year it remained within them. However, when the water receded I noticed the boiling current had badly eroded the soft soil of the embankment at the edge of our meadow, where the trees had been cleared away years ago.

There were still a couple of tall cottonwoods near the bank above the erosion. They could be felled and anchored so they would lie with the butt on the bank and the branchy top in the water, breaking the current and helping slow the washing away of the rich soil.

When Earle phoned again, I told him about the problem and he suggested that I ask Maxie to help me fall the cottonwoods and try to protect the bank. Maxie agreed, and the next day, bright and early, he came down to do the job, before the breeze came up.

He left Rex at the cabin for safety's sake, then took our big cross-cut saw and an axe and went over to the riverbank to size up the trees. He walked all around one and estimated the degree of tilt; then between us we made the undercut. The technique in felling a tree for this purpose is to keep the trunk attached to the stump with as much wood as possible, making a sort of hinge so the tree will fall with its top in the water but not be broken from the stump entirely.

Everything went well and we reached the point where the tree started to sway slightly, so we stopped cutting and stepped back to watch it. Slowly, it began to move, but in the wrong direction. With a crash, it landed in the clover of the hay field. We stood staring at it. There wasn't a breath of air moving but finally Maxie scratched his head, then declared, "It was the wind what done it!"

After all these years, whenever we miscalculate and something goes wrong, Earle and I look at each other and laugh and say, "It was the wind what done it!"

May and June were mosquito months. They were an ever-present annoyance and on muggy days were a torment, so I made a smudge for the animals to stand in. Even in the cabin they were troublesome and I retreated behind mosquito netting when reading or sleeping.

Once, in July, I went picking berries without first smearing my face with the pinetar solution and came home to get a shock when I looked in the mirror. My entire face was covered with blood from blackfly bites. These tiny flies had just come out and discovered new blood. They anaesthetize the bite and then inject an anticoagulant so the blood will flow freely. Their bite is quite poisonous and

I was feverish and unwell for several days after the exposure. The swelling finally subsided, leaving purple spots all over my face as though I had some terrible disease. It puzzled me that mosquitos and blackflies had no poisonous effect on Maxie. Sometimes he would swat one on his face, but for the most part he paid no attention to them and he never seemed to have welts on his skin. Perhaps, after a time, one developed an immunity or else tobacco smoke was a repellent.

The garden took a lot of my time and I was busy canning vegetables now they were ready to eat. There was also plenty of wild fruit: thimble berries, wild raspberries, wild gooseberries and a few wild strawberries, as well as the blackcurrants from the old bushes by the house.

With the animals to care for, there seemed no end of things to do and Saturday afternoons came around quickly. They were my reward and I looked forward to going to Maxie's to talk to Earle on the phone. Maxie usually invited me to stay for supper and at this time of year he had new potatoes and boiled spring salmon or sockeye.

Sometimes I would go early and we would sit in the cool shade of the cabin with a smudge of fallen leaves and dried horse manure smouldering in a coal-oil tin to keep away the mosquitoes and blackflies. Seated on an old apple box tipped back against the weathered logs of the cabin wall, Maxie would spin yarns, his sweat-stained hat pulled down over his eyes and the smoke from his ancient pipe mingling with the woodsy incense of the smudge. There was a peace on the land that we weren't even aware of in the quiet timelessness of those summer afternoons, but it must have seeped into our lives.

Sometimes I had been shaken by an encounter with a bear on the way up the trail, but the trembling fear soon wore off and was forgotten. There was an absence of worry and anxiety in Atnarko, and my days were filled with contentment.

However, once just before haying time, when I reached home after a Saturday talk with Earle, I found the cow and the bull had broken into the field of clover. They had eaten a large amount and were distended to an enormous size and I was terrified they would die of bloat. Modesta was grunting and I imagined even her eyes were bulging.

Running to the cabin, I found the veterinary handbook that was our standby, and read what it said about bloat. Among other things, it said to keep the animal moving. Also, if the cow went down, to use the trocar and cannula, a sort of stilleto within a tube which enveloped it all except the point. Sticking this into the correct spot in the cow's abdomen up near where the ribs meet the backbone, the stilleto is then withdrawn, leaving the tube through which the gas is expelled.

We had a trocar and cannula, and putting them in one pocket and the vet guide in the other, I raced back to the animals to put a halter rope on Modesta.

She couldn't see any point in going anywhere but I dragged her, a few feet at a time, all the way up to Maxie's. At least she was getting the required exercise. It was nearly dark when we reached there and Maxie was in bed, but he dressed and came out and listened to my tearful description of what had happened to Modesta. Lighting a lantern, he walked all around her, then solemnly pronounced, "All she's got is a bellyful."

Turning her loose, she headed for home, trotting with the bull following. As she disappeared through the gate, I saw her kick her heels in the air and go bucking down the trail. There wasn't a thing I could say to Max: I felt like a fool.

At last it was time to put up the hay. Maxie was getting a crew of Stick Indians from the interior to put up his and then they would put up ours. He was able to drag the machinery down to our place on the stone-boat.

Maxie himself cut the hay, riding the mower with the lines wrapped around the stub of his left arm. The weather was fine and the shouts of the men and the whir of the mower all seemed very exciting. The clover was heavy and the large bunches had to be tossed about with a pitchfork to facilitate drying. Maxie showed me how to do this and it made me feel like a true farmer. It was even more thrilling to learn how to pitch hay onto the load. The Indians showed me how, but I was clumsy and inept and it was years before I could handle a pitchfork full of hay as skillfully as they could. It was hot, sweaty work but exhilarating, and everyone felt happy and full of jokes and laughter when things went well. A good many of the jokes were directed at the cheechako woman "who didn't know nothing."

The air was filled with the fragrance of clover and even after the hay was dry and in the stack, one could still smell it in the morning when the sun came up. Modesta was going to give some delicious milk in the winter.

Sometimes, when it was too hot to work or there was a little time out from haying, Josephine, the stalwart young woman from Anahim who was helping with the hay, took her little boys, Oogie and Jimmy, to the slough where they dogpaddled merrily in the icy spring-fed water.

Then there were mornings when the dew was too heavy on the hay for work to begin, and Maxie would try to teach the children how to write the alphabet.

Holding down the paper with the buckskin-covered stub of his left wrist, he took the pencil in his gnarled right hand and instructed them how to make a capital R.

"First you make a straight line down, then you start at the top and go 'way to hell and gone over here and back again. Then you put a leg on it."

Oogie never learned to read or write very well but when he grew to manhood and had children of his own, he was ambitious for them to have schooling, so some of Maxie's teaching must have rubbed off on him.

Summer was almost over. September came with its quietness, and the autumn colors began to creep down the mountainsides. The haunting fragrance of woodsmoke hung in the air and there was an excitement in living. Each day I marked off the date on the calendar until Earle would return.

Before long he was home. I was proud to show him all that had been accomplished and he showed me snapshots of his wonderful new boat. It was beautiful. The inside wasn't completely finished yet but he had been able to use it for fishing and it had been a fairly good year. The building of the boat had been expensive but there was enough money left to buy supplies for the winter and to finish the boat the next spring.

16

Bear Hunt in Stillwater

EARLE had accepted an offer to guide a couple of bear hunters from Vancouver. He planned to take them to the Stillwater and asked me if I would like to go along. Modesta would be dry by then and we could get a chap to take care of things while we were gone. It would be a bit of a change for me and was exciting to think about.

Dr. Parr and his friend, Bob Ward, were due in from Vancouver on the boat about the middle of October. Before they came, Earle had to go to a farm thirty-five miles down the valley to arrange for horses, as well as to get a young man to take the animals to the end of the road and meet the hunters when they came up from the boat in a car. Then he would bring them to Atnarko with the horses and stay and take care of the place while I went to the Stillwater.

This would be the first time we had ever taken out a hunting party and I was beginning to realize what a lot of organizing and work it entailed.

The weather was beautiful when they arrived, with deep blue skies and the leaves on the birches and cottonwoods were golden. There was an autumn tang in the air and I was thrilled at the prospect of going to the Stillwater again.

Before we left, the men decided to hunt in a likely spot about five miles up the trail from the farm and Ward shot a beautiful buck with a large set of antlers. Excited over getting the deer, the men had been relaxing by the river when suddenly two large grizzlies appeared, walking over a log jam. Dr. Parr happened to be looking in that direction when he saw them, and taking aim, he killed one instantly. It had a beautiful hide.

The buck was dressed and hung in the woodshed at the farm for them to take back in the cooler on the boat, and they salted and packed the bear hide, ready to take to the tanner in Vancouver.

We were away to the Stillwater early the next morning and arrived by afternoon. It was like looking down into paradise to climb up over the "ding-blasted" trail and suddenly come out on a promitory with the Stillwater beneath us, warm and peaceful in the autumn sunshine. The sky was deep blue and cloudless and the gold of the trees was reflected in the water. Ducks and geese fed in the quiet pool near the cabin and there was fresh snow on the high peaks in the distance. It was breath-taking.

Then we descended to unpack the horses at the end of the trail where the boat was moored. Earle took the animals up the meadow and turned them loose while I ferried the hunters and their gear across the Stillwater to the cabin. We used the boat Earle had built two years before.

There was time before supper for a hunt at the upper end of the Stillwater and the men found lots of tracks and evidence of bears feeding, but saw no bears. The salmon were spawning and there was plenty of feed so probably the bears were filled for the day and wouldn't be back until morning. The men were pleased and looked forward to the next day.

During the night I woke to hear wind and rain lashing against the cabin. It was unbelievable. The weather had been so perfect. Hunting bear in wet brush is the last thing any hunter wants to do so I hoped it would let up by morning. It didn't. If anything, the rain was heavier. It rained steadily and hard all day, then again that night. By morning the river was up and muddy and there was a roar of creeks above the sound of the pelting rain.

Fall is the time for floods in the Bella Coola Valley. Surrounded by high mountains which catch the moisture-laden clouds from the Pacific, the autumn rains are usually snow on the higher peaks. During the fall the snow builds up and then sudden high temperatures, accompanied by heavy rain, flush out the snow, causing a flood. Sometimes it is minor, with a bridge or two washed out and a few farms inundated, and at times, perhaps once in fifty years, the floodwaters spread from mountain to mountain across the valley floor, creating havoc.

It began to look as if we were in for a flood. There was a deafening roar in the sound of the waters and I began to be frightened.

By the afternoon of the second day the meadow was flooded and driftwood was floating down the muddy, turbulent Stillwater. Earle decided to bring the horses over to the cabin. There was no feed but they would be safe and there would be some shelter for them under the firs and cedars. Ward went with him in the boat, sitting in the stern holding the halter rope while they brought one horse at a time, swimming through the tops of the willows which had lined the river in front of the cabin. By this time the water was almost up to the building. Then Earle noticed something strange, the Stillwater was flowing back up the valley.

This could only mean that Goat Creek, a steep mountain torrent west of us, had filled the outlet to the Stillwater with boulders and the creek was now beginning to cut a new channel and pour over toward the cabin, raising the Stillwater above the dam. We were in danger of being caught between the two torrents.

It was growing dusk and the cabin was vibrating from the rolling of enormous boulders in Goat Creek and the falling of huge trees in its path. Then water from Goat Creek began to flow through the woods and past the cabin. The horses were standing in it and it was running through the woodshed, then into the cabin. We found a shovel and dug a ditch to divert it from the door but it was only a temporary measure. Earle decided it was far too hazardous for us to remain.

By this time it was dark and still raining heavily. The roar of the water was hideous and the horses were whinnying in distress. Earle took the lantern and the two men with a tarpaulin and some of their things and rowed them through the darkness to the other side of the valley and the comparative safety of the rockslide. The lantern made only a small circle of light in the gloom and they were constantly running into driftwood, but managed to get across. Earle left them to put up the canvas and try to make themselves comfortable.

Returning for me, he loaded the remainder of the valuable equipment and some food into the boat and took one last look at the horses which would have to remain where they were for the night. It would be far too risky to try to swim them in the dark through all the driftwood. As he was checking them in the dim light of the lantern, Earle noticed the water around their feet had dropped. This was water that had been coming from Goat Creek and it meant the creek must have returned to its former channel and was no longer threatening us.

Then when we went to get into the boat we discovered the Stillwater was dropping and flowing westward again. Goat Creek, moving westward, must have left the dam vulnerable to the terrific force of the backed-up Stillwater, and the enormous pile of boulders must have washed out. For the time being the cabin was safe and certainly much warmer than the rockslide, so Earle unloaded the boat and rowed back again to fetch the men.

When he reached the other side there was no sign of them, and then he heard a voice from up a tree. Four grizzlies had splashed by in panic only a few feet from the men as they were trying to put up the canvas; they had dropped everything and climbed the tree. They were also reluctant to come down again.

Loading the men and their sleeping bags back into the boat, Earle returned once more to the cabin side, and as the boat was gliding through the inundated grass only a few yards away from where I stood in the shelter of the porch, three more grizzlies ran by between the boat and the cabin. Earle could have touched them with an oar.

There were two shaken hunters to

pacify; they had seen all the bears they wanted.

We were able to light a fire in the cabin and have something warm to drink, then we tried to get what rest we could. It continued to rain hard all that night but in the morning it began to let up. By noon the water was beginning to drop and the rain had almost ceased. It seemed a little colder, which probably meant snow in the mountains so Earle felt the worst was over and we decided to get the horses across and see if we could get home.

The "ding-blasted" trail was still there, high and dry, but as we dropped down onto the flat to the west there was no trail left. The whole terrain had changed and we tried to find our way as best we could among the trees, over logs and through holes filled with muddy water where the horses almost fell from sight.

Bob Ward had been an aviator and after a bad crash had been patched up with metal plates in several places. The horse he was riding was an old plough horse, steady but rough, and Ward was really suffering by the time we finally

307

reached Maxie's cabin and stopped to hear the news of the flood.

Maxie's place was safe and so was our farm, he said, but most of the bridges down through Hagensborg were out and the road was gone in many places. This was the last news Max had before the telegraph line went out. It was going to be difficult getting the men back to Bella Coola again.

We were relieved to see our farm undamaged and to be able to sleep in security that night. Earle took the hunters down the next morning and the young farm helper went with them. The horses had to be returned to Firvale, but Earle would still need them to carry the packs until the hunters were able to get a car.

Unless the road was badly washed out, Earle thought they might get as far as Ratcliffs in a day. If they did, they were in for a treat as Mrs. Ratcliff was one of the best cooks in the valley and sometimes could be persuaded to put up travelers for the night.

They reached the farm in time for Mrs. Ratcliff to excel herself. Telling me about it when he returned Earle said the huge dining table was completely covered with the most delicious food: roast caribou, fried chicken, all sorts of vegetables and a salad, pickles, homemade butter, hot sourdough biscuits, strawberry jam, two kinds of pie and a cake, with canned peaches and cream. Except for the caribou, everything had been produced on the farm, even the peaches which seldom grow in this country. One of the boys had just brought the caribou meat from a hunt on the mountain.

It was the same in the morning: sourdough hotcakes, home-cured ham, eggs, porridge if you wanted it, and pie and fruit. The men were reluctant to leave.

Earle was gone for four days, arriving home late one evening with a tired Maryanka, and tired himself from long days in the saddle.

Except for a few wash-outs and erosions, they had found surprisingly little damage to the trail and road on the way down until they reached a bridge about ten miles east of Hagensborg. The bridge crossed a deep gully with steep sides and it had been damaged by a sudden flush of water off the mountain. The decking on the bridge had washed away but the stringers were still intact. They were large, heavy logs about fifty feet long and hewn on top, making a level, two-foot wide surface that could be walked on. The sides of the gully were too precipitous to take a horse down and the only possible way of getting across was to walk on the stringers. Earle dismounted and led Maryanka by her halter rope. She was sure-footed and had confidence in him. Without hesitation she followed him onto the stringer and walked quietly across; the other horses followed.

A mile or so beyond this, the entire road was covered by two feet of swiftly-flowing, muddy water which obscured the road bed. Occasionally there was a hole, but nothing serious until they reached the center of Hagensborg. Suddenly, Pat, the leading packhorse, disappeared from sight in a swirling pool, head, shoulders, pack and all.

Pat was an experienced packhorse and always chose to take the lead. He was so reliable, Earle let him carry all the expensive sporting gear: sleeping bags, rifles, cameras, binoculars and clothing. There was a yell from the hunters, but Pat was out of the hole in a moment and as he went dripping down the road, Earle hoped the water hadn't penetrated the pack too far.

All through the scattered farming community of Hagensborg the road was covered by muddy river water, obscuring unexpected holes, but the deepest was the one Pat fell into. It had been made when two currents from different directions had met and set up a whirlpool, eroding the roadbed into a basin about eight feet deep.

On either side of the road the receding water had left the fields muddy and covered with scattered pieces of driftwood; woodsheds and outdoor privies lay on their sides or were washed away. A large two-holer had left the church and was lying on its side in the middle of someone's field.

Several miles below Hagensborg the worst of the flood damage ended and the men came to where there was a truck standing in the road; the hunters must have felt like shipwrecked mariners sighting a sail on the horizon. They were able to engage the vehicle to take them the rest of the way to Bella Coola, so Earle could return with the horses.

There was plenty of time on the way home for Earle to think about the hunt and realize that what he had been paid scarcely covered the cost of food and the rented horses, to say nothing of wages for hired help. Our own time and effort could be charged up to experience and never again did we take out another hunting party.

Dr. Parr sent us some excellent snapshots and a note which read, "That was the best hunt we ever suffered."

17

Herd Sire

IT was good to get back to farming again, and not long after the hunt Modesta had her second calf. It was a male and like his sire, not very impressive, but Modesta doted on him and Bonnie was fascinated. He was constantly groomed by one or the other of them until it was time for him to drink milk from a bucket and then he went into his own little pen and shelter.

Modesta accepted me as the milkmaid without hesitation and enjoyed being milked. Sometimes she would turn her head to look at me with her enormous eyes and give my cheek an affectionate slurp which felt like a rasp across the skin and left a red welt that took a couple of days to subside, but I loved it for its spontaneity.

She was milking well with this calving and we were beginning to learn a bit more about the care and feeding of cows. Also, autumn wasn't a good time of year for her to freshen and we hoped we could change the date of her next calving to spring when the warmer weather would be kinder to a large udder. This is what we planned. Modesta had other ideas.

By now we had a new bull, one that had been brought down from the interior and left at Maxie's. I don't know how our little Jerseys knew the bull was there, but in due course Modesta was interested. In December someone left the gate open and before I knew it she and Bonnie were both romping up the trail to Maxie's, bucking and jumping, and I couldn't catch up with them.

Maxie had a couple of men staying with him and I had a blurred vision of three faces peering through the window as I panted along behind the cows, rope in hand, trying to get a loop around Modesta's horns.

They were bellowing exuberantly and the bull was screaming a high-pitched reply. Then there was a crash as he broke through the corral bars and galloped to meet my darlings. Somehow I had managed to get the loop over Modesta's horns, but alas, the rope was a long one and in the ensuing melee, we all became entangled in it. I was in the middle and we were not far from Maxie's cabin, in full view of the window.

Women in Atnarko were treated with old-world gallantry, but I knew no man in that cabin was going to rescue me from the mess I was in.

Bonnie and I managed to escape unscathed but Modesta had a calf again in September.

Not long afterwards, it was Bonnie's turn to go up to Maxie's. This time I attached the halter rope before we left, and again we all romped up the trail. Having made the trip before, Bonnie seemed even more enthusiastic and I was hanging on to the rope, taking six-foot leaps by the time we reached there. Her bellowing gave Maxie plenty of time to get inside the cabin and close the door.

Hot and disheveled, I managed to hang onto the rope until we reached the barnyard, but once there, I decided to abandon the whole project and let nature take its course. Removing the halter rope, I opened the barnyard gate at just the right moment to let Bonnie in but keep the bull from getting out. Then I turned and walked past Maxie's cabin with what I hoped was poise and dignity. Two September calves.

Earle was nearly always away during barnyard crises so I was forced to handle them myself. This time he had gone to Belarko to bring up the last of our winter supplies. Among them was a hundred-pound sack of fishmeal for Modesta. It was a high-protein meal produced from fish heads and tails at the B.C. Packers plant at Namu, about seventy miles out from Bella Coola.

Having a gas boat, Earle had been fishing farther out and had picked up a sack of the meal from the reduction plant. It had a slightly over-cooked flavor but was highly nutritious and Modesta liked it. We could feed only a small amount of it at a time but it increased her milk production and gave her minerals she needed.

Back in the spring we discovered she had a craving for something she wasn't getting from the hay when we found her trying to eat a steelhead we had buried in a snowdrift for safe-keeping. It wasn't a very large one and she had most of it in her mouth, slippery with saliva, and most certainly would have choked on it if it had been a little smaller and had she tried to swallow it. After that, we sometimes cooked fish or meat for her when we had it to spare, and fed it to her to augment her limited diet. It never seemed to flavor the milk, but had it been raw, perhaps it might have.

There was a chap farther down the valley who had taken up a preemption on a large piece of land with numerous sloughs and sandbars where the salmon spawned and died. He decided to raise pigs and let them run free, feeding on the spawned-out salmon. The pigs loved it, but alas, the pork was so fishy when it was butchered, no one wanted to eat it.

With so much to do, the winter seemed to be passing quickly and Christmas arrived before we knew it. The winter's wood was split and piled in the woodshed and a dressed deer was hanging from a rafter. The same bachelors were coming for Christmas dinner. Earle had invited B.C. when he passed by his ranch while packing up our freight.

"Better come up for Christmas dinner, B.C.," he said.

"Waal, maybe I will. Come up and get a good feed. Probably get a bellyache," he replied. B.C. was accustomed to a spartan diet.

Frank came down from the Stillwater for Christmas and to stay for a few days. He had a young collie female named Jill with him on this trapping trip, and on Christmas Eve she had two tiny puppies on the mat outside the door of our cabin.

Frank had no idea she was expecting them and I was distressed that the little things had been born out in the cold, but they weren't even shivering when we found them. Jill had dried them well and had snuggled them with her paws against her warm body and long hair. We brought her in and made a bed for her in the kitchen and Frank left her with us until the puppies were old enough to be weaned. When he took Jill home with him after trapping was finished, we kept one of the puppies with us for a time.

Already we had a kitten who had been staying in the house but Jill wouldn't allow Katsa near the puppies, so we had to take him out to the barn to live. The cows liked him and I often found him sleeping on Modesta when she was lying down.

Ralph hadn't been down for his mail since the beginning of winter but about the middle of January the weather turned cold, with the temperature going down to zero F. at night, making the ice of Lonesome Lake safe for him to walk on. He came down to meet the mail with two large bundles of furs to ship out.

During supper he told us about an encounter he had with seven wolves on the lake, just after starting out from home. Ralph never embellished a yarn but told it in an unemotional, factual sort of way and he was part way through this one before I realized it was a hair-raiser.

So many books and articles claim that wolves do not make unprovoked attacks on man, but in this instance there was no question of their intent. The wind was definitely from Ralph to the wolves, so they must have scented him.

He first saw them part way down the frozen lake when they trotted out from behind a wooded promontory in single file. They circled, and then spread out in a fan shape around Ralph. He thought the leader must have weighed nearly two hundred pounds, and it broke into a lope, trying to cut him off when it saw Ralph had changed direction. He wanted to get to the trees but the wolf was heading him off, so he dropped to his knee and removed his pack, taking out a collapsible .22 rifle he was carrying in the packsack. It was the only weapon he had. Aiming at the huge wolf, he fired, but the shot failed to go off. He shot again and missed, but the noise turned the beast and it ran for the woods with the others following.

Ralph returned home for his .35 Remington and was chagrined to find there had been but one other shot for the .22. He had taken the gun along only in case he needed it when he checked his traps on the way home.

Once before, Ralph had experienced an unprovoked attack by wolves. He had been walking along the snowy trail on the trapline carrying a packsack, with his rifle in his hand. He had just lost the woolen mitten from his right hand when he had set a snare on a foot log, accidentally dropping the mitten into the running water below.

Walking briskly into the wind, he sensed something behind him, and turning, saw four wolves almost upon him. Two were already in mid-air and he shot from the hip. Had it been necessary to stop and remove his mitten, it would have been too late.

He shot one of the wolves and wounded another, but the point of the story is that the wind was from him to the wolves and there could have been no mistaking him for a deer. Ralph hated wolves wholeheartedly; not because of his own personal safety but because of their merciless and often wanton killing of deer, the story of which he often read in the snow.

As January wore on into February, a feeling of life began to return to the landscape. The snow settled and developed a hard-packed surface. In the mornings, before the sun softened it, even the cattle could walk on it without fear of breaking through the crust.

February is the mating month for coyotes and often we saw them romping and playing like puppies in the lower field. Every night we heard them yapping and howling, alone or in chorus.

The mating howl of the wolf was the most stirring. We heard it frequently, often from the rockslide near the cabin or just across the river where there was a game trail. It had greater cadence and harmony and I regretted my prejudice against an animal with such a beautiful voice. Maxie called it a moanful sound.

Jill was still with us and was wide-eyed with terror for her puppies when she heard them. We had to keep her in the house at night, not only to protect her but to keep her from barking at the coyotes and wolves and disturbing our sleep.

We had one curiously playful visitor from the wilds in March. The warm sun had melted most of the snow from the meadow and the early buds were beginning to swell. Our animals were free to roam at will in the hayfield as well as the pasture, and we looked out of the window one morning to see Maryanka behaving in an eccentric manner. She was prancing and looking toward the farthest end of the field, then holding her head high and snorting. She seemed excited and fascinated and a little afraid; we wondered why until we saw a young bull moose down there. This wasn't the season for courting and he didn't seem interested in anything but the buds of the willow bush which he was eating.

As he worked his way up toward the house we could see the new growth of his antlers. Then he finally became interested in Maryanka, who turned coy and began running around the cabin. He chased her. They made four circuits before he gave it up as a bad job and became curious about some washing I had on the clothes line. Maryanka stood at a safe distance and resumed her snorting but the moose ignored her; then he was curious about the cabin. Leaving the clothes line, he came over to the big living room window where we were and touched the glass with his nose. Motionless, we stared through the window at each other, not two feet apart, until suddenly he saw us and like a shot, whirled, and was off down the meadow at a gallop, looking back over his shoulder occasionally before disappearing into the brush. Maryanka was still snorting and pawing the ground.

We had another interesting visitor before Earle left for Bella Coola to work on his boat. It was Frank Sill, the Algatcho Indian who had camped with his family below the Stillwater the spring we shot the moose and gave him three-quarters of it.

He had come down with his packtrain as soon as he heard there was a little feed in the valley for his horses. Arriving at our cabin one day by himself, he was obviously intent on a visit. We had lunch and I shall never forget the charming way he said "Shnahlya" in his soft voice, the Stick Indian word for "Thank you."

After lunch, the two men sat by the fire and talked for a long time before he came to the point of his visit.

"More better you start store this place. Lots of people stop. First store this side Anahim."

Earle said he hadn't thought about it. Anyway, he didn't have the money. He told Sill it would cost lots of money to build a store and buy grub and clothes to sell in it.

"I borrow you money," Sill replied. "I borrow you five thousand dollars."

Earle said that was a lot of money, and anyway he didn't know anything about running a store.

"Easy," came the answer. "I tell you how. Just you look up trail and see some man come on horse. You get frying pan and fry bacon. He smell that coffee. He come this cabin, see you eat good grub, drink that coffee. Pretty soon he say, 'O.K. I buy some coffee, some bacon.'

"You say, 'You got money?'

"He say, 'No money stop.'

"You say, 'No jawbone stop. You got saddle?'

"He say, 'I got good one.'

"You say, 'That saddle got scratch. That saddle not much good.'

"He say, 'I got bridle.'

"You say, 'That bridle got black silver — not much good.' I give you one pound coffee, one slab bacon, one sack flour for that saddle, that bridle.'

"He say, 'That good saddle. That good bridle.'

"You say, 'Suppose I get that saddle, that bridle. What I do with old saddle, old bridle? Too many. No good.'

"Pretty soon he say, 'O.K. I give you saddle. I give you bridle. You give me coffee, bacon, one sack flour.'

"Next time he come he don't have no saddle, no bridle. He trade you his horse. You give him more coffee, bacon, more flour."

"Next time he need more grub he don't have no horse, he don't have no saddle, he don't have no bridle. You say, 'O.K. You cut logs.' Then you build BIG store."

Earle asked Sill to talk over his idea about a store with the Indian agent and Sill went away happy, but to Earle's relief, he never heard from him about it again.

With a year's supply of firewood split and stacked in the woodshed, Earle was anxious to get away for an early start on his boat in Bella Coola. He wanted to finish the inside of the boat's cabin before fishing started and also install a drum for winding up the net. This was an innovation that hadn't been tried in Bella Coola fishing before.

There was a power take-off from the boat engine which turned the drum at three speeds, pulling the net from the water, over a roller, then winding it up like a gigantic spool of thread. It was geared so that it could be run fast or slow, or left in neutral, or it could be stopped with a brake to prevent it unrolling whenever a fish had to be removed or the net untangled. This was going to take all the backache out of fishing and help prevent cold, sore hands.

As he did the previous year, Earle

arranged to phone on Saturdays to tell me how he was getting along and find out how I was getting on with the garden and the animals. He worried a little about leaving me alone, especially with our bull getting to be such a big fellow, but he was an Aberdeen Angus and as gentle as a kitten.

He had spent the winter at Maxie's, but with the coming of spring he came down to stay with the cows. He stood with them in the smudge I made every day during the worst of the fly season and waited for his turn to be brushed and rubbed lightly with pine tar and oil. It kept the animals relaxed and comfortable and they mooed for the smudge if I was slow in starting it.

There was so much feed, the bull spent most of his time lolling in the shade while the cows grazed. But one day, early in the summer, he disappeared. I hunted everywhere for him and finally found where he had crashed through a brush fence onto the trail, so I wondered if he had become bored and imagined he might find someone more interesting elsewhere. I couldn't think who, because the nearest cow was about eighteen miles away.

Maxie came down the next day. They had called up from the lodge at Stuie. Would I come down and get our bull? He was down there wrecking all the fences and scaring the life out of the women. They had him locked in the corral on the stampede grounds.

I couldn't possibly go down and leave the cows but Earle was due to call in a couple of days and perhaps he could come up and bring the bull home with him.

When he called on Saturday and I told him about our problem, he thought he could get up to Stuie that evening and start up with the bull. It might be dark before he got home so if I wanted to bring the rifle and a lantern to meet him it would be a help.

I raced home from Maxie's and hurried through the milking and by eight o'clock had started down the trail with the bear gun, some matches and a coal-oil lantern. The berries were getting ripe and there were fish in the river, so there were bound to be bears around.

The sun had gone behind the mountains and it was growing dusk among the trees; darker than I had thought it would be, but still I didn't need the lantern yet and I thought it wouldn't be long before I met Earle on the trail.

I whistled until my mouth became dry. Then I wished I had brought a tin pail with a stone in it. This had been highly recommended to keep bears away, but then I remembered Earle had said it only let them know where you were; the best thing to do was to be quiet and alert.

In the twilight, stumps along the edge of the trail began to look like bears and more than once I thought I saw one move. Finally, after traveling about ten miles, I decided to stop and build a campfire on a gravel bar in the open, near Mosher Creek bridge. Earle would be able to see it when he came and the bull wouldn't mistake me for a bear.

The night was filled with eerie sounds and I thought I could hear bears fishing down at the mouth of the creek where it emptied into the river. I kept piling more wood on the fire. I had no watch, but it seemed hours before I heard a sound on the trail near the bridge, and out of the blackness came the shining ring in the bull's nose.

Earle told me he had been delayed by the bull wanting to fight every black stump on the way. There was so much bear sign, the bull was as spooked as I was. Earle had stopped again at his old place two miles down the trail and searched around once more for a pack rat's nest where he found the tag end of an old candle to make a bug with. The candle had just melted through the bottom of the tin as he came across the bridge. It was daylight when we reached home.

18

Maxie's Illness

ALL during the spring and early summer, Maxie seemed unwell and there were even days when he stayed in bed or lolled on his bunk; this was unlike him.

He had taught me how to harness and drive the team, so I had been able to help him plant his "spuds" and put in the corn and other vegetables, but it was an effort for him to drag himself about, and later in the summer, I finally persuaded him that he should see a doctor.

He steadfastly refused to go to Bella Coola for fear they would put him in the hospital. "Ain't nobody ever gets out of them places alive. Them nurses, making you take a bath!" To Max, this was the ultimate indignity. I doubt if he ever took a bath. A change of clothes was considered adequate, and a splash of water around the face in the morning did the job.

However, he did shave twice a week, but aside from the fear of being forced into a bath by a nurse, he seemed to have a genuine phobia about hospitals and was convinced he would die if he entered one.

At last I managed to extract a promise that he would let me get a doctor to come up and see him once the hay was in. There were some Indians down from Anahim Lake who agreed to put up his hay, and afterwards, they would put up ours.

It was pathetic to see Maxie so unlike himself, unable to be driving the horses and being in the thick of things. But when the haying was finished, I held him to his promise and talked a young assistant doctor into coming up from Bella Coola to the end of the road on a Saturday. Then I arranged for someone to meet him with a saddle horse and bring him up to Atnarko.

Maxie alternated between moods of elation over the prospect of the doctor's visit and sinking into gloom at the thought of dying in a hospital.

A couple of days before the doctor was due, Max thought it would be a change if he had a meal of chicken instead of smoked fish, so he asked me if I would take the shotgun and go down and shoot a guinea fowl for him. I had never used a shotgun before and hated to admit it. Maxie was lying on his bunk on the other side of a short partition where he couldn't see the gun rack, so he didn't see me take the .12 gauge instead of the .410 shotgun. The shells were on a shelf adjacent to the gun rack and I took two that looked as if they might be the right size.

Maxie had given me detailed instructions on how to pick out the right bird, but down at the barn they all looked alike to me. They were noisy but tame, and

I selected one that was just a few feet away from me and aimed, pulling both triggers. The impact knocked me flat on my back with a shoulder that felt as if it had been wrenched from my body. When I came to my senses I looked around for the guinea hen. There didn't seem to be anything but a few feathers floating to the ground.

I didn't dare tell Max I'd blown one of his pet guinea hens off the face of the earth but he must have heard the shot so I'd have to think of something to tell him. I finally said I was so nervous I'd missed, but rather than try again, I'd take one off the roost after they had gone to bed. This meant I would have to come up the trail again after taking care of Modesta and the calf. I was getting worn out with going back and forth between the two places, trying to help Max. He was going to have to get well soon or have someone come and take care of him.

The doctor arrived at last, and after checking Maxie thoroughly, told me it would be necessary to take him to the hospital for tests and medical treatment.

He thought there was a kidney disorder that could be serious if it were left untreated.

How to get Max down there was the big problem. He wasn't well enough to ride a saddle horse all that distance and he couldn't walk. Then I thought of a travois. I had seen Indians go down the trail with one, and with a gentle horse, there was no reason why Maxie shouldn't be able to get to the end of the road.

A travois is a primitive carrying device made of two poles, the front ends of which are attached to either side of a saddle on a horse, while the other ends drag behind on the ground. A sling between these poles is made of some stout material such as leather or canvas, lashed securely to them.

The doctor and I found a couple of smooth, dry cedar poles at the barn and cut them to the right length, then made a hammock out of some strong canvas and attached it firmly to the poles in such a way that Maxie wouldn't slide down or roll off. Then we padded it with hay stuffed loosely into gunnysacks and tied them securely in place. We used his gentle old Blackie and a packsaddle, but it took a lot of persuading to get Maxie onto the travois.

There was a lot of muttered profanity about these so-and-so contraptions, but we finally got him on board and were away, the doctor leading Blackie and I walking behind. Occasionally one of the poles would go over a large stone, tipping and jarring Maxie, which would start up another round of muttering. I felt the need to mutter too, but after a mile or so, it began to look as if we might get there safely. Once or twice the ends of the travois wedged between large stones but we pried them through, or over, and were on our way again. I believe Maxie began to enjoy the ride before it was finished.

We had arranged for a car to come to the end of the road to meet us and Maxie was able to lie down on the back seat with his long legs folded up like a jackknife, for the forty-five mile ride to the hospital.

Going back to Atnarko, I rode Blackie on the packsaddle padded with a sack of hay. I would be all alone up there unless

337

we could find someone to come and stay at Maxie's.

When Earle and I had our customary chat on the following Saturday, he had already heard that Max was in the hospital and had been to see the doctor about him. The doctor had said that Maxie's condition was more serious than he had first thought and that Max wasn't responding to treatment. He thought part of the trouble was psychological; Maxie had given up hope when he entered the hospital and felt he had been taken there to die. They were really afraid that this was what might happen.

Earle scolded me about trying to do too much and said he would try to find someone to go up and take care of Maxie's place. He was fortunate. Within a few days Oscar Bryan and his dog arrived, and no one could have been more welcome.

Oscar was a middle-aged Norwegian bachelor with a droll wit and caustic tongue who never seemed tied down to any permanent job. He didn't enjoy work but was kind to children and animals, and he was an old friend of Maxie's and ours.

Oscar had walked into paradise. The weather was sublime and the worst of the mosquitoes and blackflies was over. Maxie's garden was in its prime, with the tomatoes and corn ripe, and plenty of new potatoes, carrots, beets and cabbage.

Everything grew well during the long summer days at this latitude. The heat from the sun was reflected from the rockslide across the trail from Maxie's garden and a spring creek kept it sub-irrigated during the hot weather.

Oscar would sometimes arrive at our place and empty a gunnysack of ripe corn and cracked cabbages over the pasture fence for the cows. They loved it and in return I was able to keep Oscar and the dogs in milk and butter. Maxie's chickens laid well, so Oscar had all the eggs he wanted and there were fish in the river. Happily there was little work to do until it was time to harvest the garden but that wouldn't be until the end of September.

Reports from Bella Coola weren't good and I was beginning to worry. If part of

Maxie's problem was psychological, as well it might be, he wasn't going to get better lying down there yearning to be home in his bit of paradise. There was something about the beauty and solitude and the very air itself in Atnarko that made one feel alive. Even the horses were aware of it when they came up the trail and out of the woods onto the open gravel bar at Young Creek, a few miles below our place. Tired after a day on the trail, they picked up speed and lifted their heads. Earle and I almost always stood still for a moment and drew in deep draughts of air and remarked about how good it was to be getting near home. So I knew how Maxie felt and wondered how I could get him back to where he could breathe the healing balm again.

The following Saturday, Earle told me the news of Maxie still wasn't good and the doctor was growing concerned that he might not make it. They had cleared up the kidney disorder but he wasn't getting well. He seemed to have lost the will to live. I made up my mind on the spot.

"I'm coming down to get Maxie and bring him home," I told Earle.

"But you can't possibly do that!" he exclaimed.

"Yes, I can" I replied. "I know I can manage. What Maxie is pining for is Atnarko. Once he gets back up here he'll get well. I'll come down on the next mail trip."

Modesta was nearly dry and Oscar could take care of her for a couple of days; he was wonderful with any animals.

I was sure I could talk the doctor into letting me bring Maxie home. Then I could get the Ratcliffs to make a bed for him in the back of their pick up and take him from the hospital to the end of the road.

If I took Blackie with me when I went down with the mail carrier, then perhaps I could get Milo Ratcliff to help bring Maxie back up the trail on the travois. It all seemed so simple.

"But you can't possibly do all this by yourself. You're not strong enough and I'll be out fishing when you come down," Earle argued.

"I'll ask Milo to help me. He'll understand."

Milo was an old friend of Maxie's. His farm was at Firvale but he also had a hunting and trapping cabin at the Precipice and stopped with Max when he went back and forth. Furthermore, he himself was aware of a man's need to live in the freedom and clear air of the wilderness, and I was sure he would help. I felt full of confidence and assurance.

Oscar agreed to stay on and take care of Max if I brought him home. There seemed only one thing left to do before the mail came up in a few days; make some sort of commode chair for Max to use until he regained his strength. Oscar and I set about fashioning one of bits and pieces of box lumber that were around the place. It wasn't a work of art but would serve its purpose.

My chief worry was whether the doctor would let Max go when I got to Bella Coola, but there was something about him when he came to Atnarko that made me feel he would understand and be willing to take a chance. Anyway, what had he to lose? Max wasn't getting well down there.

I was shocked when I finally saw Max

in his hospital bed, the sheet drawn up under his chin, like a shroud. He look so clean and white and his sunken eyes were dull and lifeless. I was really frightened and for a moment felt brash and irresponsible in thinking this man could be healed by taking him back to Atnarko.

"Hi, Max. I've come to take you home. Milo and I are going to take you back to the ranch where you will get well."

His eyes opened in disbelief and a flicker of hope passed through them, but his voice came from far away, weak and without vitality, "I'm dying. Don't let them bury me down here."

"You're not dying, Max. All you need is a mowich steak and some sourdough biscuits; and some of the Atnarko air."

"Gawd, they feed a man cream of wheat in this place!"

This was more like it. I could see the old spark beginning to glow and felt sure I was doing the right thing.

We talked a little while longer, then I went downstairs to talk to the doctor. Quite simply I said, "Doctor, I want to take Maxie home to Atnarko."

He thought for a while and then replied, quite as simply, "All right, he's not getting better here."

I could scarcely believe it, but he gave me the necessary medication and instructions for taking care of him.

Maxie was extremely weak but they managed to get him dressed and out into the back of Ratcliff's pickup where he lay on the mattress. I sat with him and listened to his comments about the blue sky and the fresh air and the *nurses*.

We stayed that night at the hospitable farm home of the Ratcliffs and Maxie had the first sourdough biscuits he had eaten since he left home. He seemed to come more alive with each slow bite.

Milo left early in the morning with his saddle horse and was almost at Belarko where I had left Blackie, by the time we reached there in the pickup. A mile or two farther on, the travois poles were still at the side of the road where we had left them on the trip down and it wasn't long before Max was settled on the sacks of hay, being dragged up the trail behind old Blackie; Milo led the horse while I walked behind.

I couldn't believe it was happening. The warm September air and the excitement were bringing a bit of color to Maxie's cheeks and his voice was losing its forlorn hopelessness. He almost sounded like his old self again and he seemed to be enjoying the adventure.

It was late afternoon before we reached the ranch. Oscar and the two dogs came out of the cabin to greet us and Rex was beside himself with joy when he discovered it was Max who was lying on the travois. He stood on his hind legs and licked Maxie's face and hand, wriggling in ecstasy. Max tried not to look touched but his hand reached out and caressed Rex's head. We managed to get him out of the travois and onto his feet and he stood there, a bit wobbly, looking about him and breathing deeply of the sweet air. Then he muttered fervently, "I'm home again!"

Oscar was a good nurse and it seemed no time at all before Maxie was able to get out of doors and walk about a bit. From then on his recovery was merely a matter of time. Oscar agreed to stay until the garden was harvested and then he wanted to return to his little house in Bella Coola. Max was going to have a friend come and stay with him for the winter who would take over his trapline, so there was nothing more to worry about.

19

The Accident

IT was nearing the middle of September and Earle would soon be home. Time seemed to stand still, and while I waited for him to return, I would sometimes walk up to Maxie's for a chat or to talk with someone on the phone. One day I had a compelling urge to go and I didn't know why.

Since my sister's death, my brother-in-law, Vincent, had not returned to Bella Coola but was living in Victoria. He had given up all plans of developing a ranch of his own but he liked working with horses and was spending the haying season with his sister, Dorothy, and her husband, Andy Christensen, on their cattle ranch at Cless Pocket near Anahim Lake.

The elevation there is about thirty-five hundred feet, and in September the air is dry and exhilarating, with the sun hot during the day, although the temperature drops to freezing at night. Autumn is the most delightful time of year in the interior and the camaraderie of the haying crew made a pleasant work-vacation for Vincent.

Sometimes I phoned Dorothy for a casual chit-chat, and the day I had felt compelled to talk to someone, I cranked the Christensen ring of two long and one short. Max was sitting outside in the warm September sunshine with Rex at his feet. Everything was peaceful.

Dorothy answered, but her voice was strained and hushed. "Isabel, there has been an accident. Vinney is hurt. I can't talk now. We need to keep the line open."

I went outside to Maxie, feeling sick

with concern. He knew nothing as he had been outdoors most of the day and hadn't heard the phone ringing.

I couldn't call Dorothy again but the suspense was unbearable. After a while the phone rang for Andy's ranch, and I listened unashamedly. Lifting the receiver, which cut down the sound between Cless Pocket and Bella Coola, I "rubbered."

It was the doctor in Bella Coola calling Dorothy to say the plane that had been ordered from Vancouver had arrived in Bella Coola about noon but it was so stormy, the pilot had difficulty in landing at the dock. It was still too rough to take off again so he didn't think he would be able to try to leave until morning. Unfortunately, the weather reports were for stormy weather the next day too. The doctor enquired about Vinney's condition and from the report Dorothy gave him, I was able to piece together some of the story. Most of the blank places I was able to fill in later. Also, I was thankful Dorothy and the doctor could hear each other well.

Vincent had been driving a team of

horses operating a mower on one of the meadows about six miles from the ranch house. There was also another team on the same meadow, driven by Domas Squinas, one of the experienced hands. It was a crisp morning and one of Domas' horses was not fully broken yet.

As Vincent's team was going through a narrow neck in the meadow, Domas's team came up behind him. Something spooked the horses and they bolted, heading straight for Vinney. Domas tried to throw his mower out of gear, but slipped and fell behind the mower, still holding onto the lines.

With the sound of the mower whirring and crashing behind them, Domas's team galloped in a frenzy, toward Vincent. Hearing the noise, he looked around and saw them coming, the cutter bar bouncing in the air. They were almost upon him when he stepped forward on the pole of his own mower to escape Domas's cutter bar. His leather shoes slipped on the dry pole and he fell in front of the cutter bar of his own machine, which was still in motion. One leg was severed just below the knee and the other leg was gashed and mangled so badly it was thought later that it might have to be amputated. The thing that probably saved his life was that he continued to hold on to his lines and to his rawhide whip. With these he was able to stop his team and then use his whip for tourniquets on both legs.

Domas finally stopped his team and tied them up; then ran to Vinney. Finding him still alive and with the tourniquets on both legs, he rode hard to his brother Louis, who in turn almost killed his horse, racing to tell Dorothy and Andy of the accident.

Dorothy, who was extraordinarily capable and efficient, gathered together disinfectant and bandages and other first aid equipment, along with blankets and a pillow, while Andy and several of his haying crew ran to the corral where they caught and saddled horses for the six-mile race back to where Vincent was lying on the grass.

After they left, Dorothy was able to get through to Vancouver to arrange for a float plane to leave immediately for Bella Coola to pick up the doctor there and bring him up to Anahim Lake. Then she called the doctor in Bella Coola and told him of the accident, asking him to be ready as soon as the plane arrived. This was an excellent plan except for one thing: Dorothy wasn't aware that a storm was blowing in the inlet at Bella Coola.

Rich Hobson, a young rancher who knew something about first aid, was visiting Dorothy and Andy and was able to help with the first aid until Jane Bryant, a hardy and capable young woman neighbor with nurse's training, arrived and took over.

By this time the men had made a stretcher out of fence poles and blankets and were trying to get Vinney back to the ranch house. Racing on her lathered horse, Jane met them and they stopped while she did some primitive but necessary surgery on the legs while they were still numb and before the feeling returned to them in force. The men had replaced the rawhide whip with two cloth tourniquets which had to be adjusted every fifteen minutes and Jane wanted to tie the arteries instead. She had nothing but the simplest instruments to do the job and there was no morphine. There would be none until the doctor arrived, and Jane's concern was that the shock and pain would prove too much for Vinney unless the doctor got there with the morphine soon.

It was about eight in the morning when the accident occurred and the evening was growing dusk before the stretcher finally reached the ranch house. Dorothy had turned one of the rooms into a hospital unit with two beds in it. The plane had not arrived and it was going to be a bad night for Vincent.

Andy's vigorous father, Adolph Christensen, phoned from Bella Coola several times and said he was going to start up with the doctor and the morphine, now the plane was stormbound, but Andy begged him not to take the doctor out of Bella Coola as the plane was already at the dock and would be able to take off the first thing in the morning. It was less than an hour's flight by plane to Anahim but would take the doctor two or three days by horse trail.

When morning came and Vinney was

still alive, three men from the ranch left early to ride over to Anahim Lake to light a bonfire on the shore as a beacon for the plane. All day they waited and tended the fire until Andy rode up at five o'clock and told them it had been so stormy in Bella Coola during the night and day, the plane hadn't been able to take off, so the doctor was still down there.

No one knew how long the plane would be delayed but the restless and frustrated men could wait no longer. They had formulated a plan: it was decided to take twelve shod horses and three of the best riders and stake out a relay of horses on the horse trail which went from Anahim to the end of the road in the Bella Coola Valley, a distance of sixty miles.

Andy phoned his father asking him to start out in his car from Bella Coola with the doctor, then pick up two horses from some farmer as close to the end of the road as they could, and ride until they were met on the trail by the first of the relay teams from the ranch.

"About time," Adolph snorted, "We'll start up the road and give her snoose!"

The car was an ancient Ford, gassed and ready. Its owner never questioned whether the tires would hold out over the forty miles of rough road but we heard later that the car was riding on rims before they came to where it was possible to get the two horses for the trail.

Dorothy phoned at last to tell me about the accident and to let me know that Adolph and the doctor would be stopping at our place to rest the horses some time during the night before going on to meet the relief horses farther up the trail.

The storm had passed and the moon was beginning to shine on the high bluffs along the trail when I heard them coming. In the still night air I could hear the sound of the horses' hooves on the trail over a mile away. It was near midnight and already Adolph and the doctor had ridden twenty-five miles and there were still another forty miles to go. We fed the horses oats, but the men were too exhausted to eat the supper I had prepared for them. They drank only rum-laced coffee.

One of the horses was a heavy

young Percheron, unused to trail work and unshod, but he had an amiable disposition and was willing. The other horse was much older and had been packed and ridden before, but he was not shod either. It was a lot to ask of them that they go still further that night but they traveled another ten miles before they were relieved.

Adolph and the doctor had two more changes to make before the last team finally raced with them into the ranch house yard and slid to a stop at the door. It was six o'clock in the morning, forty-eight hours after the accident. At last Vinney was able to have morphine to relieve the pain.

Early in the afternoon the plane from Bella Coola arrived on Anahim Lake, guided by the beacon fire; and the following day the doctor was able to take his patient in the plane to Vancouver.

Vincent survived, and they were able to save what was left of his lacerated leg. His stamina and endurance had saved his life.

A week later I woke one morning to the sound of splintering wood. Leaping out of bed, I looked out of the window to see the two horses that had started the journey to Anahim with the doctor and Adolph. They were out on the trail. Pat, the older and smaller, was standing back and watching Horsie, the enormous Percheron, with feet as big as over-sized dinner plates, draping one front foot gracefully over our fairly tall and quite sturdy gate. He was gently rocking it back and forth in a relaxed manner, as one would casually rock a cradle. It simply disintegrated beneath his weight and both he and Pat walked in. I couldn't help laughing, even though the gate lay in ruins. They must have been turned loose on the trail and were on their unsupervised way back home to the Gyllenspitz farm below Stuie.

"Well, bully for them," I thought, "They deserve a good feed, but not in the garden." Hurriedly I dressed and went out to put a rope on them. It was like walking up to an elephant to approach Horsie, but he was gentle and so relaxed. His lower lip hung down in a flap and his eyes were crinkled as if in perpetual amusement. He nickered softly as I approached and reached out his nose to be nuzzled.

"You lovable slob," I thought, "I thank you kindly for what you did."

Pat was more reserved, or maybe he was just smarter, and waited for Horsie to take the lead. At any rate, they both had a feed of oats and then I put them in the hayfield for the rest of the day before sending them on their way again. I had to rebuild the gate completely.

Not many years later, when Gyllenspitz died, Horsie found a wonderful home with another gentle old man, Thomas Astleford, who lived alone on his farm in Firvale. He was a slight man whose feet were crippled with arthritis and Horsie was just what he needed to get around on. He fed the horse so well there was a deep hollow in the middle of his enormous back in which Mr. Astleford could sit in comfort without a saddle, as though he were riding an overstuffed chesterfield. He never used a bridle; just a rope around the neck. Horsie seemed to understand everything that was wanted, and when the old chap needed to get on or off the horse they would use a stump. There seemed to be no need for orders or instruction; Horsie would edge over to the handiest stump and adjust his position carefully until it was precisely right for the rider to mount or get off. In ploughing or working it was the same, and in years to follow, I thought when we saw them together, that it was Horsie who was taking care of the kindly old man.

20

1936 Flood

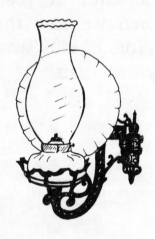

FISHING was over for the 1936 season and Earle was home at last. His quiet presence was comforting after the disturbing events of the past six weeks.

I had been able to get away for a few days, long enough to help Earle put the beautiful new boat in a safe boathouse for the winter. I didn't mind missing the fishing but it was a pleasant change to be in Bella Coola and I marveled at water coming from a tap and the luxury of a hot bath.

But we were home again and anxious to finish harvesting the garden so Earle could get started on the packing in of our yearly supplies. After that came the hunting.

I was beginning to find the hunting season upsetting. At Ralph's place and at the Stillwater, it seemed natural to obtain food from the wilds, but here at Atnarko, just a day's hike from the end of the road, we were exposed to too much hunting. There was shooting all around us during the season and the deer, who had spent the summer in safety near us, were either killed or frightened away.

One chap from down the valley, who considered himself a friend, walked through our gate one afternoon and shot a covey of grouse that had grown to maturity in the brush along our fence. He came to the door with the warm little bodies of our flock dangling from his hand and asked if the coffee pot was on. I was speechless with rage and he never knew how much he tempted providence that day.

In November the garden was safely gathered in and the ground was beginning to freeze. All the packing was finished and the animals were comfortably housed. Modesta and Bonnie had both had their calves and I was making butter again.

I loved going out to the snug little barn and milking the cows twice a day, then feeding the calves; in the evening I did it by lantern light. They mooed gently to me, and to make sure they had plenty to eat I always went back and gave them a little extra. My heart welled with affection as I tucked them in for the night.

As the days shortened in November, the mountain sides grew white with snow. The sidehills of the Atnarko Valley, facing the sun, were the winter feeding grounds of the mule deer which ranged during the summer as far back as the Itcha Mountains, north of Anahim. Then, as the snows deepened, they wandered back down into the valley again, foraging for kinnikinnick and bunch grass on the sunny hillsides facing the south.

Early deep snow during the hunting season meant a greater congregation of

362

deer in the valley, as well as up on the breaks of the mountains. Already it had snowed heavily down to the four thousand foot level when it had been raining in the valley, and the deer had come down.

It was the middle of November when a friend of ours from Bella Coola came up to stay and go hunting. The weather was cold and dry when he arrived but during the night it turned warm and started raining. By morning it was raining hard right to the top of the mountains and the men kept going to the door and looking out.

"Doesn't look good," Odin observed. "There's a lot of snow up there. If this keeps up there'll be high water by tomorrow. November's the worst month for floods."

I remembered the alarming experience we had at the Stillwater two years before but comforted myself that it hadn't flooded our farm then.

By afternoon every little gully had a torrent pouring down it and the crescendo of sound became a roar. By evening there was no let up in the rain. If anything it was raining harder and the roar became an all-pervading force from which there was no escape.

The rain continued all night, and by morning the river was bank-full of muddy water, swirling and whipping at the brush along the bank. Great logs and bits of driftwood were speeding by on the crest of the current and we could see chunks of our meadow breaking off and disappearing into the turbulence.

By noon the water was flowing around the cabin. Odin had been in floods before and he tried to comfort me by saying the farther the river spread, the less rapidly it would rise. What he said was logical but it didn't seem to be working as I could see the water rising at an alarming rate. We began to lift the furniture up onto tables and pack food to take to the fir ridge with us where Earle was making a camp. There was a small level spot, high above the swirling waters where the animals would be safe, and Earle had tied some tarpaulins between the trees to give them and ourselves a bit of shelter. He had packed a lot of hay up for them, as well as food and bedding for the three of us.

It was getting dark when the water began to flow through the cabin, so we decided to leave. There was just time for a last cup of coffee before going up onto the ridge, so to make room on the table for the cups, Odin set some of the things that were on it back down on the floor again. Among these was a square, four-gallon tin of neat's-foot oil that had three sides of its lid cut with a can opener, leaving the fourth side to act as a hinge. When we were finally ready to go out into the night, we accidentally left this half-full tin of oil sitting in the shadows on the floor.

We went out into the darkness and the roar of the flood, walking through nearly three feet of icy water. With only one lantern between us, we sloshed our way to the barn to get the cows and calves. They were standing in a little water and the cows mooed with concern for their babies.

Earle picked up one calf and Odin the other while I carried the lantern and led the way. Modesta and Bonnie, their eyes wide with fear, followed behind, splashing water up the men's backs with each step they took. It wasn't far to the ridge and once there, the calves followed their mothers up to where the bull was standing in the edge of the firelight. He was so black, only the ring in his nose and the reflection of the fire in his eyes were visible.

We stayed there that night, not sleeping, but resting and keeping the fire going. It was the only spot of cheer in all the darkness. Trees were crashing along the edge of the rushing water; the rain was still pouring down and the roar was undiminished.

It continued to rain all the next day but the level of the water was not rising so rapidly. Odin was right; as the water spread over the floor of the valley, its rise was not so alarming. There must have been two feet in the cabin by now. The root cellar was full and two feet of hay in the tall hay shed stood in water.

The men kept busy bringing in firewood, and with no pasture for the animals, they had to tie up bundles of hay and wade with them from the shed to the ridge. Getting the animals to water wasn't much of a problem but they didn't enjoy drinking the swirling, mud-filled torrent.

By the evening of the second day on the fir ridge, there were times when we thought the rain was beginning to let up a bit. Perhaps we were just getting used to it, for by nightfall we were all so exhausted by the noise and the discomfort, we were able to sleep.

In the morning the rain had stopped. Most of the snow must have been flushed out of the mountains, for the river stopped rising and at the end of the day the water began to drop. As the skies cleared we could see fresh snow on the mountains and knew the weather was turning cold; this was why the river had gone down. It was still a foot deep on the fields but was no longer flowing through the cabin, and Odin thought we should try to clean out the silt while there was water close by to do it with. He was an old hand at this sort of thing and we were glad of his advice.

Odin and I decided to clean out the cabin while Earle went up to Maxie's to see if there was news of the flood elsewhere. Odin was concerned about his home down the valley although he lived in an area that was fairly safe from flooding.

Wading through a foot of water, we splashed our way over to the cabin and stepped up onto the porch. The door was open and we stared at the mess within. The empty neat's-foot oil tin was lying on its side and the unpainted, hand-hewn planks of the floor were covered with an oily, slimy silt which left a highwater mark two feet up the walls in both rooms. It was incredible that one tin of oil could have spread so far.

Even chips of wood and debris were lying scattered about where they had floated in from outside. There was nothing to do but clean up the mess before it dried and before available water close to the house began freezing.

Odin manned two buckets and filled them with water which still flowed past the door, sloshing it over the floor, while I swept it back outside again, swishing the silt with it. It took us most of the day to do this but finally it was clean enough so we could close the doors and light both fires. It would be days before the sodden floor dried out, but at least the fires would take the chill off the air and we would be able to sleep in beds that night.

It was months before I stopped stirring up little clouds of fine silt each time I swept the floor. We never were able completely to remove the high-water mark of oil on the walls, so we learned after a while to point to it with pride to show how deep the water had been in The Flood.

Earle came back from Maxie's with the news that Maxie's cabin was safe but his hay field and pasture were under water. The telegraph line was out between Atnarko and Bella Coola, so he had no idea how bad the flood had been down the valley. However, the line was still intact to the interior. Earle had talked to headquarters at 150 Mile House in the Cariboo and they asked him to take what men and equipment he could find and try to repair the line to the west.

There was no radio transmitter in Bella Coola, and the telegraph line was in reality the lifeline of the valley; the only means of communication with the outside world. With a flood of this magnitude, the inlet would be filled with driftwood for miles out and it would be hazardous for any boat to try to navigate it until the trees and logs drifted away on the tide or were beached on the shoreline or tideflats.

After a sound sleep in beds that night, Odin and Earle took what tools we had and the roll of annealed fencing wire that Maxie loaned them and went down the valley to find the break in the line. They found absolute chaos.

The first of it was at Young Creek, a mountain stream about three miles below our place. It drained forty-five miles of deep snow country to the north and such had been the force of the water from the melting snow and heavy rain, that it had burst from the canyon walls at the entrance to the Atnarko Valley and literally torn everything in its path.

The bridge was gone; so were the trees. Ones that had grown for four and five hundred years along the mossy banks of the creek were no longer there.

Now nothing remained but gray, washed boulders for a quarter of a mile and the creek had dug itself a new channel farther west. There was no sign whatever of the telegraph line and the last pole still stood with part of the line dangling from it. Earle managed to attach one end of the annealed wire to this and from there the men strung the wire westward until they came to the shattered timbers of the bridge. Intermingled with the battered and torn logs that had been trees, the bridge had been washed down-valley and piled into a gigantic log jam, thirty feet high.

In front of it were remnants of the pile, still bobbing about in the turbulent water, and as far as the men could see, this was the only place they could cross the still-swollen stream. Quick-stepping from one rolling log to another; they managed to get across, carrying the tools and roll of wire. One misstep and they would have been swept by the current under the enormous jam.

They continued to hang the wire until at last they came to the end of the devastation, where they were able to join

371

the wires together again.

Another five or six miles farther down the valley was Mosher Creek; not unlike Young Creek, except that it did not drain quite such a large territory. It had been a picturesque trout stream, with mossy banks and overhanging trees, but it too had been scoured out of recognition where the water had burst with tremendous force from the canyon walls, leaving the same great piles of gray boulders in its wake.

Here too, the line had been swept away. The men had used up almost all the roll of wire at Young Creek but Earle knew that most of the barbed wire fences would still be standing at his old homestead; about half of them were on high ground and would be available. He estimated the amount of wire they would need, then he and Odin went on down to get what barbed wire they required, releasing it from the cedar fence posts and coiling it up as they went.

Finding the lower end of the break in the telegraph line, they attached the barbed wire and worked their way back up the valley, hanging the wire where they could until they reached the undamaged poles east of Mosher Creek and were able to join the barbed wire to the telegraph line there, restoring the service.

It was getting dusk by the time they had finished their work and neither of them wanted to take the risk of crossing Young Creek on the floating logs in the dark. Neither did they want to camp out, so they hurried, but it was too late by the time they reached the log jam. They hunted along the bank of the stream to find a standing tree that could be felled for a footlog and the only thing standing that would reach across the still-wide stream was a cottonwood, three feet on the butt.

Cottonwood is difficult to chop near the base. The grain of the wood is tough and filled with swirls and cross-grains, so the chips do not split out easily. With axes dull after a day among boulders and wire, they knew it would be a slow job but it was either chop down the tree or spend the night without blankets around a smoky campfire.

At long last the tree was down, and to their relief it spanned the creek so they were able to get across safely. I was glad to hear them coming, slugging through six inches of sticky silt which lay over everything now the water had receded. We kept a tub of water near the back door to wash our boots in before entering the cabin.

The place was warm again but had a slightly greenhouse atmosphere with all the moisture in the floorboards and the ground beneath them.

The cattle were back in the barn, but we had one serious problem; the bottom of the hay in the shed had been soaked and it was beginning to heat already. To save the rest of it we were going to have to toss out all the dry hay, dig out the wet, packed, heating hay and then replace the dry before the moisture from the steaming portion spoiled any more. Earle was perturbed when I told him about it but it was something that had to be done right away and Odin said he would help us with it before he returned home. He was anxious to get back down the valley and see how much damage had been done.

The next morning Earle went up to

374

Maxie's to check on the telegraph line and found that it was working again and messages could get through between Bella Coola and the interior. Satisfied, he returned to our hay shed and the three of us started tossing out fifteen tons of hay with pitchforks. It was a tiring job but by the end of the day we had finished and the dry hay was back in the shelter of the shed again, with the two feet of sodden hay scattered about in the clean place to freeze dry. The animals would eat any that wasn't silted or rotten, after it had dried. Hay was a valuable commodity in this country. No one ever had enough of it.

Odin left the following morning and we turned to the root cellar to bail out and remove all the vegetables. They had to be washed and then spread out to dry on the living room floor. It was a dirty, wet job; our clothes were soaked and our hands cold and muddy and I began to hate the clinging silt that seemed impossible to remove once it had dried on anything.

We were living in a sea of mud. There must have been six inches to a foot of silt on the garden and burying the grass in the pasture and hayfield. We slipped and slithered in it wherever we walked, until it finally froze and dried, then I prayed for snow to cover it.

Our raft and the ramp going down to it miraculously were still intact. Earle had anchored them well with cables and they had floated over onto the field out of harm's way. I was grateful they were still of use since the animals could not walk through the deep mud in the hollows on the path down to their water hole at the river. We had to dip water in buckets for them and carry it up the ramp, pouring it into a tub in the field.

Enormous pieces of the deep, rich soil of our meadow had been eroded and washed away. Earle comforted me by saying that the Lord taketh away but He also giveth, distributing it evenly over the face of the fields.

We needed a little light-heartedness after the flood, so when Jack Weldon came down from the Precipice to get his mail we invited him to stay over and visit for a while.

We had raised some tobacco quite

successfully from Havana seed that had been given to us, and there were clusters of leaves hanging in the attic to cure, turning from gold to brown. Jack and Earle made cigars out of them by rolling the leaves tightly while they were still a bit damp, hoping they would stick together before they were toasted lightly in the oven. Sometimes they had to use a bit of string to tie them in shape and sometimes they were so tight they had to borrow one of my fine knitting needles to run a hole through the center to get a better draft. It was extraordinary they weren't both ill with so much smoking and the only thing I liked about it was that the aroma camouflaged the smell of stale floodwaters.

To cure the leaves into suitable pipe tobacco, Earle sawed off a section of green vine maple about nine inches in diameter and a foot long. This is a sweet, hard wood, a relative of sugar maple, and difficult to split. With a huge auger Earle bored a hole in the block about three and a half inches wide and seven inches deep. Then he made a vine maple plug of the same green wood, slightly smaller in diameter than the hole, and with this he tamped in selected leaves that had been cured to a uniform brown. He sprinkled them lightly with a small amount of diluted molasses and some "deertongue," an aromatic herb we had seen advertised in the *Family Herald* and *Weekly Star*.

Tamped in with the plug and a mallet, the tightly packed leaves were reduced in size until they filled the lower half of the hole. Then Earle made a plug of dry vine maple, and as the block itself shrunk in the dry air near the stove during the next two months, the plug grew tighter and tighter. At the end of two months Earle thought the tobacco must be seasoned and ready to use and he tried to remove the plug but it was immovable. Taking a single-bitted axe, he split the block by hitting the back of the axe with a hardwood stick, and in the hollowed-out cavity was a solid round plug of delicious-smelling tobacco, about three and a half inches in diameter and three inches long. Earle shaved it with a small hand-axe, sharp as a razor, and it made some of the best pipe tobacco he ever used.

Some of the Havana tobacco plants went to seed in the garden and lived through the winter under the snow. They grew to tiny seedlings in the spring and then we transplanted them into rows where they grew exceptionally well in the hot sun of Atnarko and we harvested another excellent crop.

Earle had one other project that kept him and Jack occupied for a few days. The mail order house in Vancouver where we bought our yearly supplies each autumn sent us fifty pounds of green coffee beans instead of the roasted ones we had ordered. They were a good blend and we decided to keep them, but we would have to make a coffee roaster.

I tried using a popcorn shaker but standing over the hot stove and shaking it was tedious and not very satisfactory. Sometimes I put the beans in the oven to roast but often forgot them until they were burned to a crisp. So Earle decided to make an automatic coffee roaster with a spring that unwound and revolved a wire-mesh cage when it was put in operation by a thermostat that we had ordered. The whole apparatus was very involved and complicated but it actually worked — most of the time — and the fragrance and flavor of the freshly-roasted coffee were sublime.

It was a time of adjustment, waiting for the mind and body to recover from the nightmare of the flood, as well as giving the ever-present mud a chance to freeze.

Before long it did, and then it snowed, covering the unsightly mud and debris until spring when our resurgent spirits were more able to cope with the clean-up.

With the coming of the snow, life returned to normal. Christmas came again and the bachelors gathered at our festive dinner.

Bert Robson was among them this time. He was spending the winter with Maxie, running the trapline until Max had fully regained his strength. The son of a Hudson Bay factor, he was born on the north coast and had spent most of his life on it, fishing and trapping.

He was a perfect companion for Maxie, his colorful anecdotes matching Maxie's longer stories.

After Christmas dinner the men sat by the heater in an after-dinner glow, listening to each other's yarns as the smoke from their pipes grew thicker. It was like the other Christmases, and as I watched and listened I wished that nothing would change and that there would be other Christmases to come.

21

Fishing in the New Boat

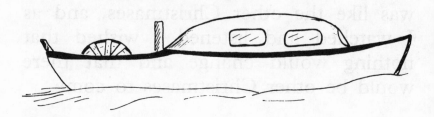

EARLE and I were relieved to be free of the concern and feeling of responsibility for Max. It was good to see him hiking down the trail with Bert, a little more slowly than before, but with his gun and packsack, going to tend some of the closer traps.

There were times when the two of them stopped on their way back for a cup of coffee or tea and a chat, but mostly they went down and back, passing by on the trail without any sign of greeting. I felt a twinge but still was happy that Max had a companion.

Sometimes we would invite them down

for a special dinner and occasionally we would take the lantern and walk up the snowy trail in the evening to visit and hear Bert's radio. But the old rapport was gone and before spring even these visits slowly came to an end.

Max no longer needed us; but it had been a relationship built on mutual need and proximity. We had helped each other because there was no one else to turn to.

Although our days were filled with activity, something had gone out of Atnarko and I was happy that Earle wanted me to go out fishing with him for the summer in our comfortable new power boat.

Bert would be gone too when fishing started up in May. He operated a collection boat for the B.C. Packers, so Maxie would be alone, but in the pleasant weather he could always get someone to come and stay with him.

Only a year before I had thought it impossible to leave the garden and the cows to go out in the boat with Earle, but this time I wanted to go and the animals were no longer a deterrent. We were going to make arrangements to leave them with friends on a farm in Firvale, so perhaps we could see them on weekends.

Everything seemed well-organized and I was looking forward to a summer with Earle in our spacious boat, so different from the cold, cramped quarters of the old cannery sailboat. In my spare time during the winter I had spun plenty of wool so I could knit sweaters and socks while we were fishing. I was even going to take my typewriter. Then in March we nearly lost the boat.

A late, three-foot fall of heavy, wet snow in Bella Coola collapsed the shed where Earle had stored the boat. A friend had phoned to Maxie's and Bert brought the message that the snow-laden roof was down on top of the boat and it was difficult to get to it to assess the damage. We imagined the worst and it was a stunning blow, but Earle left immediately, hiking down the trail to where he could get transportation to Bella Coola.

The snow had settled somewhat by the time Earle reached the boat and he was able to shovel his way in to it. It seemed a miracle that the boat stood there, still propped upright the way he had left it, with the heavy load of the snow-laden roof resting on the curved top of the cabin. It was still intact, with no damage done, except that a few of the ribs of the cabin roof were slightly depressed, but they returned to normal after Earle removed the load of snow and propped up the shed.

There were huge snowslides all along the steep sidehill where the boat houses stood and one or two of the buildings had been buried but we were fortunate that the slide nearest our boat had missed it by only a few feet. Probably this had been winter's final fling and there would be no further snow that spring so Earle returned home feeling confident the boat would be safe until we went down about the first of June.

Before long, the hot Atnarko sun had begun to melt the snow and spring was on its way. Everything came alive again and little shoots of grass found their way up through the mud on the farm. We were busy every day, still picking up debris and cleaning the mess left by the flood six months earlier. It was depressing to see how much of the deep, rich soil had been eroded at the edge of the field and we wondered how much more would go or how we could stop any further loss.

In flood, the river had a mighty force and in eons past, had wandered back and forth across the valley like a serpent, filling the low places with silt and then flowing from them to still lower areas and in turn, filling them. The river channel was forever changing and there seemed nowhere that was safe from flooding and erosion except the rocky ridges and established bedrock river banks. It made us wonder if we had been wise in choosing to make our home in such a vulnerable spot. Little doubts kept creeping into our minds, but quickly we rejected them. We loved Atnarko.

By the end of May the garden was planted and we were ready to leave for the summer. I felt like a nomad as I started out down the trail, leading Modesta. Bonnie followed close behind and Earle herded the calves into line as he brought up the rear, leading Maryanka who carried our pack with the milkpail tied on top.

It was fifteen miles over the narrow horsetrail to Belarko where we were going to spend the night and the following morning we would be on our way again for another fifteen-mile hike down the single-track dirt road to the farm in Firvale where the animals were going to spend the summer. Trees met overhead and in the shade under the tall evergreens there was a carpet of delicate blossoms and green leaves; the exquisite twin flowers, wild ginger, bunchberry, wintergreen and kinnikinnick vine. On the edge of the narrow dirt road the scars of road-building were covered with columbine, Indian paint brush, blue gentian and saxifrage. Dogbane, with its beautiful pink blossoms, grew in the dry, open spaces and near the three or four clearings we passed, wild roses were in bloom. We met no cars as the road was seldom used and since there was no wild fruit ripe yet, there were no bears. The last time I had been over the road was in a car and one missed the beauty of the trees and plants, racing by so fast.

It took us most of the day to get to the farm in Firvale and when we reached it we were glad to rest, but not before I had milked both cows and turned them out to pasture. The cows had not yet been bred again, so they would continue giving a fair amount of milk until winter when they would have a rest before the next lactation began in the spring with the birth of the next calves.

I milked them once more in the morning before turning them over to the farmer and his wife for the summer. My conscience smote me and for a moment I didn't want to leave them, but these were kindly, gentle people and I knew the animals would be well cared for.

Earle was restless to get down to Bella Coola to do some work on the boat before fishing began, and when at last we reached the boathouse on the edge of the tideflats, we could see the damage done by the heavy snow, but inside, still upright and unscathed, was the *Stormy Petrel*.

Earle decided to leave the boat in the propped-up shed until he had completed the work he wanted to do and it was pleasant to have a motionless boat to keep house in. It was so clean and bright inside the cabin and I had made some plain monk's cloth drapes to pull across the windows at night.

During the day I never tired of the view across the colorful tideflats with the slough-grass waving in the breeze, dotted here and there with driftlogs and derelict fishboats, lying rotting on their sides. There were always ducks and seagulls and the mountains in the background were still white with snow.

I missed the routine pressure of farm work and felt a little guilty that I wasn't working hard, but I helped Earle when I could and did a little painting on the boat. Sometimes I walked the mile up the shady road to the general store on the townsite for fresh supplies, carrying them back in my knapsack. On one of these trips I met a former acquaintance who suggested I might like to come to the Ladies Aid Sewing Circle the next afternoon.

Earle was noncommital when I told him about the invitation, but finally he said, "Well, if you think you would enjoy it, why don't you go?"

I had brought a skirt and blouse down with me from Atnarko and thought perhaps the wrinkles would come out of them if I hung them up overnight. I was mildly excited and self-conscious walking up the dusty road the following afternoon in a skirt. I had never been to a Ladies Aid meeting before.

There were a dozen or more middle-aged women gathered when I arrived. Dressed in summery frocks with their hair curled, they looked very feminine and I was suddenly aware of the wrinkles in my own clothes and the faint aroma of mothballs and fresh paint that followed me about as I was introduced to everyone.

In the living room a big quilt was stretched out on a frame, ready for stitching by a group of the women. The others sat about the room, embroidery in their laps waiting to begin, but not before the minutes of the last meeting had been read and a prayer offered. Then everyone joined in singing a hymn, accompanied by one of the women on a charming reed organ which she pumped with her feet.

I felt slothful and useless sitting there with not even a pair of overalls to patch or a button to sew on. The room was filled with the murmur of contented chatter but I seemed to have no part in it. I wished I had brought my knitting.

It had been years since I had been in the company of women and I began to feel stifled in this unaccustomed feminine atmosphere.

It was too soon to leave and furthermore, the kitchen table was laden with beautiful cups and saucers and plates of delicious-looking sandwiches and cakes.

I sat there in misery, trying to make polite conversation, first with one safe topic, then another, but each fell flat. Then suddenly I was aware of myself telling the story of the cows romping up the trail to Maxie's bellowing for the bull and dragging me behind them on the end of the rope.

The needles stopped and the chattering ceased and I was all alone in a starched silence, but I went on and on. My cheeks grew flushed and I longed to escape into the comparative security of a barnyard again. At last I reached the end. There were polite murmurs and I muttered some excuse about getting back to the boat. I left with what I hoped was dignity but my ears burned all the way back down the road.

I had missed the delicious refreshments; but then, the whole afternoon hadn't been exactly my cup of tea.

Before long, work on the boat was finished and Earle was able to get help launching it into the slough on a high tide. It floated like a gull and looked handsome as we went to the cannery to get the net.

Tied up at the cannery, we had several days to get used to the motion of the boat before fishing began. I was squeamish but not as sick as I had been in the cramped quarters of the sail boat and it was pleasant to have power to go wherever we wanted.

Earle had been waiting for a new net to come from Vancouver and he finally received word that it would be on board a cannery freighter that was due to arrive any time with a load of supplies and helpers for Tallheo Cannery, across the inlet.

It was a beautiful day when we heard the freighter's whistle and Earle thought we would take a run over in the boat and pick up the packaged net.

The freighter was already unloading when we tied up at the float and I stayed on board our boat while Earle went up onto the dock to enquire about his net. It was listed on the manifest but hadn't been unloaded yet, so he stood by the edge of the dock near a group of Chinese laborers, watching the heavy slingloads being hoisted out of the hold by the noisy winch.

Suddenly, on one of the return trips, when the boom was being lifted so the empty sling would clear the boat rail, something let go, allowing the boom to drop to a horizontal position about three feet above the dock. In a horrifying instant it began a sweeping motion toward the men. Earle dropped to his knees as the heavy boom swept over him. Some of the Chinamen also dropped and others leapt out of danger, but four of their companions were knocked over into the narrow passage of deep water between the boat and the piling.

Standing by was an English fisherman who had also been watching. Without hesitating or removing his clothes, he dived from the dock and swam to where two of the men were splashing helplessly in the water. He was an expert swimmer and was able to take them, one at a time, to a ladder where they were safe.

Of the other two there was no sign. The Englishman dived several times but the water was thirty feet deep and it was thought they must have struck their heads on the guardrail of the boat and been killed instantly or been knocked unconscious and drowned.

The two bodies floated to the surface the next day. The corpses were recovered from the water and then taken to an empty shack by the Chinamen who wanted them to be buried at sea so their souls would be free to swim back to China; but first, the drowned men would have to be dressed in new clothing. Their compatriots didn't want to dress them so the Englishman volunteered to do it.

New clothing was bought at the

cannery store; boots, socks, underwear and suits. It seemed important that everything be new, and when they were ready, the bodies were carried down and placed on the deck of a sailing boat, together with some ropes and rocks.

The cannery laborers stood in a silent group watching the boat as it sailed out of sight with the bodies. The Englishman had agreed to take them out into deep water and attach the heavy rocks so they would sink to the bottom.

We were still there when he returned to the cannery and Earle talked to him, finding him to be an interesting chap who was there only for the fishing season, to replenish his finances before continuing his way around the world. He was an experienced sailor and fisherman and something of an adventurer.

Earle asked him how far out he had taken the drowned men.

He answered without hesitation, "Just around the point, out of sight. Seemed a waste to leave new clothing on cadavers so I took off the underwear and socks. Nobody will recognize them and they'll do me for next winter."

Earle had noticed that he spoke Chinese fluently, and when he asked him about it, the Englishman replied that he had lived in China for a number of years and had been employed as a collector of customs. The government didn't trust their own nationals and thought the English were more honest.

The tragedy of the drownings cast a pall over the excitement of going fishing. Men stopped and asked Earle about the accident, then gathered together to talk about it again over a cup of coffee.

I was saddened, and wondered whether the dead men were married and if they had families in China who were waiting for money that would never come.

22

Rivers Inlet

THE official opening of the sockeye
season usually began at six o'clock
on a Sunday evening about the
middle of June, following a trial "set" by
the Department of Fisheries to determine
the imminence of the run.

Earle and I purred away from the
cannery in the afternoon so we would
be in a choice place to put out the net
by the time the signal bomb reverberated
down the inlet. We were independent
of the towline now but I missed the

drama of its departure. However, it was exciting enough to round Dead Man's Point, beyond the dock, and run into the afternoon waves which sent spray up over the bow.

Burke Channel is one of the windiest inlets on the coast. Running like a fjord forty miles inland from Fitzhugh Sound, it is about three miles wide in most places and the wind is funneled through the high permanently snow-capped mountains of the Coast Range.

Before it reaches the head of the inlet, Burke Channel is divided into two arms, South Bentinck and North Bentinck. Most of the salmon swim into North Bentinck Arm on their way to spawn in the Bella Coola River and its tributaries. It is in this ten-mile stretch that most of the gillnet fishing was done in sailboats. Outside the comparative shelter of this arm it is usually windier and rougher and the less sea-worthy boats rarely ventured into it during sockeye weather when the west wind began to blow with regularity by ten o'clock each morning.

To fish successfully during the daytime, it was necessary to have a net as much the same color of the water as possible, so most of the linen nets were pale grayish-green when the boats were fishing sockeye within the glacial-silt area.

The density of the silt is determined by the temperature of the weather. Usually in July when the weather is hot, the Bella Coola River is in full spate and gray with pulverized rock which flows out from under moving, melting glacial ice. Fed by tributaries draining the huge glaciers that are part of an enormous ice field, the main river rises almost to flood stage, turning the inlet gray for ten or fifteen miles out. Then, as the silt settles to the bottom of the inlet, the clouded waters gradually clear and farther out they become green again, turning at last to the black-green of the sea.

Not only did the high water of hot weather bring out glacial silt, it brought down whole trees and stumps from eroded banks, as well as dislodging debris from the tideflats during high tides. It was a sorry morning when a fisherman woke to find his net entangled in the branches of a tree, rolling lazily back and forth in a gentle swell.

To the casual observer, a fisherman's life is an easy one, something like a holiday away from home and farm chores. Actually, the opposite is the case and a successful fisherman works hard at the job. He is constantly on the alert, noting the water currents, the color of the water, the state of the weather, and determining the course the schools of salmon will take.

Each species has its own time of return from the ocean but the runs overlap, and while a fisherman is still using his spring salmon net, a few sockeye may appear so it is a matter of judgment when it is more profitable to change nets, as the much smaller sockeye go right through the large mesh of the spring salmon nets.

The spawning migration of the Bella Coola sockeye begins with a few stragglers in the inlet, or a small school, by the first part of June, reaching the peak of the run by the last part of the month. This may vary from year to year, just as the size of the run may vary, but the main body of the run lasts for about two weeks, then the fishing gradually tapers off until it is time for the humpback run.

The sockeye is generally regarded as a four-year fish, the mass of the run returning at maturity, to spawn in the place of their origin in four or sometimes, five years' time; although there are some that return in three, or even six years.

They spawn in areas where there are lakes, laying their eggs in the gravel beds of the streams which feed the lakes, and when the eggs are hatched, the fry swim downstream to the lakes where they live for one or more years before leaving to swim out to the ocean. Should a freshet, or flood occur during the autumn following the laying of the eggs, the spawn could be washed out or buried beneath silt, so that a good hatch might not necessarily result from a large number of salmon reaching the spawning grounds.

The Pacific Coast salmon begin their spawning migration somewhere out in the North Pacific, approaching the coast in large masses, but as they swim toward their own spawning area they begin to break up into smaller schools. Seiners, which catch them in purse seines in the ocean and in the mouths of inlets, are partly responsible for the break-up of the mass, so by the time the salmon begin their run into the inlets, they are swimming in small schools, usually near the shore.

If a gillnet fisherman has the good fortune to intercept one of these schools he is able to estimate its size by the number of fish he catches in one set. If it is a good catch, he estimates how far the remainder will travel in a day and then decides where to set his net to catch more of them as they pass a specific point farther up the inlet.

At night the fisherman does not often move his net, but in the daytime he sets it, then watches the corks to see if they begin bobbing which indicates a caught fish. If enough start bobbing within an hour, he leaves it. If no bobbing occurs, he picks up the net and sets it again in a different place.

Seals are an ever-present menace to gillnet fishing, particularly spring salmon, and every fisherman has a rifle. In the sailboat days, the cumbersome boat was rowed along the net and the fish removed before the seals had time to eat it, and if the fisherman was too late, it was maddening to find nothing left but the head, still caught in the mesh. With the advent of the gas boat, dinghys were either towed behind the boat or carried on board, and they facilitated "running" the net.

About two weeks after the beginning of the sockeye season in Bella Coola, the Rivers Inlet run began.

The mouth of Rivers Inlet lies about forty miles to the south of Burke Channel on which Bella Coola is situated. The two inlets are somewhat parallel, but Rivers Inlet is shorter and wider. The long Owekino Lake at its head seems like a freshwater continuation of the inlet, except for the short stream at the outlet which separates them. The lake is fed by innumerable creeks and rivers which make ideal spawning grounds for sockeye and the run was almost always large. Fishermen from all over the coast went there for the best two weeks of the sockeye season, and as there was a good run expected this year of 1937, Earle decided to go too.

This would be an exciting experience

for me and I zealously helped Earle prepare for the trip. We stocked enough food to last us for a couple of weeks, as well as getting an extra supply of coal-oil for the lanterns and gas for the boat.

Everything was battened down and we were away with the outgoing tide early Saturday morning. It would take us two days to reach the head of Rivers Inlet, the goal of most of the fishermen, where they hoped to make at least one set in the salmon-filled waters at the boundary on Sunday night.

Until now, our sailboat fishing had been confined to the familiar waters inside Ten Mile Point. Beyond that, I had seen little of the inlet but as we rounded the point, I could see the wild and rugged aspect of the shoreline for ten miles farther out. Earle said there was very little safe shelter in a blow on either side of the inlet below Ten Mile until the boat reached the bold promontory of Masachiti Nose and rounded it into the usually quiet waters of Labouchere Channel, which led to Dean Channel on the north. But we weren't going that way; we were going straight on down Burke for another thirty miles to the open waters of Fitzhugh Sound.

Masachiti Nose had been named by the Indians for the "angry" waves that broke on its worn, rocky bluff, and the winds that came all the way up the long channel. It would be an awesome spot in gale and I was glad we were on the opposite side of the inlet and would continue our course down the long, unbroken stretch beyond.

A swell had begun, the harbinger of the day's wind, and as little wavelets began slapping at the boat, I wondered how rough it would get. There was a shelter at Quatna Sound, about a third of the way on our course, but it would throw us off schedule if we had to stop there. Beyond that, there was another inhospitable run until we reached Restoration Bay, about two-thirds of the way to Namu. It was off this bay that we had an encounter with a whale.

In spite of my forebodings, the water was not unduly rough, so Earle let me steer while he attended to something out on the stern deck. I was enjoying the rhythmic swish of the bow into the waves when suddenly, the whole boat lifted and moved sideways. For a moment I thought we might have hit a log or a submerged reef, but there was no violent impact; it was more of a gliding motion. I made an involuntary outcry, then Earle called out, "Whale!"

From the stern of the boat he could see its enormous body beneath the water, moving away from under the boat. It had approached from the stern quarter, behind his back, but he had a clear view of it as it swam on, to emerge and blow some distance beyond us.

I was shaken, but Earle assured me that had it intended to attack we would have received more than a gentle nudge. "Very likely it was emerging for air and we happened to be in its way," he explained.

His voice was assuring, but I was aware that he knew whales were equipped with sonar. Why, I wondered, did the whale come to the surface beneath the only boat in sight? Our boat was gray and streamlined, not at all like the other boats in appearance; could the whale have mistaken us for one of its kind?

I kept a wary eye for whales the rest of the way into Namu, at the mouth of Burke, where we intended to spend the night. Sure enough, just north of it we saw a pod of four whales surfacing and blowing but they were far enough away so that we were in no danger. It was a relief to turn into the safe harbor and tie up to a float for the night.

Namu is the Indian name for whirlwind, and the bay was named because of the strong winds that blow into it both summer and winter. There had been a cannery there since 1893, and a large, modern plant was now in operation with a full crew, so there was a great deal of activity and boats were coming and going constantly. It was probably not the quietest place to spend the night but it seemed safe to me as it was doubtful whether whales would enter the bay.

We left Namu early the next morning to travel the open waters of Fitzhugh Sound before the wind came up. Even without the wind there was a bit of a sea, and halfway to Rivers Inlet the waves coming up the sound from the south were met broadside by a swell that rolled in from the ocean through a pass between Hunter and Calvert Islands. It created a choppy sea whose waves had no direction except up. We were tossed first one way, then another, and anything not tied down in the cabin landed on the floor. Fortunately it didn't last long and within an hour we were back into the rhythmic swells that rolled up Fitzhugh Sound.

They began to grow larger but the boat handled them well, and then after we had passed close by the picturesque Addenbroke Lighthouse, with the surf surging over its rocky base, I was relieved to see the shoreline had broken up into safe-looking bays and inlets; then we came to the archipelago of islands that marked the entrance to Rivers Inlet.

Earle steered the boat through a narrow passage between some tree-covered islands, which brought us into Schooner Pass, an arm of Rivers Inlet. Toward the far end of the pass we came to Provincial Cannery, one of the many canneries that were dotted all around the inlet.

Rivers Inlet Cannery (R.I.C.) was

located at the head of the inlet, near the outlet from Owekino Lake, and this was where we were heading. It had been the first cannery to be built in Rivers Inlet and was constructed in 1892 in the most favorable location. Fortunes were made from the easily accessible salmon that milled about in the waters of the entrance to the spawning grounds, and other canneries soon sprang up: Brunswick, Beaver, Provincial, Goose Bay, Wadams, McTavish, Good Hope and Strathcona. The Rivers Inlet sockeye are larger than the Bella Coola ones but the canneries paid the same per fish for them, so it was a profitable enterprise.

On we went, past the cannery with its crowded floats bustling with Sunday afternoon activity, up through the quiet waters of the inlet whose gentle mountains seemed so much lower and less formidable than those of Burke Channel. There were boats everywhere and we even passed some of the fishermen who had already chosen the place where they wanted to make their first set and had tied their boats to overhanging trees jutting out from shore.

Finally we reached R.I.C. and the scene resembled a regatta, with boats crowding the floats, each flying the colored flags of its own cannery. Motors were running and boats were pulling out after gassing up and buying supplies at the cannery store. Most of them were headed for the boundary which we had just passed about a mile out from the head of the inlet. All along the boundary, from one side of the inlet to the other, boats jockeyed for position trying to hold them against the moving current.

There were so many boats and so much confusion, I begged Earle to go farther out to set the net but he still wanted to make at least one drift on the boundary.

We went to the side of the inlet where the current ran out more swiftly and where most of the boats were waiting. One short drift here would catch more fish than a night-long one elsewhere, Earle explained, as the outflowing current carried back the sockeye from within the boundary where they were milling around before going on up to the lake.

Earle pulled away and waited until the

worst of the frenzy had died down. He made me stay inside the cabin but I watched, fascinated by a scene I could never have imagined.

At six o'clock the signal boomed and pandemonium broke loose. Boats roared around seeking a place, sideswiping each other, while men shouted and cursed above the din of engine noises mixed with the roar of wooden corks banging like machine-gun fire as they ran out across the gunwale in a frenzy of speed. It was a madhouse and in the hysteria, men corked each other by throwing their nets too close, or even across someone else's net. One young chap in an open power boat ran amuck with his throttle wide open, dashing aimlessly in and out among the other boats, scraping their hulls and running over nets. It reminded me of a little boy I had seen once at a children's birthday party, so overcome by excitement, he ran around and around the room with his eyes crossed and his tongue out until someone stopped him. I began to wonder how long it would be before someone tried to stop this young man, possibly with a gun. Perhaps they were shooting already; the sound of a shot would not be distinguishable in the bedlam.

Earle finally had his chance to set the net and he stayed on deck watching, while we drifted slowly out the inlet on the fast-moving tide.

After dark, lights were everywhere in utter confusion and it was necessary to use a highpower flashlight to determine where a net lay or to illuminate one's own if a boat threatened to set a net too close and cork it.

There was no sleep for anyone that night but by morning the hysteria had died away, although there was still a restless moving about of boats. Bleary-eyed men were pulling in their nets and counting the catch. We had made a good one, but one night at the boundary was enough for us and Earle decided to fish farther out the inlet. We were tired, and after delivering the salmon to our own B.C. Packers' collection boat which stopped at the boats flying the company's flag, we found a quieter place to put out our net so we could have a sleep.

When we woke we found we had

been corked by another net, so Earle pulled up and we looked elsewhere for a place. Men from other areas seemed to fish by a different set of rules and lacked the courtesy of the Bella Coola fishermen who were all acquainted with each other.

The following night, well after dark, we were corked again but Earle was weary of picking up and resetting his net; this time he decided to leave it, hoping the two nets might drift apart. Instead, they drifted closer together. Earle checked the net from time to time with the flashlight but finally gave up and turned in for a sleep. When he woke in the morning, our neighbor had gone and so had most of our fish. We were beginning to wonder just how profitable this trip was going to be and understood why some of the older fishermen preferred to remain in the quiet of the Bella Coola area for the entire sockeye season.

Friday evening arrived at last and Earle thought we should go somewhere quiet where we could relax. He knew of a sheltered inlet near the mouth of Rivers, on the south side, about an hour's run from where we were, and since we had plenty of supplies, we started out.

About halfway there we began to hear a strange roar above the sound of the engine and Earle went out on deck to investigate. He was just in time to see an enormous spout of water jet thirty feet into the air along the shore at the mouth of a narrow channel not far from where we were. It was the notorious Skookum Chuck (Strong Water) and he slowed the engine to watch. It happened once again and then we noticed the tremendous force of the current emerging from the channel; forceful enough to carry all the way across the inlet. The roar, not unlike the sound of a huge waterfall, came from somewhere out of sight in the Skookum Chuck channel.

Looking at the chart we could see that this was the outlet from a tidewater lake about two miles inland. There was a sharp bend in the channel, part way in, and Earle thought perhaps the tremendous force of the water flowing out from the lake might set up a whirlpool in the bend, that continued whirling out to the entrance where a submerged rock or some irregularity in the bed of the main inlet propelled the water upward. The jet was about twenty feet wide and powerful enough to toss a good-sized rowboat into the air, We made a wide detour around it and felt the force of the current as we crossed it on our way down the inlet. Earle looked again at the chart. A circle of red marked the spot and also in red were the numerals, 17,000 H.P.

We found a beautiful sheltered bay just inside Draney Inlet where there was no wind and it was quiet. On the way in we passed a picturesque, wooded cove where a hand-logger had his home on a float. He must have had a wife for there were curtains and flower boxes at the windows of the shack and two tubs of hydrangeas standing near the door. Not far away, on the edge of the float stood a blue heron on one leg. The serenity of the scene suddenly made me think of Atnarko.

Earle was filled with curiosity about the source of the tremendous noise in the Skookum Chuck and wanted to return the following afternoon to do some exploring on the slack low tide. He asked me to check the time in the

415

tide book. On the slack tide there would be enough time to go part way into the passage and back out again safely before the current started running swiftly. It was important to be cautious and go in only at slack tide, before the tide started flowing in again. Earle had heard that boats had been caught in the channel by the immense force of the inflowing water and were never found again.

As we approached the mouth of the Skookum Chuck the following afternoon there was no sign whatever of the disturbance of the preceding day. It was so peaceful, the turbulence might never have existed. Earle checked his watch and announced that the tide was just about low slack and we would be perfectly safe for a little while. It was only about two miles in to the lake but he didn't intend to go that far.

Slowly we nosed our way into the mouth of the forty-foot wide channel. Trees overhung the water and the scene was a picture of utter tranquility. Frequent turns in the course opened up new vistas but obscured any view of what lay still farther on and we saw no sign of what caused the noise we had heard. I was on deck enjoying it all as we glided along with the engine throttled down. Then I noticed the trees along the banks were gradually beginning to move faster and faster. At the same time, Earle called from inside the cabin where he was steering, "Something's wrong! Did you check the tide table carefully?"

My heart stopped beating. There was no room to turn a thirty-foot boat quickly in a forty-foot channel, so Earle threw the propeller into reverse and we stopped our forward movement, then began to move backward very slowly. But only for a few moments; the boat was moving forward again. Earle increased the speed of the engine until it roared but there was no responding movement of the propeller. We were moving forward faster than ever.

Leaving the steering wheel, Earle shot out of the cabin and yelled to me, "Get up to the bow and stand ready with the painter! But hang on!"

Swiftly he put the oarlocks in place and inserted the oars. Rowing with all his might, he gradually turned the heavy boat toward shore where there were some overhanging sweepers. As we passed near one sturdy enough to hold us, I managed to toss the painter around it and make it secure while the boat swung around with its bow pointing back out the channel again.

I started to breathe once more.

Earle put out more ropes and we were safe for a little while. His face was still pale and his hands shaking when we went into the cabin to turn off the engine and get out the tide book.

"Are you sure you looked at the right date?" he inquired.

I hadn't. My carelessness had nearly cost us our boat and possibly our lives. Earle never mentioned it again.

Perhaps we might have been able to back out of the channel if the propeller hadn't failed. Earle thought at first we might have lost it but before long he found out what had caused the trouble. The mechanic who had installed the engine had imperfectly connected a joint in the shaft. When Earle had thrown the propeller into reverse, the strain on the joint had finally loosened the key holding the two pieces of shaft together and broken the union. Earle was able to put it together again and it held until he could have a properly secure job done when we reached a machine shop.

It was still frightening to remain in the swiftly running current but the water was not turbulent on the ingoing tide and at slack tide we were able to leave. I was thankful to be far away from there by the time the water started shooting into the air again. I wanted to go home to Atnarko.

On Sunday night fishing resumed again but we were well away from the boundary when we set our net. The catches were still good but toward the middle of the week the peak of the run had passed and boats were beginning to leave the inlet.

Earle decided we would start back to Bella Coola after delivering our fish on Thursday morning, then try to get to Restoration Bay before evening. The bay was only about ten miles inside Burke Channel and there should be time to set the net there for the night. The bay itself had a good shelter but was too shallow for a gillnet, so we would have to fish out in the channel. I couldn't help remembering that it was near where we had the encounter with the whale.

After leaving Rivers Inlet, we stopped at Namu for gas and to buy a fresh beefsteak at the cannery store. By the time we reached Restoration Bay it was dusk enough for the light-colored net not to be too obvious in the clear water, so we were able to set it before having our evening meal.

It was quiet, and with the net out, we settled down to the delicious beefsteak and then we intended to get some rest. As we relaxed in the cosy cabin we both became aware of a distant roar which seemed to be coming closer. It sounded like wind, but we were not alarmed as we could always go into Restoration Bay for shelter.

It was still light enough to see so Earle went out on deck to investigate. He stood there for a few minutes and then called back to me, "Come quickly and see. It's a tide rip."

Unfortunately it was heading toward our net. We stood on deck and watched the long, curving lines of bubbling and hissing water with their loads of debris, coming together and meeting with a roar, then diving into the depths as though propelled by a tremendous force. In no time our net went with them.

Earle reached for the axe and stood ready, but the buoyancy of the boat was greater than the powerful force of the tide rip pulling on the net. Although we could feel the strain on the cork line, it held, or we should never have seen the net again.

Presently the turbulence passed and as the roar began to diminish, the boat steadied itself. There was no sign of the net, although the corkline was still taut over the stern of the boat.

Earle started up the engine and slowly the drum began to drag the twisted rope of net from the depths. It was an unspeakable mess, filled with jelly fish and seaweed, and pierced with uncountable pieces of driftwood of every size which would take hours to remove. Earle detached only the largest sticks as the drum laboriously brought the net over the stern. We anchored in the bay for the night and slept without a care, or any fish either. There was no telling how much damage had been done to the net nor how long it would take to repair it, so we left early the following morning for Bella Coola to get the net up on a rack.

Back at the cannery floats again I yearned to go up the valley to see how my little cows were getting along but Earle needed me to help put the net up on the rack so we could clean and repair it. Furthermore, we had no transportation, so I was going to have to content myself for another six weeks until fishing ended.

The net was in an appalling state and it took us two days to clean and mend it, finishing just in time to go fishing on Sunday night. It had been badly damaged but Earle thought it would do for humpback fishing. Fishermen often did this with their older and weaker sockeye nets, since humps were about the same size as sockeye; but they were softer and weaker and easier to hold in the net.

The humpback run was beginning to come in by the first of August and there were days when both species were in the net at the same time. At first I found it difficult to distinguish between them but soon learned that sockeye were slightly trimmer and were a greenish blue on the back, with tiny black specks, whereas the humpbacks were a metallic blue on their backs, with black blotches and the males of the humpbacks developed a characteristic hump on their backs as they neared the spawning grounds. The flesh of the humpback salmon was much softer and paler than the sockeye but, caught out in the cold salt water of the inlet, they were delicious. However, lying in the fish boxes of the boats in hot weather, humpbacks soon lost their texture and flavor.

Occasionally there would be an unpredictably large run of humpbacks, due perhaps to perfect spawning conditions two years earlier, or else the absence of customary predation in their feeding grounds out in the Pacific. Whatever the cause, the massive runs usually came as a surprise and suddenly the entire inlet, from the ocean to the head, would be filled with salmon. This was going to be such a year.

On Monday morning there were unusually large catches of humps in every net in the inlet. Excited reports spread with the packer that this was going to be a big run.

By Tuesday several nets had sunk with their loads of fish and had to be pulled up by the winches on the packer. Our boat was so full of fish there was very little freeboard and Earle eased into a cove with a shelving beach so we would be safe in case a wind came up while we were waiting for the collection boat.

Even running day and night, the canneries were unable to handle the catch and packers were sent to take away loads of fish to other canneries outside the inlet, some as far away as the B.C. Packers' plant in Steveston, near Vancouver.

In the hot, windless summer weather the uncanned fish softened quickly and began to smell, but fishermen continued to arrive. As word of the extraordinary run began to spread, gillnetters from up and down the coast poured into the inlet, eager to get in on the bonanza.

Finally a daily quota had to be imposed

and most of the fishermen needed to put out only part of their net for a short while each day, and anything in excess of what the packer would take had to be thrown overboard or taken in to the dock where it was given away to anyone who wanted it. People from up the valley took home gunnysacks full of fresh fish to can or give to their neighbors. Women throughout the valley were working around the clock, cleaning and canning fish in glass sealers while they were still fresh. There was no electricity so canning was done on wood-burning kitchen stoves in the hot weather. Each batch of sealers had to be boiled for four hours.

On the weekend Earle helped one chap pull his net from the boat up to a mending rack that stood on the cannery dock, and as the net dipped through the water in the short distance between the end of the boat and the rack, it picked up more than four hundred fish. Taking time to remove the struggling salmon only slowed down the process so that still more fish were caught, and people were asked to come and help themselves to the growing pile beside the rack.

With the imposed daily quota and the weekend closure, so many spawning salmon were left uncaught they filled the river and its tributaries until the streams were black with layer upon layer of fish. Peering down from a bridge, it looked as if one could walk on them. Ravens and eagles and gulls were so filled with fish they were unable to fly when approached, and the whole valley reeked of rotting salmon. Everyone longed for a wind that would blow it all away.

We met the mail carrier after his bi-weekly trip to Atnarko and he told us that the all-pervading stench was everywhere and the river water was so filled with particles of decaying fish it was not fit to drink.

Although it was against the law, there were homesteaders who collected the spawned-out fish from river bars to use as fertilizer for their gardens. Decayed in an earth-covered pit, then mixed with soil, they finally lost their odor and became a rich source of plant food.

The extraordinary run of fish was over in a couple of weeks and fishing slowed to normal. The visiting boats left the inlet one after another, but during the weekends of the heavy run the area around the cannery floats had been a solid mass of boats, their masts a gently-swaying forest of flag-bedecked poles. Boats were tied to boats, four abreast, with nothing between but a protective bumper of bunched-up net covers, or rare, discarded automobile tires.

Not all of the boats were harvesting fish. There were several expensive-looking cabin cruisers fitted out as traveling stores. The most popular with the unmarried fishermen was the one selling men's clothing. Young men blossomed out in sharp-looking shirts and jackets and were measured for tailor-made suits, to be delivered by mail later.

Women flocked on board the one selling hardware and came away with pots and pans and kitchen gadgets that were different from the ones available in the Bella Coola general store.

It was only a short distance away to a boat carrying dry goods. They had racks of coats and dresses as well as bolts of cloth and sewing accessories and there

427

was even a small mirrored dressing room on board.

On the outer fringes of the throng were two mission boats, of different denominations, and some distance apart. They had less traffic on their gangplanks, but they must have had some, because occasionally we could hear the reedy notes of their harmoniums playing hymns.

At the far end of the float, past the mission boats, was a glamorous cabin cruiser, discreetly curtained and operated by a slick-looking skipper wearing a jaunty nautical cap. He had a deckhand and a crew of six heavily-mascaraed young women.

There was a harvest for everyone.

23

Storm

AS fishing returned to normal, the visiting boats left the inlet and the effluvia of rotting fish diminished. There was plenty of time during slack periods for boats to gather in sheltered bays for a coffee mug-up. It was a time of waiting for the shorter days and cooler weather of the coho season.

The regular westerlies of the early summer had died away but the weather remained hot, so the no-see-ums and bulldog flies were troublesome out on the inlet.

The no-see-um is the tiniest of the insect pests in the north and one is scarcely aware of its presence, but the welt from the sting can be very troublesome with itching and inflammation which lasts for days. The bulldog is an enormous fly, about an inch long, that is slow in its approach and rather stupid, so that one has plenty of time to swat it. However, a bite from one can be extremely painful and bleeds copiously. Between these two pests, much of the joy was taken out of the quiet days of August.

One weekend we went into the hotsprings in South Bentinck Arm. They had been discovered years before by a trapper who built a log cabin and somehow managed to get an enormous enamel bathtub into it. Over the years the tub had become encrusted with minerals and was impossible to clean, but no one ever seemed to suffer ill effects from soaking in it. In fact, the waters were thought to have curative qualities and many an old bachelor had gone out there to help clear his "rhumatiz."

Earle told me about the time he had stayed there for a weekend, years before, hoping to cure a cold. He was fishing a sailboat at the time and had left it anchored out from the long, shelving beach, wading to shore in his high rubber waders. The bathtub was there then, long enough so a man could lie comfortably submerged, adjusting the temperature of the water from the spigots which piped in both hot and cold water from springs.

The trappers who had built the shack and installed the tub were no longer there and the place was open to anyone who wanted to use it.

Earle soaked in the mineral water long enough to help his cold and when he was ready to leave he was surprised to find his sailboat aground on the sandy shelf, exposed by the receding tide. Walking out to it, he propped it upright on the keel using sticks from the beach, then he climbed on board for a nap while waiting for the tide to come back in.

An hour later, he woke to find the tide had gone out farther still, but was beginning to turn. It came in with terrific speed, rising as much in an hour as it normally did in six hours. There seemed no explanation for this except that in the vicinity of the hot springs there might be some sort of fault in the earth's surface, causing a disturbance in the tidal flow. Earle was never able to find anyone who had witnessed this phenomenon, nor has he heard of it since.

After hearing the story, I kept one eye on the tide while we were there, but nothing unusual happened. I had no "rhumatiz" to cure and felt slightly parboiled after a bath in the hot water, but I loved the quietness of the place and enjoyed picking the wild berries along the fringe of the woods.

Not all weekends were so peaceful. One Friday we came in from fishing a little early, and after putting the net in the bluestone tank and cleaning up the boat, we were relaxed and were walking slowly up the ramp from the floats to the cannery dock when suddenly we became aware of angry shouting from inside the cannery. It grew louder above the clatter of the machinery; then bursting through a wide opening in the wall near us, came a tall young Bella Coola chap, staggering under the assault of two Chinamen. The one on his back had an arm around the lad's throat, choking off his wind, and the one in front was pinning down his arms so that he was helpless. Behind them followed the other Chinamen, chattering excitedly and brandishing their bloody fish knives.

Earle waved me back and strode toward the struggling men. Pulling off the Chinamen, he demanded, "What's the trouble here?"

The one who seemed to be the leader answered in English, "All the time this man make trouble for my men. He pull their hair while they work. They don't like it. Now he call me son of a bitch. I fight."

"Well, those are fighting words all right," Earle agreed. "But just one of you at a time."

The frightened lad had regained his wind and had tottered over to the corner of the dock where he slumped into a piling. He could have made a run for it but he continued to sit dejectedly while the leader walked over and stood in front of him, taunting him to fight. Finally the

Chinaman struck him on the side of the head with a blow that made it rock. He hit him several times, then changing hands, struck him on the other side.

"That's enough," Earle stated. "Apparently he doesn't want to fight."

But the others weren't satisfied. The excitement flared up again and they began to wave their knives and move forward. Earle was facing them and I began to fear for him as he held up his hand to stop their advance. Clearly they weren't satisfied yet and they renewed their shouting and the brandishing of knives.

I was shaking with terror and thought of trying to go for help, when just then, sauntering placidly along the dock came a very stout, middle-aged Indian woman. With a perfect sense of timing, she shuffled into the open space in front of the Chinamen. "You want fight?" she asked and began a mimicry of boxing, doubling up her fists and jabbing them at an imaginary opponent. It was so ludicrous, it broke the tension and one by one the Chinamen began to laugh. Everyone laughed. Then the men turned and walked slowly back to the gutting tables.

My knees were weak as Earle and I walked with the subdued lad to the sanctuary of the mess house. The following day his father came down to our boat. He shook hands with Earle and said fervently, "I want to thank you for saving my son's life."

Earle gave a little smile and replied, "Perhaps we should be thanking that clever Indian woman."

September arrived at last with early morning mists that burned away by noon. The mysterious stillness of early autumn settled over everything so that one could almost hear the silence. Sounds carried across the water from far away, and near the shore it was startling to hear the crash of a coneflower dropped in the woods by a squirrel.

Early autumn was a haunting time and I woke each morning with the feeling of excitement and anticipation that most people experience in springtime.

I kept thinking of Atnarko and the farm, but there were two more weeks of fishing before we could store the boat for winter and start up the road for home. The summer had been an over-long holiday for me and I was weary of it. My role on the boat was a passive one, for it was Earle who made decisions and directed the fishing. On the farm we shared the responsibility as well as the work.

Many of the fishermen would have liked to fish longer at the end of the season so they could pick up the good runs of coho that came in after the middle of September, but both the men and the cannery managers were afraid of the sudden, violent storms that came then, usually associated with the equinox.

Most of these storms were from the west, but in 1926 one came without warning from the east. An Arctic air mass descended on the valley with frigid winds funneling down mountain passes and roaring out over the inlet, bringing a drop of temperature and blinding particles of snow that blew horizontally. The storm struck the inlet with a suddenness that left fishermen helpless in sailboats which were soon covered with frozen spume whipped from the surface of the water.

The whole inlet looked as if it were smoking.

One fisherman was caught as he was changing ends on his net, rowing the sailboat from one end to the other. He never saw his net again and his boat was blown six miles down the inlet. It was tossed about on enormous waves through freezing mist before he was able to steer into a shelter.

Another less fortunate fisherman had his wife out with him on an end-of-the-season holiday. Their boat drifted for miles out the inlet before it finally capsized in the heavy seas. His wife was swept away and drowned, but somehow his hand became jammed in the centerboard of the upturned boat and he was held captive and unconscious as the boat drifted on down the inlet. He was found, still alive, by the crew of the collection boat that was searching for survivors when the storm abated. They rescued fishermen holed up in shelters for twenty miles out the inlet. Some of them had lost their nets and all of them were cold and suffering from exposure.

A week later the freezing east wind struck again. This time it was even worse and lasted longer. There were eighteen nets lost in this second storm. Men began to run out of food as well as fuel for their lanterns and cook stoves. A collection boat ventured out to bring in what fish boats it could and as it returned with its towline of buffeted sailboats, they rounded Dead Man's Point, within sight of the cannery, where they were exposed to the full force of the wind. It was too much for them and they had to take refuge in the comparative shelter of Clayton Falls Bay until a second collection boat was sent to their assistance. In tandem, the two packers were able to bring in the ice-covered sailboats.

These two storms left an indelible impression on the fishermen as well as the cannery management. It was the canneries who owned most of the fishboats and the nets, so each year thereafter, the fishing season closed a little earlier. The men regretted losing the late coho runs, but now the middle of September became the accepted closing date for the fishing season in Burke Channel.

At last the fishing was over for the year and our boat was safely stored for the winter. Earle had rented a different boathouse this time, one that was safe from snowslides.

It was a day's work to take the boat up the slough and winch it into the shed at high tide. It had to be dragged far enough up so it would be above the extra high tides that came during the winter and then secured in an upright position so it would be safe from toppling over and cracking its ribs.

24

Making a Riding Saddle

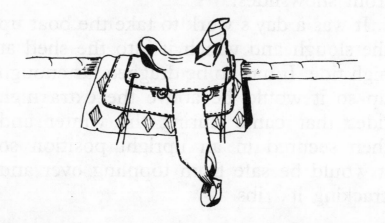

WITH the boat safely stored for the winter, we left Bella Coola with the mail carrier on his trip to Atnarko.

Ole Nygaard had been carrying the mail for a number of years and his warm, friendly personality was a link between the settled communities in the lower part of the valley and the almost unknown hinterland of Atnarko.

Driving along in his truck, the three of us chatted tirelessly all the way to

Firvale where we had left the animals. As we arrived Ole made one last remark, "You still have a long way to go to get home. Why don't you move down the valley to live?"

Oddly enough, we heard the same remark from Milo Ratcliff when we saw him at Firvale, but I was more interested in my little Jerseys and left Earle talking to him as I went to see the cows.

My heart welled with affection when Modesta gave my face a slurp with her long tongue as I scratched her ears.

When I returned to Earle he told me that Milo had been telling him about some land that was for sale, about five miles to the east. It was part of the former Seventh Day Adventist settlement, and the site of the original Firvale. There were three quarter-sections for sale, all owned by different people who lived somewhere else. One of them was Frank Sill, the Interior Indian with the large family to whom we had given the moose meat at the Stillwater. He had loaned the former owner money and the Department of Indian Affairs had finally foreclosed on the mortgage for him. I couldn't help

441

wondering if he had tried to get someone else to start a store.

The fences on all of the places were falling down and the clearings were free pasture for the horses and cattle that were turned out by farmers to forage during the summer. The Interior Indians kept their horses there too when they camped in the edge of the woods nearby, on their annual fishing trips to the valley.

Milo wanted Earle to see the places before we left, so we drove up with him in the afternoon. On one of the preemptions there was a beautifully built, two-story hewn log house and a large barn. The view was magnificent, but the clearings were small. The other two quarter-sections were side by side, their combined hay fields making one large clearing, separated only by a few strands of broken barbed wire fence and some lovely birches. Down in the far corner of the westerly holding was a hay shed and an old log house that was still habitable. It stood in the curve of a spring creek and seemed a secluded and pleasant place to live. It also had a magnificent view of the mountains. We were assured that the area had been flooded only once within the memory of the settlers, and that was when the whole valley had been filled with water from mountain to mountain. It probably would never happen again.

After showing us the land, Milo asked Earle why he didn't take an option on all three of the places and come down from Atnarko so we could have a real farm that would support us without having to leave and go fishing every summer. As I wandered off to pick a few apples in the neglected orchard, I heard Earle promise to think it over. I had found my bit of paradise on the farm in Atnarko and had no interest in living elsewhere.

The following day we walked with the animals up the fifteen miles of tree-shaded road as far as Belarko where we were going to spend the night. The road wound through giant evergreens, interspersed with cottonwoods and birches already turning golden in this dryer end of the valley. We had been walking through the heart of the Coast Range where the mountains carried their snow all year round, but in September it had melted from some of the glaciers, exposing masses of blue ice. Here and there we saw breath-taking vistas of the mountains through openings in the trees or when the road came out onto a bluff overlooking the winding river.

By the time we reached Belarko we had passed the highest mountains and were now on the east slope of the Coast Range near the junction of the Atnarko and Talchako (Whitewater) Rivers which joined to form the Bella Coola River.

Clouds from the Pacific dropped their moisture on the snow-capped mountains to the west and in this drier atmosphere the trees were not so large. In the sparsely-thicketed woods it had not been difficult to blaze a horse trail and most of the one we would be following the next day had been made to begin with by deer and bears wandering through the valley.

As the trail turned into the narrower Atnarko valley, it was not far from the river anywhere along the way. There was evidence of bears feeding on spawning salmon every time we neared the river or one of the creeks. The fish were plentiful and often the bears tossed them out onto the bank and ate only the throats, leaving the rotting carcasses for the ravens and eagles. The smell of decaying fish was everywhere near the river, but as we came out of the woods into the open area of Young Creek, a few miles before reaching home, we escaped the odor for a little while and breathed the sweet air that came from the clear, flowing water of Young Creek which did not harbor spawning salmon. This was always the place where we stopped for a moment to draw in great draughts of fragrant air, and then moved on again, invigorated. The magic always worked.

We were home at last. The cows were in such luscious pasture I feared they might bloat but they were tired from their walk up from Firvale and spent time resting, which may have helped prevent it. They bulged, though, and looked as though they were in an advanced state of pregnancy.

An unoccupied log cabin can accumulate a lot of mice in three months and we were busy for a few days setting traps to catch them. Gradually the musty, mouse-scented air grew sweet again with the wood fires burning in the kitchen stove and living room heater. There had been no one in the cabin all summer except Ralph who stayed there when he came down for the mail. Even when we were there he would often sit all night reading the mail and answering letters, dropping off to sleep sitting upright in the chair, letting the light burn low. I scraped little mounds of candlewax from the oil cloth on the kitchen table where it had dripped from his midnight candles.

By the time we arrived home there were beginning to be light frosts at night and we were anxious to dig the root vegetables in the garden. There were still some useable cabbages, enough to make sauerkraut, but most of them had split and rotted. Nearly all the leafy vegetables had gone to seed, but there were plenty of turnips, carrots, beets and potatoes.

We were going to miss all the canned fruit I had preserved the summer before but we could buy some apples from old B.C. and would have to include cases of dried raisins, apricots and prunes with our order for winter supplies. The wooden cases they came in were well made and useful for mouse-proof storage boxes. Several times we had received Australian raisins in mahogany cases with dovetailed corners and Earle had made me a beautiful sewing box from one of them.

With the good feed, the cows picked up in their milking so we had enough milk to make butter and cheese again. There were enough glass sealers of meat in the root cellar to keep us going until the hunting season began. Also, I had canned enough salmon during the summer in Bella Coola to keep us in fish all winter.

Maxie came down to see us; he looked well and was expecting Bert back in Atnarko shortly. They were going to spend the winter together again, running the trapline. In the spring they were going to cut cedar logs and drag them in to make a separate cabin for Bert, near Maxie's on a rise of ground overlooking the river and beautiful meadow. The meals would still be prepared in Maxie's cabin but Bert would have a spacious place of his own where he could entertain his friends in a cabin filled with his books, hunting equipment and trophies collected over the years.

Bert and Maxie got along well. In many ways they were very much alike, but it was Bert's stronger presence that gradually dominated the Atnarko scene and it was he who restored the sporting atmosphere that had existed with Mark Marvin in the early days of Atnarko.

It was wonderful to be home again and things soon settled into a quiet routine. It was as though we had never been away. The root vegetables were dug and safely stored in the cellar and Earle was preparing to pack in our supplies. After that he wanted to spend a few weeks making a riding saddle before he went hunting.

The saddle was for a young Hagensborg chap named Johnnie Olson whom Earle had met out on the fishing grounds. Johnnie longed to be a cowboy. His only dream was to "ride the hurricane deck of a cayuse," but he had no saddle, nor a horse to put one on. He had traded something for an old pair of chaps and Earle had promised to throw in his army spurs, along with the saddle. Johnnie was going to pay for the saddle in the spring by helping Earle cut wood and build fences.

Earle had been wanting to make a good riding saddle for a long time and had all the necessary material ready to do the job. He thought he could finish it in time for Johnnie to ride on his first packhorse job when he went to work for Lester Dorsey, a cattle rancher at Anahim Lake, helping him pack in a lot of ranch equipment as well as winter supplies.

Earle made a beautiful saddle, covering it with rawhide, soaked and stretched over the frame so it dried smoothly. He used the same well-fitting saddle trees he had made for the packsaddles, and the horn was attached to the flaring pommel, patterned after a bucking saddle, with a good grip for the knees. It was really comfortable to sit in and Johnnie was a happy cowboy the morning he stopped in to get it. I was sorry the spurs didn't jangle.

The packtrain filed by with their empty packsaddles on their way to the end of the road, Lester leading the first of the string of horses and Johnnie bringing up the rear, slapping the rein-ends against his leather chaps and yelling, "Yahoo!" His dream was coming true.

Lester had some awkward packs to put on the horses at the end of the road and we expected it would be late afternoon the following day when he returned to Maxie's place with them. Just before dusk we saw him go by, leading one packhorse with the rest of them following, tied head to tail.

Johnnie should have been following close behind with the rest of the animals but there was no sign of him. It grew dark and we kept listening for the sound of horses' shoes striking rocks on the trail. When he didn't show up we began to worry, and then Earle said, "Probably he's stopped at B.C.'s for the night."

There was a sharp frost that night and the ground was covered with hoarfrost before we went to bed.

In the morning we heard Johnnie coming. There was a knock on the door and he staggered in, half frozen, his eyes dark holes in a haggard face, and in a voice hoarse from fatigue and shouting, he croaked, "Coffee!"

It took him a long time to thaw out, but at last he was able to tell us that it had been late when he finished packing his horses at the end of the road, and instead of tying them head to tail as Lester had done, he had tried to herd them up the trail. Lester had gone on ahead and usually horses will follow the fresh scent of other horses but these animals were tired and knew they had a green rider. As it grew dark they turned off into the brush, one by one, until Johnnie was all alone, shouting up an empty trail.

He had no idea of where to find the horses, so tying his own to a tree, he huddled against the trunk of it to wait until morning. He had no axe or matches so was unable to light a fire. At daybreak, hungry and stiff with cold, he searched for the missing animals and rounded them up onto the trail again.

As the warm room and hot coffee thawed him, Johnnie stopped shivering and the color came back into his cheeks. Setting down his cup he spoke, "Earle, that is a wonderful saddle. I liked riding it and I am going to work for you next

451

spring to pay for it." Then with an air of finality the words burst from him, "But to hell with horses!"

Johnnie kept his word and worked for the saddle in the spring but he had lost his ambition to be a cowboy. Later, he sold the saddle to Jack Weldon who found it to be the most comfortable saddle he ever rode and he never used any other as long as he could ride a horse. He died at ninety-two and in his will he bequeathed the saddle to Earle.

During the winter the Weldons came down from the Precipice to get their mail and spend a few days with us; then Ralph came out in January after the lake was safely frozen. Frank was trapping all alone at the Stillwater, and came down for the mail almost every mail day.

But it was the deer that kept the snowy trail broken. After the deep snows and intense cold of the past few winters, we were having a relatively mild one for a change and the deer were able to get about with ease in the shallow snow on the sidehill and up under the bluffs.

Down in the sunless valley bottom I sometimes stood watching them as they moved about up in the sunshine, feeding on the exposed bunchgrass and kinnikinnick.

One day, after watching them through the window, I remarked to Earle, "I can't remember what it feels like to be in sunshine."

"Well, let's go and find out," he replied.

The following day we took a lunch and climbed the steep sidehill behind our farm, following a deer trail up into the sunshine. It was like entering another world.

There were even some small birds up there, and at noon when we sat on a bare rock in the sun to eat our lunch, it was warm enough to soften the edges of the snow that lay against the dark background.

For a little while we were set free and our whole world was bigger and wider and brighter. We were reluctant to descend into the dark cavern of the valley where our tiny world seemed so much smaller than it had been before we left it in the morning.

It was something that occupied my

mind for days after the outing. Did man need an occasional escape from his daily routine to help keep it in true perspective, or was he happier not being lifted out of the narrow confines of his life? I was never sure, but after that, whenever it was possible, I found myself escaping the bonds of our restricted ways and climbing into the sunshine for a little while.

25

Milk Fever

SPRING came again and Earle was making plans to go to Bella Coola in time to install the new engine in his boat before fishing began. We hoped the calves would arrive before he left.

In the hot sun, the feed in the pasture grew rapidly and the cows' udders filled out, but still the calves didn't come. It began to look as if there would be a tremendous supply of milk when they did arrive and Earle made inquiries about getting a pig. It also became obvious that the two cows, who had been bred in Firvale, would freshen about the same time.

Early in May, when the feed was luscious and high in food value, the cows had their calves within two days of each other. Then, both of them came down with milk fever.

This is a disorder we had never needed to be concerned about as the cows had always freshened on fall pasture, or hay. But in the spring of the year on milk-producing feed, good milk cows were vulnerable.

Milk fever is caused by a sudden withdrawal of calcium from the cow's body in her effort to produce milk. It affects heavy milkers within a short time after calving, and the animal staggers and goes down and rapidly loses consciousness. The head is turned back against the flank and there are rigid corduroy creases in the neck. Our handbook on the treatment of farm ailments told us this, and it also told us to call a vet.

The prescribed treatment was to pump air into the udder with a milk fever pump. I didn't fully understand why this worked but unless it was done, the cow would soon die. There was no time to get a pump from down the valley, even if there was one available, so we were on our own and Earle would have to make one.

Only a few months before we had bought an Aladdin lamp that operated on fuel pressure made by pumping air into it with a pump about the size of the ones used for bicycle tires. Earle thought he could make a tapered tube from a piece of copper cut from an old copper tea kettle and solder it to the end of the pump. If the edges were smoothed off carefully with a file and whetstone it would not injure the milk duct when it was inserted into the teat.

He went to work while I carried out canvases and poles to erect a shelter from the hot sun for Modesta. Bonnie had gone down and was lying unconscious in the shade of some trees but Modesta was out in the open where the sun might become too hot for her. Although this disorder was called milk fever, the book said the temperature of the cow dropped, so some sunlight might be beneficial, but to be in the direct glare of the sun all day might not be. My mind was too terrified to reason. It was unbelievable that both cows should be afflicted at the same time.

I kept running back to the house to see how Earle was progressing.

"Are you nearly finished?" I asked each time.

"Just a few minutes more," Earle would reply. "Be patient."

Patient! Fear was pulsing adrenalin through my body, but there was nothing we could do for the little cows until the pump was finished.

At last it was complete and Earle boiled the end to be inserted in the teat while I prepared some swabs and an antiseptic solution.

The book gave explicit instructions on how to use the pump and how to tie the end of each teat with tape afterwards to prevent the loss of air.

"It says to inflate the udder," I read to Earle. "How do you know how much air to pump in? Their udders look full now."

We pumped air into all four teats of Bonnie's already milk-distended udder until I thought it would burst. She was totally unconscious but was still breathing.

Modesta's udder was even larger, but Earle pumped air into it as well until I begged him to stop before he injured it. Then we returned to Bonnie. She had opened her eyes. It was incredible; I couldn't see how the treatment could possibly work so quickly, but the book said it would. In fact, it was the only thing they knew of that would. Within an hour Bonnie had staggered to her feet.

Modesta still was unconscious when we returned to her. Since she was older and produced more milk, perhaps she needed more pumping, so Earle untied the tapes on her teats and pumped again. Before long there was a movement of the eyelids and I went limp with relief.

We carried water and hay to them both and by now Bonnie was up and moving around, her udder distended to an enormous size.

Modesta had regained consciousness but was still down, so we left her, letting her take her own time about getting up.

In the morning she was still down.

The following morning there was still no change. And every morning after that, for the whole month that we nursed her, she still was unable to get up. Each morning at daybreak I went out, sure that this was the day I would find her up, but there was no change.

At first, we tried lifting her with a sling made of gunnysacks attached to stout cedar poles with breech straps made of more gunnysacks to keep her from slipping out when we lifted her with ropes and pulleys, but she just hung there from the tripod of cedar poles. We massaged her legs and tried to exercise them, but nothing worked. After that, I kept her bathed and clean, putting fresh bedding under her and changing her position frequently by rolling her from side to side.

The weather grew hot but the shelter I had erected over her kept her comfortable on the slight rise where she lay catching whatever breeze there was. Her appetite was good and she drank well. She just couldn't get to her feet.

For a whole month I cared for her, spending all my spare time out there, brushing her back and massaging the crippled legs. She kept trying to get up, and in the mornings her bedding would be scattered where she had kicked her legs in an effort to get on to them.

Earle had to leave and I was alone in a dark cloud of fear that went everywhere with me. I think he knew that Modesta would never walk again but I kept hoping that a miracle would happen. One morning, just a month after she had gone down, she was moving her exposed hind leg when I heard a crunching noise from somewhere near the stifle joint, the one that might correspond with the human knee. After that she made no effort to move, and intuition more than knowledge, told me that this was her end.

My Modesta. The one animal I had loved unreservedly since I first saw her. Beautiful, gentle and affectionate, there was a rapport between us that never existed again with any other animal, no matter how fond I was of them.

Slowly I walked up the trail to get Maxie. Aching with grief, I knew then that this was the beginning of the end of our life in Atnarko.

Max came without being asked locking Rex in the cabin. My heart turned over when I saw him reach for the rifle.

All the way back down the trail I tried to convince myself, and Max, that it was probably my imagination that had heard the noise. "Very likely it is nothing serious," I told him. But we both knew without doubt when we examined Modesta, that the stifle joint was dislocated and there was nothing we could do for her.

I stroked her lovely head once more and walked blindly to the house. Even with the door closed and my hands over my ears, I heard the rifle shot.

Maxie went home for the team while numbly, I began to dig the grave. We buried her not far from where she lay, on the rise of ground overlooking the farm where she had given us so much joy and happiness.

26

Firvale Cloudburst

THE months following Modesta's death were painful for me but gradually I agreed to Earle's plan to sell the boat and take an option on the three unoccupied farms in Firvale, and within two years we had left Atnarko and were living in the old log house on the westerly quarter-section.

Nothing about these places felt like home to me and I didn't especially like them but they had great potential as a farm where we could support a number of cattle and have a large market garden.

They were surrounded by magnificent scenery and the fact that Alexander Mackenzie had been at a loss for words to describe the beauty of this area on his historic trip into the valley in 1793, meant nothing to me.

He descended into the valley on a game trail down the steep mountainside on the north of our clearings, and in his diary he wrote:

Before us appeared a stupendous mountain whose snowclad summit was lost in the clouds; between it and our immediate course flowed the river to which we were going. — Nor was it possible to be in this situation without contemplating the wonder of it. Such was the depth of the precipice below, and the height of the mountains above, with the rude and wild magnificence of the scenery around, that I shall not attempt to describe such an astonishing and awful combination of objects of which, indeed, no description can convey an adequate idea.

There was no difficulty in obtaining options on the two quarter-sections still owned by the Seventh Day Adventists, but the third farm, the most favorable of them all, was the one owned by Frank Sill, the Algatcho Indian. The Indian agent in Bella Coola managed to contact him but he replied that he didn't want to sell. When he was told it was Earle Edwards who wanted to buy, he changed his mind saying, "Good man, that one. Maybe he make store that place."

Earle put the money from the sale of the boat into good farm machinery and made a deal with Milo to exchange work on the interior of his house for the use of his work team in the spring.

We moved into the habitable part of the old house. It was a picturesque spot at the bend of the creek, but there was scarcely time to admire the scenery. It took us three months to repair the fences and plough and disc the ground for three acres of potatoes.

We were able to buy the seed from Milo and he offered us the use of his horse-drawn potato planter. Potatoes grew well in the valley and the price was stable. With the growing market in the interior and the pulp mill town of Ocean Falls out on the coast, we would be able to sell enough to pay for the farms in a couple of years.

We had bought another milk cow as a companion for Bonnie and besides the cows and two calves and a yearling heifer, we had a gregarious pig called Lulu. We still had our old flock of laying hens and we bought one hundred purebred leghorn pullets. The list wasn't very impressive, but in our disorganized state the care of that many animals entailed a lot of work. We had to go to the spring creek for every bucket of water we used, and the cows were usually at the far end of the vast brush pasture when I went to bring them in at milking time.

Our car was still at Anahim Lake and would have to be driven back to Vancouver, then brought up the coast on the deck of the steamboat before we could have it to use, so we were without our own transportation.

Now that there was someone living in old Firvale again, we managed to have the former weekly rural postal service restored, and by putting up the red flag attached to our mail box on the side of the road, the mail carrier would pick up our grocery order along with the outgoing mail and deliver the groceries to us on his next trip. He charged a nominal fee for this service but I'm sure it was never enough to pay him for all the trouble involved.

In the warm, rich soil of the sheltered area near the house, plants grew rapidly. Grass was several inches tall there when it was barely poking through the ground in the exposed, winter-browned areas elsewhere, so we planted a limited early garden nearby and then our main crop went in adjacent to the potatoes, farther away.

By the end of May all the planting was finished and we were beginning to relax a bit. I even put on a dress occasionally.

On the fourth of June, Earle went up to the potato patch garden to put in a few more carrot seeds before it started to rain. There were thunder clouds gathering near the mountain tops and before long we heard the first of the thunder. Earle just made it back to the house before the rain came. It was a deluge. I have never seen so much rain in such a short time. We stood in the shelter of the porch and watched the downpour congratulating ourselves that the last of the planting had been finished in time.

By mid-afternoon the storm had passed and we were feeding the pullets when we saw Milo Ratcliff's son, Norman, splashing his horse through pools of water on our lane. He seemed agitated, and without dismounting, called to us, "You'd better get out. Burnt Bridge Creek is flooding and heading this way. It's on your fields now."

Earle and I looked at each other in disbelief. This must be a hoax; it couldn't be true. Then we looked at the creek and saw it had risen alarmingly and was filled with yellow mud.

Norman called again, "Get out while you can! Your bridge is floating. I've got to get back across it."

"My God, the potatoes!" I cried to Earle, "And the animals! We'll be trapped!"

The house and hay shed stood in the bend of the creek on the lowest

468

portion of the two quarter-sections. The flood waters were entering from the highest part of the farm, after tearing down from Burnt Bridge Creek, a mile farther up the road. Our whole place would be inundated with fast-flowing water and it would be deepest where we stood. The only escape was across the already floating bridge on the winding lane leading to the road and higher ground.

We grabbed halter ropes and started out across the pasture to get the animals. They were already on their way in, sloshing through the water that was filling every hollow and depression and spilling over, carrying debris along with it.

Earle caught Maryanka and I put a rope on Bonnie and led her while the others followed. The bridge was still there, but floating, and for a moment I hesitated about taking them across but Earle led the way with sure-footed Maryanka, and Bonnie followed. I turned her loose and ran back for the others, driving them across ahead of me.

The two calves were still locked in the calf pasture and I raced back for them while Earle went to move the pullets from their flooded pen. The water was up to their necks when he got to them. There was only one place to put them; grabbing gunnysacks, he stuffed them full of sodden pullets and carried them up the stairs of the house to the empty bedrooms and turned them loose.

By this time I had caught the calves, tying one to each end of a long rope — the only one I could find — and started leading them toward the bridge. This began to look like a game to them, and entering into the spirit of it, they took off at a gallop in the wrong direction. I was wearing dress shoes which had no traction but I hung on until the calves reached the edge of the advancing water where they stopped suddenly and I shot forward as though fired from a catapult, measuring my length in the muddy water. I had on a flowered cotton summer dress, but the print was no longer recognizable and all the hair pins had fallen from my long hair.

The water sobered the calves so I was able to lead them to the bridge, and the cows' mooing on the far side lured them across.

Suddenly, I thought of the pig. Racing back to the house, I found Earle sloshing around in the flooded pen, trying to catch her. Between us, we cornered her, and carrying her upside down by the legs, she wriggled and twisted and screamed as though she were being murdered. Halfway across the disintegrating bridge she had a spurting, fluid bowel movement all down the front of my dress.

Earle returned across the bridge just as it began floating downstream. He called to me that he would stay with the pullets until the water went down. I was on my own with the animals, but they were safe.

Away from the nightmare of the flooding waters, I began to be aware of the warm June sun and the flowers and the washed green leaves along the side of the road. Lulu scampered ahead and the calves frolicked along the road while the cows browsed as they walked. I followed slowly behind with Maryanka, trying not to think of what had happened to us.

I began to wonder what Mr. Astleford would think of having us turn up in his farmyard, but he had almost unlimited pasture and I was sure he would take us in.

Also, there was one thing in my favor, I was wearing a dress.

Thomas Astleford lived alone on his large farm, the last of the Seventh Day Adventist colony that had settled in this area. He kept a few head of cattle and his old mare, and Horsie, the enormous Percheron that had made the midnight ride with the doctor years before.

When we first moved to Firvale, Mr. Astleford had ridden up on Horsie to make a formal call on Earle. They knew each other from before the First World War when Earle bought butter from the Astlefords. Hearing that we had come to live in Firvale, Mr. Astleford had come to renew the acquaintance, but the real reason for the visit was to ask Earle to make sure I wore skirts and not overalls.

It was one of the edicts of the founder of their faith that women wear skirts modestly covering their boot tops. I often wondered what it must have been like for his womenfolk to help on the land with long skirts dragging in the mud, but I respected him enough to try not to let him see me in overalls. Occasionally we would meet while I was wearing them and I would hide behind a tree and converse with him while he sat on Horsie. He was a bit of a martinet and I think it gave him a lot of satisfaction to see that he was getting things in hand.

"Well, he is going to be pleased that I am wearing a dress this time," I thought.

Lulu grunted cheerfully as she ran to meet Mr. Astleford when he came to open the gate to let us in. He began to laugh, and whether it was at such a charming little porker or at the sodden milkmaid, I never knew.

There was nowhere for me to stay in the tiny, one-room cabin, but friends arrived before nightfall and took me home with them. There was plenty of pasture for the animals and Lulu would stay with the cows.

Staying with our friends, I borrowed slacks and had to remember to take along something to wrap around me to conceal them when I went to milk the cows and feed Lulu the next morning.

It was a week before the water dropped sufficiently to allow us to take the cows back to a fenced pasture on the upper part of our place. The pasture on the lower portion still had water standing on it with hummocks of brush making little islands everywhere. The grassy sod bounced and undulated as we walked over it and the beautiful, level potato patch was torn by gullies. All the seed and top soil were washed away; Earle sank in mud to the tops of his gum boots when he went near it, and the vegetable garden was still under water. The muddy water had cleared so that we could see a golden squash blossom in full bloom beneath a foot of water. After all our effort, there wasn't so much as a head of lettuce left growing when the ground finally dried out again, and by then it was too late to replant.

In one cloudburst all our hopes and dreams had been washed away. I was devastated and wanted to escape to a land where there were no floods and no problems, but Earle was made of sterner stuff. Already he had begun to plan for the future.

The flood had been caused by the cloudburst flushing out the springtime-softened snow at the head of Burnt Bridge Creek, bringing it down all at once and creating a lake behind a dam formed by a landslide. Overloaded, the dam had burst, releasing a wall of water that tore out the west bank of the creek near the road, sending the creek coursing through the woods and down the road to our farm a mile below. Rubble had spilled across the hay field and some of the fence posts were torn out, but this could be cleaned up and repaired. It was where we had ploughed the three-acre potato patch that the damage was irreparable — the top soil had gone.

"We'll just have to keep the fields in pasture and hay," Earle observed. "If we don't plough the sod, the water won't do so much damage if it comes again. Anyway, the government will have to dyke the west bank of Burnt Bridge Creek to protect the road."

I could understand the logic of it all,

but secretly I wished I could run far away. I was also suffering from a sense of guilt over having encouraged Earle to sell his beautiful boat, otherwise we might have been able to go back to fishing.

"We'll drop the option on the other two quarter-sections and concentrate on the higher, dryer one where we can raise sheep and beef cattle," Earle went on. He was undaunted by the disaster. It seemed more like a challenge to him, but I was overwhelmed with gloom.

However, Earle's optimism soon worked its magic and the next twenty years were filled with happiness and fulfillment for us both. We had very little money but a great sense of security; and there were plenty of animals. It grew to be a soul-satisfying time for me. Somewhere in my life there had been planted a love of animals and here on the farm in Firvale it reached fruition.

27

Grizzlies in the Orchard

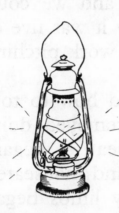

AS summer advanced, the fields gradually dried out and it began to look as though we were going to have a bumper crop of hay. Jack Weldon came down from the Precipice with his team to help us with the haying and when it was finished, Earle was going to return with him to the Precipice and help with the haying there where the grass matured later because of the higher elevation.

As if to make amends, the weather

was perfect — hot and dry. There were days when it was even too hot, with the mercury soaring above 100°F. and we had to take refuge in the closed house or cool root cellar during the heat of the day until the temperature cooled off in the late afternoon and we could go haying again. One day it was five o'clock before we could start work pitching the hay on the wagon.

I had learned how to toss hay with a pitchfork and enjoyed doing it, but in the unusual heat, I began to feel ill. I was dizzy and nauseated and when I sat down my limbs began to tremble and jerk uncontrollably. Earle and Jack diagnosed the trouble as heat prostration and took me back to the house on one of the horses. It was several days before I felt completely well again, and after that I was always careful to have extra salt in my food during the hot weather.

One day, when the haying was almost finished, and Earle was getting things in order so he could leave with Jack for the Precipice, we saw a Stick Indian riding up the lane. He remained on his horse by the gate and called, "Hoy, this place."

Earle went out to speak to him and I heard the Indian say, "Just now, glizzly bear he stop that place," gesturing toward the orchard. "Some more he stop that pasture."

Earle thanked him and came back in, looking concerned. The bears were probably eating apples in the old orchard and wild berries in the pasture. This is where I went twice a day to bring in the cows for milking and I was going to be alone while Earle went to the Precipice for two or three weeks. Bears were something we hadn't thought of, and neither of us was happy about their presence.

"We'll have to do something about them," Earle said thoughtfully. "There's a full moon tonight and they will probably be out in the orchard feeding again."

Jack had an old .25-.35 he had brought down with him and Earle had his trusty 8mm Lebel. They planned to go up to the orchard when the moon rose and wait for the bears in a small log structure nearby. It was a very low building and must have been used as a chicken coop or a pighouse years ago. There were no

479

windows and the door was missing.

The more I thought about Earle going bear hunting in the moonlight with someone else, the less I liked it, and finally I suggested to Earle, "Why don't you take me with you and let Jack stay here? Maybe he will lend us his gun." Both of them protested but in the end I had my way.

The August moon was full and it seemed as bright as day when we started out through the pasture, carrying both guns as well as extra boxes of ammunition. We also took along a couple of quilts since there was some hay nearby that we could toss inside the hut to make a bed while waiting for the bears.

It was so quiet as we stood there in the moonlight watching for the bears; the only sound we could hear was the murmur of the river nearly a mile away.

My slacks were soaked from the heavy dew on the long grass we had walked through, so I took them off before rolling up in my quilt on the soft hay. From inside the tiny log shelter we watched the moonlit orchard through the open doorway, but we were tired from a hard day and before long, drifted off to sleep. The last thing I remember was seeing a tuft of bear hair caught on a nail that stuck out of the doorjamb.

I don't know how long we slept, but something wakened me. I was sure I saw a movement in the doorway, and then it was gone. It may have been a dream, but I nudged Earle and then placed my hand over his mouth to keep him from making a noise. Silently we crept out through the opening with our guns to see a large grizzly with a cub about fifty yards away from us, walking toward the trail over which we had recently come. There were some wild raspberries there and it looked as if they were eating them.

Earle fired a shot or two in her direction and I added a few to try to scare her, but she and the cub showed no signs of alarm and it flashed through my mind that hunting grizzlies at night was a foolhardy thing to do.

We stood there in the moonlight for some time, watching the two animals, when we both heard the crack of a twig breaking behind us in the direction of the orchard. Whirling around, we saw another bear, standing on its hind legs not more than thirty feet away.

My heart gave an enormous thunk and Earle swung the rifle to his shoulder, but through the peep sight the bear was only a blur in the landscape. He pulled the trigger but the bear showed no signs of being wounded as it dropped to all fours and took off at a terrific speed through the barbed wire fence. We heard the strands screech and ping as they parted.

How were we ever going to get back home, I wondered, and began to shake, probably as much from cold as from fear. Glancing down at myself, I discovered I had been standing there shooting at bears in lace-trimmed silk panties — my slacks were still inside the hut.

When I went back in to put them on, Earle asked me to bring out the boxes of ammunition and it was startling to hear them rattle like castanets when I picked them up.

Earle reloaded and I stood there beside him watching everywhere for more bears. I held the .25-.35 carefully, with the barrel pointed toward the ground, when suddenly there was a loud report.

482

Somehow, I had managed to fire the gun, missing Earle's toes by only a fraction of an inch.

Except for the menace of his own wife, Earle was enjoying himself and wanted to go closer to the orchard. The moonlight was so brilliant we had thought the whole scene would be as clear as day but beneath the apple trees, the shadows were black and we could see nothing.

I was afraid to go under the apple trees, but was more afraid of being left alone. So, hanging on to Earle's coat and walking backwards, I guarded the rear while Earle advanced slowly toward the trees.

We stopped every few seconds and listened, then went on again, a few steps at a time.

Nearing the trees, Earle stopped suddenly and whispered, "What's that?"

At first I heard nothing but the pounding of my heart, then I heard the sound of crunching. It was unmistakable; somewhere in there a bear was eating apples. I could have run without stopping, all the way home, but the old sow and her cub were still on the trail, picking berries.

"Don't shoot!" I begged Earle in a hoarse whisper, "Let's go back to the shack."

But Earle had spotted the bear. It was standing on its hind legs in the shadows, eating apples from a low bough. Undisturbed by our presence, it was as though we weren't there, or there had ever been a rifle shot or flashes of light from the gunfire.

Once more Earle swung the rifle around and fired in the direction of the bear which dropped to all fours and took off through the fence as the other had done.

By this time I was close to tears as I begged Earle to go back to the hut. Back there, he boosted me onto the roof and then climbed up and sat beside me on the ridge, smoking his pipe and talking in his quiet voice which always had a soothing effect on me. I felt secure up there and gradually my heart began to beat normally again.

It was a false sense of security, for any one of the bears could have stood on its hind legs and swept us off the ridge with one swipe of its paw. Earle didn't mention this to me until later.

Suddenly, we both saw the fifth bear. It had entered the orchard at the end farthest away from us and was on all fours, walking rapidly in our direction in the moonlit path between the rows of trees. We could see it clearly, moving purposefully toward us, and there seemed no question whatever of its intent.

Earle slid to the ground, and sighting along the rifle barrel, took aim as carefully as he could. There was a terrible explosion as the gun went off, and the bear turned and ran with a crash through the fence like the others.

Five grizzlies! We hoped there were no more as we stood debating whether we should risk trying to go back home through the pasture or whether we should crawl into the quilts and spend the rest of the night in the hut.

A movement at the bottom end of the field caught our attention and in the distance, riding toward us on his saddle horse, was Jack Weldon. He carried a coal-oil lantern and something white fluttered from his coat pockets.

Back at the house he had heard the

first fusillage of shots, then there was a pause, followed by a series of three shots close together. Jack was sure it was a signal for distress.

He had crawled out of bed and dressed; lighting the fire, he had put on a kettle of water to boil. Then taking a sheet, he tore it into strips to make bandages and put them in his pockets. Then he lit the coal-oil lantern, not because he needed it to see by out of doors, but because he didn't want us to mistake his horse for a bear. Finally, he caught his horse in the pasture and rode the rest of the way to rescue us and administer first aid.

No one could have been more welcome and we laughed in relief, but Jack didn't find it amusing.

"Aren't you hurt?" he enquired in disbelief.

He was piqued all the way back to the house, whether because he had missed out on the adventure, or because we had no need of his first aid. But I was never so glad to be rescued in my life.

In the years to follow, as we acquired sheep, and our cattle multiplied, we had constantly to be on the alert to protect them from predators. It was the age-old conflict of the homesteader against the natural inhabitants of the woods, and although I was upset by the killing of a predator, I never questioned our right to destroy it. I hated what they did, not only to domestic stock but to the deer as well.

Now that I am older and farther away from the pioneer life, I find it distressing to talk or write about hunting and killing and would rather delete such stories from this book, but since it is an account of frontier life, they must be told.

28

Sheep

AFTER Earle returned from helping Jack at the Precipice, we went to work preparing winter quarters for our pullets. The old living room wing of the house would make a warm and pleasant place in which to house them when they started to lay that fall. It was never going to be used as a dwelling again, so we put roosts and nesting boxes along the log walls and litter on the floor. There were windows for light and a door to the outside as well as one into the large kitchen-living room where we lived. We lit a coal-oil lantern in the mornings and evenings to encourage their egg-laying, for eggs were going to be our only source of income that winter and the best was none too good for the pullets.

We had rebuilt the bridge that floated from its moorings in the flood but still our dwelling was some distance from the main road. This added to our feeling of isolation, and during the first winter in Firvale, we had very little social life.

We still had no radio or telephone, but during the long winter evenings we read and oddly enough, it seemed companionable to have the cheerful pullets close by. In January we had other company — the lambs started to arrive.

Earle was following through with his plans to stock the farm with animals and in the fall he sent to the government experimental farm in the Fraser Valley to buy six pedigreed, Horn Dorset ewes. They arrived on the steamboat, individually crated, and we had them brought up by truck to the farm. They had been bred and it was obvious from their trimmed feet and clean, clipped fleeces that they had been well cared for.

Earle had a pen ready for them near the house where they would be safe from predators. They were sheltered from the wind and snow and slept on soft beds of straw. Each day when we fed the cattle, we picked out the finest clover hay for the sheep and brought it over in a bundle from the shed.

In the Horn Dorset breed, the females as well as the males have horns; slim, curving, graceful ones, whereas the males have massive, coiled ones like those of mountain sheep. We liked the horns, they made convenient handles and kept one from grabbing the wool, which must have been painful for the sheep.

When they first arrived they all looked alike to us and except for some slight variation in the shape of the horns, it was difficult to tell them apart; but before long we became aware of their individual characteristics.

We discovered their personalities were as different as those of humans, and this is when we started giving them names. When the flock grew in time to number seventy-five or more, we could still identify each one, although Earle was always better at it than I was. By that time however, we gave names only to the favorites.

We were proud of our sheep, and their pedigrees were impressive, but the papers didn't tell us the one thing we wanted to know — when we could expect the lambs to be born.

One cold January morning, Earle bundled up to go out and feed the animals but he was back in again within minutes. His voice was excited, "Slip on your coat, I want to show you something."

In one corner of the sheepfold were two of the most beautiful little lambs, curled up together in a pile of hay with their mother lying protectively beside them. It was right out of a story book. The only thing wrong was that there should have been green grass and sunshine instead of snow, but the lambs were dry and fluffy and full of milk. They didn't seem to notice the cold.

The other ewes lambed a few days apart and soon there were ten little balls of wool bouncing around the enclosure, bunting each other. We spent hours watching them. Everything they did was fascinating and nature had endowed them with more than their share of charm. They grew quickly and at ten days they began to chew their cud. I shall never forget the first time we saw the look of utter concentration and surprise on a lamb's face as it burped and had its first cud to chew. It happened with them all, followed by the expression of pleased satisfaction when it happened again and again.

The only thing I didn't like about sheep was their odor. No matter how clean we kept their beds or how well we clipped the soiled wool tags around their tail and udder, there was always an odor that transmitted itself to one's clothing. The lambs were irresistible and we picked them up and held them every time we went into the pen, so that we must have smelled like sheep ourselves most of the time.

One night we decided to bring some

of the lambs into the house. We didn't dare bring them all in for fear they would get out of control and hurt themselves, so we brought in just three, the largest and gentlest. Dimming the coal-oil lamp so they wouldn't be disturbed by the bright light. Earle sat in the rocking chair holding a lamb in his arms, rocking gently. In the warm kitchen it gave a sigh of contentment and was asleep in no time.

Earle remembered a painting in his Grandfather Graham's New England farm home; it was of an old Scottish farm kitchen with the family gathered about the fireplace, and in the background there was a door open to the byre where the horse and cow were tethered, enjoying the warmth and companionship; and in the foreground were some sheep. Sometimes I think we would have been happy with such an arrangement ourselves.

Not every evening was so tranquil and idyllic. Several times during the winter the Arctic air roared down Snowshoe Pass, the narrow canyon not far from us that cut through the mountain and funnelled the bitter wind into the valley, dropping

493

from an elevation of six thousand feet. There were days on end when it roared down the pass and buffeted the house until I wondered how anyone could have built in such a place. One night it screamed in such fury I feared for the safety of the animals and in the morning we saw the hayshed roof lift with each gust of wind. I helped Earle put a cable over the ridge from one side of the shed to the other, anchoring it to tree stumps. Then we took Maryanka and the cattle up the meadow to a thicket of heavy timber where they could find shelter from the relentless wind.

At the beginning of an Arctic air onslaught, cold air would pour over the mountains rolling the snow with it. One could watch it coming down the mountainside like an ocean wave. Then it struck with a breathtaking force and one was blinded and smothered in a blanket of snow so fine and driven with such force, it penetrated the hair of the animals until it reached the warm skin where it melted and froze, forming a cake of ice along their backs. After the storm had passed we took the currycomb and scraped the particles of ice and snow from their hides so they could be dry and warm again.

By spring, it wasn't difficult to decide where we wanted to build our house and barn. The upper end of the easterly quarter-section was not only drier but was far enough away from the pass so that very little of the wind reached it. Up there, the first phase of the storms rarely lasted more than twenty-four hours and then the air was still while one could hear the wind roaring like a train out of Snowshoe Pass to the west.

January passed and February brought longer days and more sunshine and by the end of March, the last of the snow had disappeared. Earle spent several days tramping through the woods looking for suitable cedar logs and shake trees for our barn-building project. Not far from the hay shed whose roof we had fastened down with a cable, he ran across a gigantic windrow of uprooted cedars and firs, one against the other in a diagonal line between the barnyard clearing and the main road. It must have been three-quarters of a mile long and forty feet wide, blown down like ninepins by the Arctic wind.

Earle found all the building material he needed on the upper place and Mr. Astleford brought Horsie up to drag in the cedar logs for the large barn and hay shed, but not before we had gathered the material for a turkey brooder house.

We were going to try our hand at raising turkeys. Earle thought they could forage and do well on the drier land where we were going to build the barn. The day-old chicks would come by boat from Vancouver and we would have to keep the brooder house down where we were living until it was time for us to move to the upper place. So it would have to be built on skids, and later, we could drag it across the fields. It was to be of light construction with cedar shake walls and a roof nailed to a peeled pole frame.

It was a busy time for us. The days were never long enough but we were as happy as larks to be settled in our minds about what we were going to do and where we were going to build.

Earle arranged to exchange work with a couple of men who were strong and experienced and were able to help him with the barn. In between caring for the animals and preparing meals, I helped peel cedar logs and the lodgepole pines to be used for stripping on which the shakes were nailed for the roof.

The central part of the barn was to be large enough to store forty tons of loose hay on a floor that would be elevated three feet from the ground in case there should ever be another flood. A roof would extend from the central portion on three sides. On the north would be the walled sheep fold, on the west would be the stalls for the cattle, and on the south the sheltered loafing shed for them, open to the winter sun and with feeding racks against the hay. On the fourth side there was to be a sloping incline up which we could drag the hay from the wagon with a huge hay fork attached to a cable pulled by a team.

The barn was in a beautiful setting of birch trees which made a park-like shelter for the animals and not far away was a spring which stayed open the year round.

It was amazing how quickly the barn went up and I could hardly wait for work to begin on the house. But the men who were helping had to return to their own farms to do the spring planting and Earle said it was time to plough and fence our own vegetable garden. The house could wait.

"We are going to have to put up some sort of shelter to live in," I argued. "How can we possibly spend the summer running back and forth from one end of this flat to the other, tending the garden and putting up the hay? We simply must have some sort of place to live near where our work is. Furthermore, it is much too damp down in the lower quarter for the turkeys and the sheep."

Then we both had a bright idea. We were going to need an incubator house for hatching turkey eggs the following spring, so why not build another structure like the little brooder house and camp in that for the summer.

We had been able to buy a cast-iron cook stove like the one at the Stillwater, embossed bunches of grapes on the doors and all, and we could line the walls of the little house with heavy building paper, glued to the shakes. With double-decker bunks and a drop-leaf table in front of the window it would be snug and compact.

It took only a short while to build the incubator house and I rather liked it because I could stand in one place and reach everything I needed to prepare a meal. It seemed cramped only when guests came, but during the summer we could entertain them out of doors.

We intended to spend only the summer in the shack, but with the increasing pressure of work, there never seemed time to build a house. Whenever I complained, Earle would remind me of how comfortable we were and of how little time I had to waste on housekeeping. Furthermore, he had read somewhere that one could always judge the success of a farmer by the relative size of his barn and house. A big barn and a small house was the criterion. I believed him, but thought we carried it a bit too far.

Before winter came we did make one improvement, we added a bedroom. The turkeys no longer used their brooder house, and all we needed to do was drag it alongside our dwelling and cut a door between the two structures, then line the walls with insulation. It doubled the size of our living quarters and dispelled some of the tension that was building up each night when it was time for me to climb into the upper bunk to go to bed. This procedure lacked dignity and besides, it was hot and stuffy up there and I didn't like it.

The new room was tiny but charming, with space for our books and a clothes closet as well as a desk in front of the window. The little house was warm and cosy and we lived in those two rooms for more years than I care to remember.

The turkeys stole their nests in the brush the following spring, so there was no further need for either an incubator or brooder house.

With only skid logs for foundations, we banked the house with soil which would freeze in the winter and anchor it to the ground. Then, to make sure we didn't go bounding across the meadow in a strong wind, Earle guyed the north side with stout cables attached to buried logs.

It didn't take long to dig a well in such deep, rich soil. At fifteen feet we struck an underground spring that poured into the excavation with the most beautiful water we have ever tasted.

Earle lined the well with spruce lumber and built a three-foot curbing on top, with a hinged lid to keep little children and mice from falling in. There was an overhead pulley with a rope and bucket attached which I could use to draw the water from the well and then pour it into the waiting house bucket.

I enjoyed going out there for water. In all the years we lived there, it was only during severe weather that I didn't stand at the well for a few moments and gaze at the beauty of the mountains around us.

The well was fairly close to the house and there was one time when I was glad it was. It was winter and there was a sheet of ice on the flat top of the well curbing where I rested the bucket after drawing it up from the water. The lid was open and something told me I should have closed it when I saw two young cats playing and chasing each other outside. I heard a splash as I sat

501

sewing in the house and knew instantly what had happened. A cat had leapt onto the icy well curbing and skated on over into the depths. It was splashing around helplessly with nothing to cling to when I dashed out.

Earle was away, and there wasn't time to fetch a ladder, so I lowered the well bucket carefully and partially filled it with water until the top was low enough for the cat to climb on, then I guided it with the rope over to the side of the well where a two-by-four was nailed around the inside of the lining. With its hind legs on the edge of the bucket and its front ones clinging to this precarious perch, I secured the rope and then raced to get a ladder. As soon as this was lowered into the well, the cat climbed onto the rungs and came up by itself. My erstwhile pet gave me a baleful look as it emerged over the top and took off for the barn. A sodden cat is not a beautiful sight at best, and this one had absolute loathing in its eyes.

I baled water for hours before I thought it was clean enough to use again.

During the summer Earle attached a

lock to the lid of the well which we kept closed when we had visitors. Children were fascinated with the water in the deep hole and wanted to throw things into it. I had a horror of their falling in, and ran to lock the lid when I saw a car drive in on Sundays.

This was the day for visitors in the summer. We were thirty miles from Bella Coola and it was a pleasant drive up the tree-shaded road on a hot day, especially when the corn was ripe.

It was hotter and dryer in Firvale than farther down the valley, and with unlimited barnyard manure and sufficient sub-irrigation, the garden flourished and the corn and tomatoes and cucumbers were always ripe before those of the lower part of the valley, nearer the sea.

Each year we planted a large patch of corn to sell, and when the golden ears were ripe there was a constant succession of cars turning into the driveway on the weekends.

They made Sundays a nightmare, and I could scarcely straighten my back by nightfall after spending the day stooped over in the rows of corn, pinching each cob to feel if it was plump and well-filled. Picking it, I piled it on my other arm and when I had a load, carried it to the end of the row and dumped it in a wheelbarrow or clothes basket which I took to Earle who trimmed and counted the ears. Fortunately most of the corn ripened about the same time so there were only a couple of Sundays when we worked steadily all day, with scarcely any time out for meals, stopping only when it grew dark.

After the corn, there were other vegetables for sale — squash, tomatoes, cucumbers, carrots, potatoes and cabbages. There was a market for everything we could produce; the only limitation was our ability to handle it all.

During the first summer on our own place, we had the good fortune to have a friend who wanted to make the trip to Anahim Lake over the horse trail, and then drive to Vancouver and come back up the coast on the boat. He agreed to bring in our car in exchange for its use during his holidays. We were delighted, and having it to use after his return facilitated our hauling of supplies and marketing of produce. It also gave us a bit of a change from incessant farm work and we were able to have an outing now and then. Not that it decreased the work, we just got up earlier in the morning and worked harder so we could do the chores and prepare the market produce before driving over the thirty miles of rough road to Bella Coola.

Sometimes I was so tired before we started that I would rather have stayed at home, but it was an outing and we would see friends. We were nearly always tempted to stay somewhere for supper, so it was late as we drove up through the village of Hagensborg, past houses with their cosy evening lamps lit.

The narrow dirt road on up the valley seemed interminable, and when we did reach home, we were met by a reproachful milk cow and a bawling calf. The pig would be squealing and the sheep had to be counted and locked in the fold. By the time the eggs were gathered, I hated everything about farming and longed only to fall into bed.

In the morning we were in our own little world again and happy to be there.

29

Fall Fair

I N the quietness of the farm, we slept soundly every night. The house was some distance from the road and we wouldn't have heard a car even if one had gone past in the night. Except for picnickers on Sundays during the summer, there were few cars traveling the narrow road during our first years in Firvale. The nearest neighbor to the east was ten miles away, and to the west, with the exception of Mr. Astleford, it was five miles before there were any other farms.

It was peaceful and idyllic and I hoped it would always remain that way, but the winds of change were beginning to blow.

There were always people who wanted the valley to stay as it was, and others who could see the advantages of progress and yearned for a road out of the valley the way a blind man yearns for sight. To one faction, a road over the mountain would be a release from imprisonment, and to the conservative element it might be the opening of the flood gates to hordes of settlers flowing down the new road into our Shangri-la.

Tired of waiting for the government to build a road out of the valley, the energetic Board of Trade in Bella Coola conceived the idea of building one themselves. This is a saga of enterprise and daring, hard work and little money, but on the fourteenth of September, 1952, exactly twenty years from the time we crossed Charlotte Lake on a raft, a bulldozer started ploughing a roadway through the trees from Anahim Lake to Bella Coola. At the same time, another one started up out of the valley to meet it.

After overcoming almost insurmountable obstacles, a road was finally pushed and blasted through, and in the course of time the government assumed responsibility for it and improved and maintained it so that it became British Columbia's third outlet to the coast. Traffic flowed freely over it and the valley accepted the change it brought, and on long winter nights there were no longer heated debates about whether or not a road would be good for the valley. Such as it was, it had become a fact accomplished.

Before the completion of the road our own car had been brought around by way of Vancouver and up the coast by boat. It was a pleasure to have it again and once a month during the summer we made the arduous excursion to Bella Coola.

Having transportation, we planned to attend the Fall Fair for the first time; we even decided to enter some of our vegetables.

The coupé was laden with the best from the garden. I even took along an antique pitcher to hold an enormous cluster of deep blue delphiniums, and my grandmother's priceless, heavy copper preserving pan, filled with ripe tomatoes which overflowed among the other colorful vegetables.

We had never taken part in a fair before and didn't know anything about the value of points in a competition, but we thought our vegetables were beautiful and arranged everything in a display like a still life composition. It won the two dollar first prize and we were as proud as if it had been a fortune.

More than that, we were bitten by the Fall Fair bug, and every year from then on, we ravaged the garden for perfect specimens to take down the bumpy twenty-five miles to the fair.

Everything had to be cleaned and trimmed and carefully packed to withstand the trip. This was Earle's job. I dug or cut the vegetables and brought them into the woodshed to him.

After I had dug a hundred pounds of carrots and selected six roots, Earle would exclaim, "Is this the best we have? Could you go back and get some more?"

Two days of this, and the garden was a shambles. None of the vegetables was as perfect as we thought it should be but it was the best we had and we took it.

We were tired and irritable by the time everything was packed and loaded, and we were late getting away as the chores had to be done before we left. Saturday was the big day of the fair but the entries had to be in not later than ten o'clock on Thursday night so the judges could have all day Friday to judge them.

Thursday night was the best time of the whole fair for us. Only dedicated participants were there, collecting their entry tags and attaching them to the plates that held the specimens, then finding their place on the display tables and putting them in the right class. One had to be careful to count and re-count the number of small vegetables on a plate. One bean too many or too few would disqualify the entry.

We left the arrangement of the vegetable collection until the last. There was a prize for a collection of twelve or more different varieties. These added up to an impressive number of vegetables, three potatoes, six carrots, twelve string beans and so on, for twelve varieties and everything in this display had to be identified with a label.

There were volunteers who spent the evening helping where they could, and friends who had finished earlier would saunter over and offer to help as well, but it was a meticulous job that one preferred to do alone.

There was a camaraderie about this part of the fair, a fellowship of kindred souls who loved showing what the valley could produce. Even the people we passed on the way down in the car waved in a special way, as if to let us know they were aware of where we were going; as though anyone could mistake our goal, with the overloaded car bristling with cornstalks and the front seat so filled with potted plants, I could scarcely see out.

All the way down the road we talked gloomily about the poor quality of our entries and the glaring blemishes that would be sure to disqualify them. Some we even left behind because we didn't feel they were good enough; and in the rush, some of the perfect specimens, packed and ready to go, were accidentally left in the woodshed. But on Thursday night, when the vegetables were set out and the arranging was finished and we were so tired we were reeling, there was usually just time enough before the doors closed to take a quick look at the other entries. Our vegetables didn't seem so bad after all, and we were sorry we hadn't taken down everything we had.

On the way home we talked over the entries and tried to guess whether we would get a first, second, or third prize and whether we had a chance to win the vegetable trophy. It was cheering, but we were never entirely right. Most years there was a different judge from outside the valley, with different standards, which added an element of chance.

For twenty-five years we took part in every fair and as we grew older, we kept saying, "Never again!" But we kept up an interest in one way or another, never missing the Thursday night involvement.

30

Precipice Sheep

LATE one autumn, Jack Weldon sent word from the Precipice that he was going to sell his sheep and wanted to know if we would like to buy them. The wolves and coyotes had been killing them and he had only a dozen left, including the ram.

Earle decided to go up with Maryanka and get them before it snowed. The weather had turned cold and the clouds looked gray and threatening. He could ride from Firvale to Maxie's at Atnarko in a long day, and from there to the Precipice in another. On the way back with the sheep it would take him twice as long but there was a cabin at the Sugar Camp, halfway between the Precipice and Atnarko, where he could camp and feed grain to the animals, then go from there to Maxie's, then B.C.'s or Belarko, then home.

It was dusk as Earle approached the Precipice and was beginning to snow. He hoped it would be only a flurry but in the morning there was a blanket of two feet over everything and it was still snowing. Earle hesitated about starting out with the sheep but Jack was anxious to get rid of them, so with Maryanka breaking the trail and Earle shouting at the reluctant sheep he managed to start them moving toward the Sugar Camp. It turned out to be one of the most arduous experiences of his life.

The wool on the sheep kept them afloat in the snow and their legs were unable to reach bottom. Maryanka took the lead but Earle had to lift each sheep and toss it forward on the trail through the deepest snow. It took him all day to travel the ten miles from the Precipice to Sugar Camp where he had left the grain on the way up.

It stopped snowing the following morning as Earle left the Sugar Camp and the snow on the trail gradually diminished as they descended the mountain until there was only a foot in the valley bottom and the sheep were able to move along more easily. Earle was able to get as far as B.C.'s before dark, but there was one obstacle that almost stopped them. An unbridged creek ran across the trail at the upper end of the clearings and the sheep refused to cross. Maryanka went through it, stepping off the icy bank and climbing out on the shelf of ice on the other side. The creek was not very deep but was too wide for the sheep to jump.

The mare stood patiently waiting on the far bank while Earle stumbled back and forth among the snow-covered boulders, trying to keep the sheep from getting around him and starting back up the trail again. Finally, in desperation, he grabbed the one nearest the creek, and putting one arm under the neck and the other around its rump, he lifted it and tossed it with a mighty heave into the middle of the creek from where it jumped through the flowing water and out onto the ice on the other side.

With one across, Earle was able to drive the others into the water. One at a time, they leapt high into the air and landed with a splash in the middle of the creek, scrambling out as the other had done.

It was a traumatic experience for the tired sheep but a few yards farther on they were fed and safely housed for the night.

The next day was a long but comparatively easy one through only six inches of snow, and by nightfall they were home. I heard them coming as I was finishing the evening chores and there was much bleating and bunting after I opened the gate and the two flocks mingled together. There was no mistaking them, the Precipice sheep were of a different breed and had been used to a less sheltered life than ours, who looked like pampered darlings beside these shaggy newcomers.

Apparently the ram had had a rough

life; he wanted to fight everybody and everything. Several times as I bent over the outside feed trough, filling it with a bucket of grain or some chopped vegetables, I found myself sailing over it to make a three-point landing in the snow on the other side. It might have been serious if he had struck me on the head but his attacks were always from the rear.

Having him so belligerent took some of the pleasure out of going into the sheepshed, and one day Earle finally got fed up with being battered about. He waited until the ram began licking his lips and squaring off for a run at him, and as the ram charged, Earle stepped to one side and grabbed his horns as he passed, flipping him over onto his back and holding him there, petting him. This loss of dignity was too much for the ram. Earle had only to do it once again before he was cured of bunting us. Over the years we had a number of rams and we observed that the ones we raised ourselves were always gentle and could be trusted, whereas the ones we bought were unreliable and quarrelsome.

A ram with a massive set of horns can be a menace, especially if he catches you in the middle of nowhere, armed only with an empty bucket. This happened to me once when one flattened a bucket against my shins before Earle rescued me. It was painful and I was frightened, but I had a greater horror of being struck on the head, so I developed the habit of glancing around to see where the ram was before bending over in the sheepshed.

When I sheared the sheep in the spring, I did it in a box stall and the sheep that were going to be sheared were tied up so I had no fear of being bunted while I was concentrating on the shearing.

Shearing sheep was always done during the first hot weather in spring. A sheep's wool is filled with an oily substance, commonly called "yolk," from which lanolin is obtained. When warm, this is fluid and facilitates the cutting. In cold weather the yolk stiffens to the consistency of putty, making it difficult to push the shears through the fleece. Sometimes on chilly days I had to lubricate the shears with coal-oil.

Unfortunately, Earle had injured his

back since moving to Firvale and was unable to do the shearing but he helped me catch and tie up the sheep to be sheared. I always did the clipping with a pair of high-grade dressmaker's shears instead of the conventional sheep shearing ones which were too large for my hands.

I loathed the job. It was hot, dirty, tiring and bruising work, and I thought of nothing but pictures I had seen of big, brawny shearers who casually dumped a sheep on its rear and zip, in four minutes the whole fleece was off and rolled in a bundle.

We did hire a chap to help us with shearing the first time, but to our distress they emerged from the shed with their skin in bloody ribbons, so we thought of an excuse for me to take over and from then on I did the disagreeable job myself rather than have the animals cut.

I wasn't strong enough to sit them down in the approved position for shearing, so at first we stretched them out flat on their sides on a platform, but I was so slow this was hard on both the sheep and the operator. Finally we settled on the safest and easiest method, tying them by the horns in the corner of a box stall where there was no room for them to move around. Starting at the back of the head, I snipped a parting down the center of the back. From there, I cut the fleece down on either side, shearing as close to the hide as I could, but careful not to dig the point of the shears into the delicate, flexible skin. I took great pride in not nicking them and giving the sheep a smooth haircut.

Sometimes the ewes fought to the bitter end. There were some that would have liked to kill me if they had been able to get loose, and my own temper was sorely tried. I was often tempted to trim the troublesome ones like a French poodle, and only pride in my work stayed my hand.

Other ewes were placid and gentle, chewing their cud while I clipped. Turning them loose, all of them seemed relieved to be free of the hot, cumbersome blanket they had been carrying. Some of them were startled by the white apparition that was suddenly part of themselves; others jumped into the air with joy and cavorted out to join the flock in the pasture. They were unattractive without their coats and even startled the others, but before long they were covered with a downy new fleece again.

It took me an hour to do each sheep, although when the flock increased to seventy-five, I grew more proficient with practice and could do a gentle sheep in forty-five minutes.

Earle came out frequently to see how I was getting along and to bring me something cool to drink, or sharpen the shears. At the end of the day I was so bent over, sometimes he had to help me straighten up. I walked stiffly to the house and stripped off my outer clothing on the porch, but no amount of soapy water would remove the odor from my hands. Disagreeable though it was, I was proud rather than relieved to have finished the job.

We tried to manage to have the lambs come in the spring, about the time the snow disappeared. It was safer to have them at the barn where we could watch them, and Earle built some maternity pens in one end of the sheep shed where the ewe could lamb in privacy. What was more important, it kept the lamb from straying and being contaminated with the odor of some other ewe. In her excited state, a ewe would often reject a new-born lamb that she had just dried and bleated over lovingly, but which had wandered away while she was occupied with the delivery of a second one. This was a disastrous situation and one that took patience and wile to overcome. Sometimes it was necessary to tie the ewe to prevent her from harming her own baby.

Once we had a young ewe with a single lamb that had wandered off and somehow come in contact with an alien scent and we had to pen the ewe and remove the lamb to save its life. We kept it in an adjacent pen, going out every two hours to let it nurse its mother who had to be held. We tried everything we could think of, including dabbing cologne on the lamb's rump and the mother's nose but instead of persuading her to accept the lamb it only made her sneeze as though she had hay fever. For two weeks she fought and tried to kill the lamb each time it nursed. Just when we were ready to give up she suddenly accepted it for no reason we could understand, nearly wearing out the poor little thing with her loving ministrations. She talked to it and licked it incessantly and was the most attentive mother in the flock.

Sometimes there were problems in the delivery of the lambs. It was like a miracle when everything went well and the lamb emerged into the world alive, with the ewe reaching around to lick it, talking to it with a soft, throaty sound, keeping it up all the while until the lamb was dry. It never failed to move us; but what filled us with wonder was watching the little fellow totter to his feet and find his way to the udder. How did he know where to look for it?

When there were lambing problems, there was no vet in the valley and we were on our own. This is where my small hands were an asset. I would have to go in alongside a protruding head to find a missing foot and bring it forward so the lamb could be born properly.

There was only one correct position for a lamb or a calf to be born and that was with both front feet lying alongside the head. It was always a relief to see both front feet and the nose together when the new arrival started to be born.

Once, when we were being swamped with the arrival of new lambs, Earle and I were both in the sheep shed when the ewe I was with had triplets. She had delivered two beautiful lambs when the third started to appear. I called excitedly, "She's having a third one!"

"Don't stop her!" Earle called back.

Nature has provided ewes with equipment for feeding only two lambs at a time.

I loved caring for the sheep, but there were three jobs in connection with sheep raising that I detested — shearing, cutting off the lamb's tails and castrating the male lambs.

We used bloodless emasculators, a sort of pincers, which crushed the cords without cutting the skin. It was momentarily painful but bloodless and less of a shock to the lamb than using a knife.

We used pincers for docking, too, clamping them on the tail and holding for a few minutes to allow the blood to coagulate before cutting alongside the pincers. Most of the time this method was completely bloodless, but still it was painful and I suffered with each little lamb. It was my job to hold them and I felt like a betrayer.

31

Mr. Jones

ONE of the most delightful things that happened to us was being given a puppy. He was a cross between a purebred Airedale and a Collie, a blend of intelligent aggressiveness and gentleness that was perfect for a farm like ours.

We brought him home when he was six weeks old, a tawny ball of irresistible puppy that we fell in love with. Even at that age he displayed the characteristics that made him an outstanding dog as he grew older. There was an innate dignity in everything he did and we named him Mr. Jones. There was never any need to reprimand or punish him, and we always spoke to him softly, in a low voice. If either of us ever did speak to him crossly he was upset for a long time. This sensitiveness must have come from his Collie sire, while his Airedale mother gave him courage and stamina.

The first night away from his brothers and sisters we held him in our arms a lot, and when it was time to go to bed I let him sleep beside me on my bed, getting up a couple of times during the night to take him outside to let him run around on the grass until he relieved himself.

The second night he had a bed on the floor near mine where I could reach down and pet him when he grew restless. We put a hot water bottle under his blanket and covered him with an old sweater. Again I took him outside during the night. After that, he went to the door and whimpered gently whenever he needed to go out and never once did we have an accident in the house.

All his life he slept inside the house.

To have left him outside would only have disturbed our rest because there were always predators and he would have barked at them. There was scarcely a night when we first lived in Firvale that we didn't hear coyotes or wolves.

When he grew older, I took Jonesie everywhere with me as I roamed the countryside, picking berries, hunting the cattle or bringing in the sheep, or just walking over to the river enjoying the beauty of the woods. He was my nose and ears, telling me about bears long before I was aware of any.

Only once did I regret having him with me; this was when he was still a roly-poly puppy and I carried him most of the way to a patch of wild ginger I wanted to gather, about a mile or so away through the woods.

Jonesie was tumbling about, investigating a squirrel cache under some tall fir trees and I was bent over, intent on gathering the herbs when something made me look up; ambling toward us on a game trail was an enormous black bear. Ordinarily I had little fear of black bears but suddenly I realized the pup might have looked like an appetizing morsel to this one.

It hadn't seen us yet, and fortunately Jonesie hadn't seen him, but the pup was halfway between the bear and myself still digging out the squirrel hole. The bear continued coming and at any moment Jonesie was going to see it and let out a yip, then get himself killed by attacking the bear or else turn and bring the bear to me. There was only one thing to do — hastily I scrambled forward until I reached the pup, then grabbing him in my arms, I muffled his mouth with my hand while I turned and ran for the shelter of the first tree.

Dodging from tree to tree, I kept as many as I could between me and the bear until I had courage enough to look back and see whether we were being chased. There was no sign of the bear and I never knew whether we frightened him or if he even saw us, but he was only twenty feet away from Jonesie and must have caught his scent.

Jonesie lived a charmed life. Before he was old enough to develop discretion, his fearlessness led him into one brush with death after another. Once, when he was almost full-grown, we took him with us to look for the cattle. We had debated many times over whether we should make the dog heel when he was with us in the woods or let him roam free. It seemed more sensible to let him run ahead and intercept any predator we otherwise would have run across unexpectedly. Certainly Jonesie was happier to be free.

On this particular day we were following a cattle trail through the woods toward an old clearing and the remains of an orchard. It was August and we should have remembered about the apple trees and kept Jonesie with us, but by the time we heard his bark, it was too late.

We heard the bear crashing along the trail toward us with the dog barking at his heels. There was just time to step aside as the bear raced past and we could have reached out and touched it. Intent on getting away from the dog, I don't believe it saw us and Jonesie must have taken it half a mile away before he returned, panting and victorious. He had saved our lives.

Another time Earle took his axe and

went to check the fence at the farthest corner of the pasture where the creek ran through tall ferns and brush. Jonesie went along and both of them discovered fresh wolf tracks in the soft mud at the same time. Jonesie dashed into the gigantic ferns before Earle realized the danger and started to call him back when he heard the ominous sound of teeth snapping together, followed by a yelp. He strode toward the sound just as the frightened dog emerged from the ferns with a huge black timber wolf at his heels.

The wolf was only seven or eight feet away from Earle who was armed with nothing but a single-bitted axe but he swung it up ready to drive it through the beast's head, when the wolf swung in an arc and disappeared in the ferns with Jonesie in pursuit.

Before Earle had time to grab him the dog was .gone. His Airedale hunting instincts had taken over and he was in full cry. Earle listened fearfully to the excited barking as it ascended the mountainside for a quarter of a mile and then there was silence, followed by a triumphant howl from the wolf. Earle never expected to see Jonesie again but presently he heard him panting through the brush, returning without a scratch and looking pleased. The wolf sat on a knoll overlooking the farm and howled for half an hour.

I listened with concern as Earle related the encounter. There was something familiar about his description of the wolf that rang a bell in my mind.

"Do you suppose this was the big black dog I met in the woods not long ago?" I asked.

I had gone one evening to bring the sheep home from their day's grazing in the old clearing through the woods across the road. Jonesie was with Earle and I was alone sauntering along the trail under the tall cottonwood trees. It surprised me to find the sheep wending their way home by themselves, but I still had to go to the clearing to make sure none had stayed behind. About halfway there I looked up to see a large black dog walking slowly behind the sheep, following them in. We were less than twenty feet apart when he saw me and stopped.

I wondered who he belonged to. We had no near neighbors and no one we knew had a dog that looked like it. At any rate, he shouldn't have been running loose so I scolded him, and said, "Bad dog! Go home!" in an angry voice.

He stood there and made no effort to move. It occurred to me that this might be a Stick Indian dog from the interior that didn't understand English.

"Its-tsaw!" I cried in a threatening manner. This is the Indian word for "Go! Get out!" It is uttered with a hissing sound and almost impossible to pronounce by someone not born to the tongue, but I tried it.

That didn't work either and we stared at one other until I began to feel uneasy. There was something bold and menacing about the animal and he must have weighed about one hundred and fifty pounds.

Without taking my eye from him I slowly crouched down and picked up a heavy stick. Standing up, I waved it at him, shouting, "Shoo!"

In an instant he whirled and loped through the trees. There was something graceful about his movements, but until Earle described him, I thought my encounter had been with a dog.

All that summer we were beset by predators. Often we heard the wolf howl from the mountainside and saw his footprints in the damp mud near the creek. There was also a large grizzly with a two year old and an eight month old cub. We saw them frequently and they seemed to be around at the same time as the wolf.

We began to lose lambs, and one day a ewe with her twin lambs came limping in from the pasture. Both her hams had been torn out and Earle had to destroy her. I began to loathe wolves.

We locked the sheep in the sheepfold every evening. It was near the house, with access to water and the barn, and the enclosure was well-fenced.

About three o'clock on a dark, drizzly morning, I was suddenly awakened by the sound of sheep rushing from one end of their enclosure to the other, crashing into the wall of the barn in the dark.

Earle was a sound sleeper, so without taking time to wake him, I grabbed the flashlight and raced out in my bare feet and nightgown with Jonesie ahead of me. Opening the gate to the sheepfold, I stood there trying to get the flashlight to work when the sheep thundered past on their return to the other end of the enclosure. As they passed beside me, Jonesie let out a roar and lunged at something in the rear of the flock — something that had almost run into me in the dark. I yelled at it and a moment later heard the sound of wire squealing as the creature went over the fence.

I ran back to the house, woke Earle and lit a lantern. In warmer clothing I went out again to find three of our finest, almost full-grown lambs with their throats cut. Nothing had been eaten; there was just a hole in the throat.

It hadn't been a wolf — they were inclined to hamstring the victim and rip open the abdomen and eat the liver and tender parts first. But they did choose the finest, fattest animals, and they also killed wantonly. However, this was different and looked like the work of yet another predator.

In the morning Earle drove down to

Milo Ratcliff's and phoned the game warden in Bella Coola. He promised to come up in the evening and spend the night in his car, with the carcasses of the sheep in line with the headlights so he could switch them on suddenly and shoot the predator when it came back to feed.

The poor chap spent the long night out there in the freezing cold, and at four o'clock in the morning he knocked at the door, stiff, shivering and hollow-eyed from his vigil and sorely in need of a cup of coffee. There had been no sign whatever of the predator and the warden decided to call the predator control officer in Williams Lake and ask him to come in.

The following evening Earle climbed into the hay loft with the rifle and kept watch until it was too dark to see. Then during the night the animal returned and with one of the forty-pound lambs in its mouth, it jumped over the five-foot, pagewire fence of the sheepfold. We couldn't find a trace of the carcass anywhere but we did find a track. It was a cougar!

It wasn't until Mr. Lesowski of the Predator Control Branch came all the way from Williams Lake with his hounds that the cougar cache was found. The cougar had carried the dead lamb over the rocky hillside into the woods and covered it with leaves and twigs.

Mr. Lesowski discovered the regular route of the cougar, a circuit beginning on a trail starting up the mountain near Burnt Bridge Creek, a mile above our place. He set a foot snare attached to a toggle, which is a small log the animal could drag for a short way before getting tangled in the brush.

It was three weeks before Mr. Lesowski came back to inspect the snare. The cougar had been caught by one foot and had almost chewed its way through the toggle. In a short while it would have been able to get away but Lesowski shot it and when we saw the body I was surprised that it was not larger. It was amazing that an animal its size had the strength to jump over a five-foot fence with a forty-pound lamb in its mouth. It was also extraordinary how beautiful it was, with silky, tawny hair.

During the autumn we lost more sheep, and then a full grown steer. The grizzlies and the wolf seemed to be operating as a team and we never knew which one did the killing, but the bears were enjoying the spoils. I ran into the three of them feeding on the remains of a sheep they had dragged into the edge of the brush in the pasture. The wind was blowing and the sound of it in the trees covered the noise of the bears until I was so close I heard bones crunching.

It was frightening and depressing to have lost so many animals and we realized we were going to have to do something about it.

Ralph had brought down a steer all the way from Lonesome Lake to butcher at our place. The men finished the job in the morning and while the carcass was chilling in the shed, Earle took Ralph to Bella Coola on business.

Before they left they rolled the offal onto a low sled and dragged it behind the car over to the old clearing through the woods across the road from us. There they dumped it on the far side of the field, opposite the unused barn. Earle was intending to walk over when he returned in the evening, to see if the grizzlies were there.

It was growing dusk by the time the chores were finished and still the men had not returned, so I locked Jonesie in the house, took the rifle and hurried through the woods to the clearing.

The bears were there. They were a magnificent sight in the evening light. The sow was a silver-tip, her hair rippling over powerful muscles as she walked with slow dignity among the scraps of meat. The two year old and the cub were tearing the remains to pieces.

It was a breath-taking scene and I was fascinated by their beauty, but these were the animals who had been preying on our stock. Or, were they the scavengers and the wolf the killer?

For a moment I hesitated, then raising the rifle to my shoulder in the shelter of the barn, I shot the sow and the two year old with one bullet each. They dropped where they were.

Sickened, I couldn't shoot any more and let the cub escape to the woods where he climbed a tree. In the morning

Earle found it and put an end to its life. It was too young to have survived alone.

I never used the rifle again. Even on walks where there might be bears, I went without it. Jonesie was going to be my protection from now on.

Later, the wolf was shot in a pasture farther down the valley, and after that our troubles ended. Never again were we so harassed by predators as we were that year. The frontier had been pushed back a little farther.

32

Bambi

OUR life in Firvale wove itself into a homespun fabric of happiness and hard work, drama and tranquility. Through it for a little while, like a bright silver thread, ran the blithe spirit of Bambi.

One Sunday evening in June a car turned in at our gate on its way back down the valley. Friends were returning from a trip up the road and they came to the house with a tiny fawn in their arms. It was trying to be motionless, as if it were in its hiding place in the woods and my heart flooded with protective love as I took it from them and held it gently.

The umbilical cord was still intact, so it couldn't have been more than a week old. They had found it entangled in a roadside brush pile and there were no deer tracks anywhere in the soft sand that had been washed clean by rain during the night. The mother had either been killed or this was one of twins and had been left behind when it became entangled in the brush. Rather than let it starve or be killed by predators, our friends brought it to us.

We took it to a box stall in the empty barn and draped gunnysacking across one corner so the little animal would feel secluded. Fortunately we had bottles fitted with rubber nipples which we sometimes used for feeding lambs and I prepared warm milk, but it wouldn't drink. We knew nothing about doe's milk but ewe's milk is much richer than cow's so we added a little cream to the whole milk in the bottle.

In the morning it still refused to drink and we knew it must be hungry, so I tried feeding it with my finger in a saucepan of warm milk. This worked. Probably it had been the flavor of the rubber nipple it hadn't liked. In a couple of days it was drinking from the pan without the aid of my finger.

It gave little mewing sounds as it drank the milk and bunted frequently as though it were nursing its mother. This spattered the milk and I had to wipe its face dry after each feeding.

There was something else interesting about the feeding process. There was an area at the inner corner of each eye that appeared to be a fold in the skin but which opened up as a hairless, saucer-like depression while the fawn was drinking. We never understood the reason for this, but the gentle squeaking and the opening of the glands, as well as the raising of her tail like a signal flag, continued as long as we fed Bambi. She was a mule deer with a black-tipped tail which stood straight up in the air while she was drinking, with the hair spread out like a fan until the milk was finished.

For the first two weeks I went to the barn and fed her every two hours but as she grew we were able to increase the milk and lengthen the time between feedings and she soon began to eat a little crushed grain and the tender clover I cut for her. Before long we were able to bring her over from the barn to the dooryard which was enclosed by pagewire fencing so she could not escape, although when she first came she crawled through a four-inch square in the mesh. It seemed incredible that she could go through anything so small but something had frightened her.

We had a pet lamb we were feeding with a bottle and as Bambi grew older they were good company for each other in the dooryard. Then I brought in a calf from the pasture, and during the summer we added Coffee and Cocoa — engaging young goats that came from an over-populated lighthouse island off the coast. Earle called this my "frothing maelstrom of dumb chums" but I loved having them there. They were safe and I could watch them.

Bambi grew amazingly and was highly intelligent. She had discovered how to twist the wooden knob on the door and open it. Often she did this and came into the house to greet me in the morning, resting her head under my chin in a demonstration of affection. Sometimes she stood half in and half out of the doorway, nibbling apple peel that dropped as I pared the fruit for sauce or pie.

One day I had been picking raspberries when friends drove in on their way to a picnic and asked me if I'd like to go with them. It was a temptation as Earle was away, but I had jam to make. However, they persuaded me and I crushed the berries and mixed them with sugar, putting them in a large shallow bowl, out of the way on a chair in the bedroom.

We took Jonesie with us and left the gate locked so Bambi, Coffee and Cocoa and the calf would be safe. It was a delightful picnic and I was home in time to milk the cows.

As I opened the door on my return, I was appalled at the mess inside the house. In the middle stood the calf, facing the door and chewing her cud with her long tail draped over the bowl of raspberries on the chair. Bambi was nowhere to be seen but it was evident she had opened the door and had come in with the calf, then left, with the door closing behind her.

Between them they had tipped over the pitcher of buttermilk that had been left on the table. I imagine Bambi must have left about this time, but someone ate the bouquet of flowers on the table, tipping over the vase and spilling the water. Judging by the tracks, the calf must have moved back and forth between the two rooms before taking up the position in the bedroom, facing the door with her tail in the sweetened raspberries.

In the warm house the sugar had drawn the juice from the soft, ripe berries and the calf's tail had made several complete revolutions through the shallow pan because the sticky mess was over the bed and on the walls and ceiling. It was unspeakable, but I was thankful it was the calf rather than the excitable goats that had been locked in for they might have harmed themselves trying to get out the window.

This brought an abrupt end to my

dooryard menagerie. Only Bambi remained and she was free to roam wherever she chose. The goats and the lamb went into the sheep pasture while the calf joined the cattle. I missed them but even I had to admit it was getting to be a bit too much.

There had been one advantage in having the pets together in the enclosure — they were all in one place when the carloads of children arrived to see them on Sundays, to have their pictures taken petting Bambi or sitting beside her as she lay on the grass. Nothing in the world is lovelier than a deer languidly stretched out, chewing its cud or sleeping. Coffee and Cocoa were inclined to frolic around and bunt with their stilleto horns which scared the children but Bambi was always gracious and dignified, submitting to endless petting.

The goats tolerated attention until the cookies ran out, then they would take off together and were usually found lying on top of the visitor's car, chewing their cud and watching the activity. If the door of the car had been left open they curled up in comfort on the back seat.

With the animals feeding in the far pasture, Sundays were no longer a day of rest for me. I walked miles to bring in Bambi and the goats for the children, and after each carload of visitors had left, the animals returned to the pasture again so I would have to go and get them when the next carload arrived.

We never worried about Bambi harming anyone, for during the summer she was gentle and affectionate. But in the fall and early winter when she was almost full-grown, she grew boisterous and we had to watch her.

I had taught her to stand on her hind legs to reach for a special treat that I held high in my hand, and she towered above me. We didn't realize this was how deer stood when they fought with each other, rearing on their hind legs and striking their opponent with their sharp, pointed hooves.

As autumn advanced, Bambi developed the habit of racing at top speed to the far end of the meadow and back again until she was breathless and panting. She did this regularly once a day and I suppose this was nature's way of giving her the exercise she would have had in the wild. She could jump a five-foot fence with graceful ease.

One day Earle was walking through the pasture to mend a fence the bears had broken and Bambi came racing up behind him, rearing and striking him painfully on the shoulders with her hooves. After that we watched her carefully, especially when she was running since it seemed to excite her.

Bambi was free to roam at will but she never strayed very far from the farm. The area was extensive and there was such a variety of feed there was no need for her to go outside the fences. Nevertheless, when the hunting season began, we posted "No Shooting" signs on the place and put notices on the road about a pet deer, as well as attaching a red collar around her neck. But there were many nights when I lay sleepless, wondering if some harm might befall her. It was an immense relief when the hunting season ended and Bambi was safe again.

She grew sleek and fat as autumn approached and loved to come out into the garden with us as we harvested the vegetables. Carrots were her favorites and we wiped off the small, tender ones for her to eat as we dug the crop.

When she had been young we had a lot of trouble keeping her out of the growing garden. Every time Earle found her there he picked her up and carried her out while she protested with tiny squeaks. Finally he made the garden gate higher and this discouraged her.

During the winter when the snow was deep, she had her daily run on the trails the cattle kept open. She loved the snow and curled up in it for a nap, usually where she could see all about her, but at night she chose to sleep, sheltered and safe, in the bed of hay we made for her on the porch in front of the window.

The porch seemed to be her favorite spot and we cleared it off except for her bed and an orange-painted captain's chair which we used as a manger for her food. It seemed just the right height for her, as the principle feed of the mule deer is brush, although they do graze on short grass and clover in the spring. She stood feeding at the chair a good deal of the time, eating hay or peelings or grain or licking salt.

Smokey, the cat, adored Bambi and climbed up on the chair each morning to have her face washed by the deer. The cat loved it but winced when Bambi became too energetic. If the licking stopped, Smokey would reach out with her paw and gently tap the side of Bambi's face, then settle back and wait for her to start washing again. Sometimes Smokey would stand on her hind legs and wrap her arms around the deer's nose and wash her, but most often the process was the other way.

As Bambi increased in size the porch seemed to grow smaller, and often as she stood eating at her manger we had to push her sideways a little so we could enter the door. When Jonesie wanted to come in the house and she was in the way he waited patiently for her to move, then when the time was right he would duck under her and open the door and come in. He was a fair-sized dog, and before winter came Bambi had grown so much, he could walk under the bridge of her abdomen without difficulty.

The latch on our door was homemade with a simple round birchwood knob which lifted a lever when it was turned and allowed the door to open outward. Jonesie learned at an early age how to turn the knob with his teeth and as the latch released, he pulled the door toward him opening it a crack, then hooked his paw in the opening and pulled the door the rest of the way, enabling him to enter.

Bambi must have learned how to do this from watching him because from the time she was able to reach the knob she opened the door easily. Often in the mornings she came in to waken us, mewing for milk.

We continued to feed her in a saucepan long past her time of need for milk because of the pleasure in feeding her. Jonesie would share it with her, putting his head in the pan beside hers to make sure she drank up the last drop, then licking her chin if she had spilled milk on it.

Each afternoon Bambi came to the door for a special treat. Sometimes I would pretend to be stupid and not know what she was there for, then she would lick my chin and nibble the buttons on my sweater, then nibble my ear, and then by that time, if I still hadn't understood, she would give an impatient little mew and quite a vigorous nudge with her nose. When she saw me reach for the jam jar she would dance about on her dainty hooves and put her tail straight up in the air. When she was eating jam, or rather, flipping it into her mouth with her tongue, she talked with an exquisite sound, half-way between a hum and the sound of a contented bee in a bottle.

With the colder weather her coat grew thicker and darker and she grew sleek and fat. We often wondered if she would wander away and join her own kind in the wilds when the mating season came but we never saw any indication of her wanting to go; only the compulsive daily run on the snowy trails.

Jonesie spent much of his time in Bambi's company, but kept a wary eye on her when she was racing or in an exuberant mood as she had caught him a couple of times on a narrow trail in the deep snow and struck him playfully with her front hooves.

When Christmas came there was no room in the little house for a tree so I cut some small firs and tied them to the posts supporting the porch roof, making a bower for Bambi. On Christmas Eve they were laden with powdery snow.

Earle and I rested in the cosy warmth of the kitchen and talked about other Christmases.

"Do you recall the Christmas at Ralph's?" he reminisced. "You've changed a lot since then. Do you remember how frightened you were of the snow?"

"I was afraid of a lot of things in those days," I replied.

"Remember coming across Charlotte Lake on the raft?" Earle went on.

"And hiking through the woods in those awful longjohns," I added. "Didn't you suggest I sew some ruffles on them?"

"I guess there hasn't been much time for ruffles, has there?" Earle reflected.

No time, or inclination, I thought. Our lives had been filled to the brim.

Earle reached over to put more wood on the fire. "It seems a little colder tonight," he observed, "I wonder if it's stopped snowing."

Drawing the curtains aside, he exclaimed, "Look, it's cleared and the moon is shining. Come and see!"

Turning down the coal-oil lamp, we looked out through the window. Secure in her bed of hay was Bambi, lying in the moonlight surrounded by the snow-laden Christmas trees, and in the distance were the majestic mountains, calm and still.

The beauty and wonder of it filled us with an overpowering awe as we stood there gazing out. This was a Christmas we would remember.

THE WILDERNESS WALK
Sheila Bishop

Stifling unpleasant memories of a misbegotten romance in Cleave with Lord Francis Aubrey, Lavinia goes on holiday there with her sister. The two women are thrust into a romantic intrigue involving none other than Lord Francis.

THE RELUCTANT GUEST
Rosalind Brett

Ann Calvert went to spend a month on a South African farm with Theo Borland and his sister. They both proved to be different from her first idea of them, and there was Storr Peterson — the most disturbing man she had ever met.

ONE ENCHANTED SUMMER
Anne Tedlock Brooks

A tale of mystery and romance and a girl who found both during one enchanted summer.

CLOUD OVER MALVERTON
Nancy Buckingham

Dulcie soon realises that something is seriously wrong at Malverton, and when violence strikes she is horrified to find herself under suspicion of murder.

AFTER THOUGHTS
Max Bygraves

The Cockney entertainer tells stories of his East End childhood, of his RAF days, and his post-war showbusiness successes and friendships with fellow comedians.

MOONLIGHT
AND MARCH ROSES
D. Y. Cameron

Lynn's search to trace a missing girl takes her to Spain, where she meets Clive Hendon. While untangling the situation, she untangles her emotions and decides on her own future.

NURSE ALICE IN LOVE
Theresa Charles

Accepting the post of nurse to little Fernie Sherrod, Alice Everton could not guess at the romance, suspense and danger which lay ahead at the Sherrod's isolated estate.

POIROT INVESTIGATES
Agatha Christie

Two things bind these eleven stories together — the brilliance and uncanny skill of the diminutive Belgian detective, and the stupidity of his Watson-like partner, Captain Hastings.

LET LOOSE THE TIGERS
Josephine Cox

Queenie promised to find the long-lost son of the frail, elderly murderess, Hannah Jason. But her enquiries threatened to unlock the cage where crucial secrets had long been held captive.

THE TWILIGHT MAN
Frank Gruber

Jim Rand lives alone in the California desert awaiting death. Into his hermit existence comes a teenage girl who blows both his past and his brief future wide open.

DOG IN THE DARK
Gerald Hammond

Jim Cunningham breeds and trains gun dogs, and his antagonism towards the devotees of show spaniels earns him many enemies. So when one of them is found murdered, the police are on his doorstep within hours.

THE RED KNIGHT
Geoffrey Moxon

When he finds himself a pawn on the chessboard of international espionage with his family in constant danger, Guy Trent becomes embroiled in moves and countermoves which may mean life or death for Western scientists.

TIGER TIGER
Frank Ryan

A young man involved in drugs is found murdered. This is the first event which will draw Detective Inspector Sandy Woodings into a whirlpool of murder and deceit.

CAROLINE MINUSCULE
Andrew Taylor

Caroline Minuscule, a medieval script, is the first clue to the whereabouts of a cache of diamonds. The search becomes a deadly kind of fairy story in which several murders have an other-worldly quality.

LONG CHAIN OF DEATH
Sarah Wolf

During the Second World War four American teenagers from the same town join the Army together. Forty-two years later, the son of one of the soldiers realises that someone is systematically wiping out the families of the four men.

THE LISTERDALE MYSTERY
Agatha Christie

Twelve short stories ranging from the light-hearted to the macabre, diverse mysteries ingeniously and plausibly contrived and convincingly unravelled.

TO BE LOVED
Lynne Collins

Andrew married the woman he had always loved despite the knowledge that Sarah married him for reasons of her own. So much heartache could have been avoided if only he had known how vital it was to be loved.

ACCUSED NURSE
Jane Converse

Paula found herself accused of a crime which could cost her her job, her nurse's reputation, and even the man she loved, unless the truth came to light.

BUTTERFLY MONTANE
Dorothy Cork

Parma had come to New Guinea to marry Alec Rivers, but she found him completely disinterested and that overbearing Pierce Adams getting entirely the wrong idea about her.

HONOURABLE FRIENDS
Janet Daley

Priscilla Burford is happily married when she meets Junior Environment Minister Alistair Thurston. Inevitably, sexual obsession and political necessity collide.

WANDERING MINSTRELS
Mary Delorme

Stella Wade's career as a concert pianist might have been ruined by the rudeness of a famous conductor, so it seemed to her agent and benefactor. Even Sir Nicholas fails to see the possibilities when John Tallis falls deeply in love with Stella.

MORNING IS BREAKING
Lesley Denny

The growing frenzy of war catapults Diane Clements into a clandestine marriage and separation with a German refugee.

LAST BUS TO WOODSTOCK
Colin Dexter

A girl's body is discovered huddled in the courtyard of a Woodstock pub, and Detective Chief Inspector Morse and Sergeant Lewis are hunting a rapist and a murderer.

THE STUBBORN TIDE
Anne Durham

Everyone advised Carol not to grieve so excessively over her cousin's death. She might have followed their advice if the man she loved thought that way about her, but another girl came first in his affections.